An Accidental
CUBAN

✤

JOAN MORAN

BEWARE THE PATIENT MAN

CONTENTS

CHAPTER 1
The Get

usk was settling on the seaside city of Cienfuegos. The indigo light descended into violet darkness as Harry's work began. It was his favorite time of day, especially when he observed an unusual light mist dancing inside the sticky humidity that engulfed the plaza. It looked like sparkling wine.

Harry was a hustler in the Plaza Martí. It was where he ended up at twenty-seven, but it wasn't where this tall, handsome, physically imposing young man was going to be for long. He had plans, not just for him, but for his family. He was leaving Cuba for good. It was his dream since he returned from the States ten years ago, and he was ready to expedite his escape with a solid, well-thought-out plan that would take his wife and daughter to a new life in America. As soon as he could find an opening. Or a possibility.

It was all he could do to keep his energy focused and balanced as he moved around the plaza from customer to customer, translating and facilitating business deals. Harry also recommended his Uncle Ray's restaurant and steered tourists to Airbnb apartments that paid him a kickback. That was his gig, and he was good at it. Yet, every night he felt as if it was his last night in the seaside city of Cienfuegos.

After years of indoctrination and brainwashing as a young student on the inglorious Cuban revolution, its paltry party-line, and ongoing hero-worship of Comrade Fidel and his chaotic exploits, Harry was convinced that dreams were forbidden on the island.

Dreams were like weapons turned against Fidel's government, because dreams could lead to rebellion. Then, there would be freedom. For centuries, Cubans had been dreaming the dream of freedom. Harry couldn't wait any longer.

As was his custom at the start of working hours, he watched two old Cuban men sit at a table in front of the Sonrisa Bar, mouths closed, eyes downcast, slowly preparing for an evening of drinking. Harry saw them every night, staring at their beers as if waiting in anticipation for a horse race to begin. The race never started because no one was going anywhere in Cienfuegos. Except Harry.

A weathered, wrinkled, dark-skinned Cuban man nightly spread his cards on a wooden table preparing to play solitaire with uninterrupted steadiness. He sat in front of a tall, narrow faded green door to the far right of the Sonrisa's entrance. The cardplayer was a self-contained man who spoke to no one and displayed only a hint of body movement. He seemed to move into stillness without effort or thought. Harry swung his right leg over his beat-up bike and peddled to the old man's table. When he stopped, his brakes squeaked. The old man did not look up, continuing to lay out his cards with the precision of a skilled surgeon. When the cards were aligned exactly in a perfect row, the old man nodded his head in reverence as the game began in earnest. He flipped the first card over in his deck and spread his lips in a Mona Lisa smile. All was well as the solitary game began.

Harry pivoted to the opposite vantage point, to the colonial-style arches draped in the yellow half-tones and shadows from the lights above the arcade. Sturdy colonnades stood out in bas-relief as they supported the two-story structure, complete with wide mezzanines common in colonial architecture. He was pleased that Cienfuegos still retained the purity of his youth and was not some decaying barrio in Newark, New Jersey, where he once lived as a teenager, in what felt like another lifetime ago.

A young couple at the center of the plaza were fighting like birds of prey strategizing the next move. The woman pointed toward a restaurant centered between two colonnades in the far-right arcade of the plaza. The man dragged his feet to the outside of Manuel's restaurant and studied the menu. The woman flipped her chestnut mane and followed. A few exchanges took place, which did not turn out well, and the woman indignantly walked away. The man followed, passed her, and took control of their trajectory. The argument continued.

Harry recognized the situation. Travelers together too long, frustrated at coming to consensus every day, what to eat, where to go, how to get there.

It was Harry's moment. He peddled up the side of a long colonnade so as not to be seen. When he braked, the squeak was palpable. Timing was everything in a negotiation, but Harry calculated that taking a quick moment to fix his brake with spit and glue was important to his sales pitch. He got off his bike, looked at it in disgust, set down one knee on the stone floor, adjusted the bike chain and brought the back brake into alignment. Efficiency and speed just like those Formula One maintenance guys. All of thirty seconds and that included brushing off dirt from his shirt and pants. Not bad.

The couple looked around trying to decipher the noise. Harry circled the plaza and positioned himself away from the couple to take advantage of their confusion and indecision. The night was young. The hustle was on.

Harry knew his place in the hierarchy of the plaza. Even though he wasn't on top of the business pyramid, this Cuban national could negotiate with the best of the old pros. He had street smarts but wasn't arrogant about it. His cousin in Newark called it *street cred*. *And it's not fair you look like Leonardo DiCaprio, you lucky bastard, and you've got no fucking Cuban accent.* The dude from New Jersey got the advantage of people wanting to touch his coat of many colors. Mario used to say to him, *Shit, man, you don't even know you're studly the way you dress so casual with that GQ look and blue fucking eyes and blond mind-fucking hair.*

Harry positioned himself so he could hear snippets of the couple's conversation.

"What kind of food was on Manuel's menu?" asked the young lady as she watched her male companion trudge toward the Sonrisa, his Laker tee shirt clinging to his back with sweat, his shorts slung unevenly over his waist, and his sandals flopping loudly against his heels. He led with his head, shoulders slumped. Poor Silas. He kept promising to work out. Paula wished with all her heart that Silas would dress less like a twenty-year-old start-up tech geek and more like a thirty-year-old professional. She propelled herself toward him with her long, lanky legs and wondered why she stayed with him.

"The usual Cuban fare," said Silas. "Chicken, chicken, chicken. Rice. Plantains. Let's go back. We can split a dinner."

"I'm hungry," said Paula, with more than a tinge of resentment. "I want my own dinner for a change. We didn't have lunch. You said we didn't have time."

A small group of teenage boys and girls were huddled together on a circular concrete bench that surrounded a statue of José Martí, the infamous father of Cuban Independence. The boys waved their flip phones in the air to get Internet service, switching positions randomly, or walking around aimlessly determined to make phone contact.

"That must be their only entertainment," said Paula.

"That and drinking. Nothing to do at night around here." Silas lost interest and continued walking toward the Sonrisa.

"Hey! Wait up," said Paula as she ran to catch up and take hold of his arm. "You know how that bugs me. It's rude. Let's go back to the other restaurant and forget sharing a damn dinner for once. Stop being so cheap."

6

Harry circled the couple and stopped behind them. His brakes squeaked again.

"Sorry if I startled you, but are you looking for a place to eat?" asked Harry.

Paula laughed with surprise. "God, you must know you're a double for Leonardo DiCaprio, right?"

"I get that a lot," said Harry. "I saw you looking at Manuel's menu, but I've got a better suggestion. My Uncle Ray owns a restaurant on a side street next to the Sonrisa, and his food is amazing. And so is the singer, Alma. You've never heard a voice like that anywhere in Cuba, or anywhere else on earth."

Silas and Paula were speechless as they took in the handsome, blond, blue-eyed matinee idol straddling a beat-up bike. The resemblance to a young DiCaprio was a striking contradiction to the plaza backdrop. Or were they extras in his movie?

Silas said, "The brakes on your bike made the noise we heard."

"Sorry about that. I'm Harry Cisneros. Pleased to meet you." His English was crisp and delivered rapidly.

"Nice to meet you, too," Silas said. "I'm Silas Marner."

"The name of the book?" asked Harry with amusement.

"My mother thought it would be cool. The kidding never stopped."

Paula offered her hand enthusiastically. "I'm Paula McBride. Where in the world are you from? You have a New York or maybe a New Jersey accent. Of course, you know that. But, I mean, what are you doing in Cienfuegos?"

"I live here. I spent three years in New Jersey with an uncle and cousins when I was fourteen. I left the States when I was seventeen."

"Why did you return to Cuba?" asked Silas.

Harry scoped out the plaza like a slow-motion camera. He never missed anything that appeared in the landscape. Opportunities in the making. He believed in the probability that everyone chose his own destiny by making conscious decisions. When accidents happened, dreams fade. That only happened to him once. And it won't happen again.

"See those kids hanging in the center? Shades of my youth before I left for the U.S."

Paula wanted to find out everything about Harry. He seemed intelligent and aware of himself. He must be married to a beautiful and talented woman. She wanted to ask a million questions. She didn't want to be intrusive. Maybe they might eat together, extend their evening together, and she could get his full story.

Harry said, "My mom lives here."

Paula replied, "It's wonderful to meet a local."

"Let's go see your Uncle Ray," interjected Silas. "I'm starving."

Harry hopped on his bike and led the way through the plaza parallel to the elaborate grilles on the balconies with their refined metalwork. He slowed to notice the increased activity in the outside patio. A few local men stared at the American tourists as Harry led them up a hill adjacent to the plaza. Nothing new. Nightly occurrences.

Silas kept up with the bike, and Paula was jogging so as not to miss the conversation.

"I hear Cuba is changing," said Silas. "Things are getting better. What do you think?"

"Not fast enough." Harry deflected. "My Uncle's restaurant is the best in town, but it's a secret to tourists. Probably because it has no name and no sign. But I wouldn't steer you into something that's not great. I don't even get a kickback."

Paula looked around with excitement. "Where is it?"

"Here." Harry was standing in front of a faded black door that needed paint and a sign. He rapped on the door with his knuckles in three short bursts. A thin, young man in a white waiter's apron opened the door and motioned them inside. The waiter acknowledged Harry with a slight bow, then walked through the dining room and disappeared into the back of the restaurant.

The dining room was small with an ambient yellow light that created warmth and familiarity. It looked like a painting by the Flemish artist, Pieter Bruegel, depicting a lively and unsentimental scene that enticed the viewer to settle in. The beautiful Alma, with the translucent white skin of a china doll and black liquid eyes, was singing a lovely Spanish ballad, *Sabor A Mi*, on a small wooden stage just big enough for Alma and her accompanist, a man in his early sixties, tanned, wrinkled, with long, gnarly, veined hands so compromised it seemed impossible that he could play his acoustic guitar with forceful resonance. He echoed Alma's mezzo vocals with sonorous tones.

"Locals eat here. That should tell you something about Uncle Ray's place." Harry relaxed and listened to Alma with reverence, as did the rest of the patrons.

"The waiter will find you a seat. Uncle Ray never turns anyone away."

The same thin waiter returned and cleaned the table.

"Okay, you two. Have fun. Maybe see you later." Harry headed toward the front door. "Enjoy the food and music."

Alma was beautiful, straight out of the Romantic period. She had perfect pitch. Paula was taken away by her presence. She wondered if Uncle Ray was anything like Harry.

"I'm betting the food is terrific," said Silas as he sat at a small wooden table with bamboo place mats. "Even the chicken smells great."

The restaurant scene and Harry's working hours were just beginning. He had laser focus. Evenings in the plaza were unpredictable, but the translation work could be lucrative. Locals needed favors and tourists asked for help navigating Spanish. Less attractive were his friends who shilled for Harry's services and expected a piece of the action. Hands were always out in the plaza.

Harry steered clear of the large middle-aged man in a white Panama hat sitting at a table on the far-left side of the outdoor patio. He was a drunk and a mooch. As the man struggled to get up, his hat fell off his head. He bobbed and weaved to catch its descent. An elderly Cuban woman, heavily made up with apple red cheeks, sagging skin, and perfectly coifed bleach blonde hair, gingerly picked up the hat and flirtatiously gave it back to the man. He thanked her with a nod and nonchalantly walked into the bar. Her eyes flashed with embarrassment for the man's lack of attention. She nervously straightened her hair and looked around to see who noticed the man's slight. No one was looking. No one cared.

If Harry was anxious about the way his life was unfolding, he gave no sign of it. He didn't carry around bitterness like he did when he returned to Cuba. His mother needed him home to work and make money. He thought it wasn't fair and carried a chip on his shoulder. Defensive and angry. He still thought about Newark and his uncle and cousins. He wanted desperately to return even though he knew Newark was not the best of American cities. There must be a better U.S. city to live besides Newark, maybe Miami, where all the Cuban exiles created their own mini Havana.

Unrealized dreams. Impulsive choices.

He had a wife and child to support. And it has been ten years since Newark. His uncle was older, cousins out of the house. Who would sponsor his family? What would be the reason?

Harry could smell that freedom. He needed that freedom just as much as the Cubans who immigrated to the U.S. in the sixties and the Mariel boat people of the nineties. They had it right. The young and the old got on rafts, ramshackle watercrafts made of tires and oil barrels that could burst in the middle of the journey. The rich could afford speedboats or get student visas for their children. Some got lucky with fake marriages or conning a lonely American woman to marry. If Harry didn't have Kobe and Katrina, he would have taken that chance and headed for Miami on a makeshift boat a decade ago.

Juan Juan walked up to Harry as he leaned his bike against the Sonrisa. A squatty man, late twenties, with dark beady eyes, he handed Harry a beer with his short fat fingers. He was too tall to be considered a hobbit, but he could pass for one if he had bigger ears. Juan Juan and Harry grew up together, but they were polar opposites, not just physically, but how they did business in the plaza. Juan Juan was a slight of hand guy, secretive and a grinder, a *guido* as cousin Mario called a wannabe who hid behind aggressive masculinity and vanity. If Harry had been hustling in the plaza when he came back from Newark instead of working in the cigar factory, he would be top honcho in the plaza. It didn't matter. Juan Juan was a classic *poseur*.

"You're late." Juan Juan was dressed in a pressed striped shirt and creased denims. "Where's your manners?"

The blue horizontal stripes on Juan Juan's shirt made him appear even shorter. Harry shook his head with disgust, dug into his pocket, and gave Juan Juan a few kooks.

"No dollars?" Juan Juan asked. "I thought we talked about this." He took out a white handkerchief, blotted the sweat off his face, cleaned his hands, and slicked back his dark mane. He looked around the Sonrisa patio to see if anyone was watching him. No one noticed, but he pulled out a notebook anyway, trying to look business-like.

"No time to get them changed," said Harry.

Harry took a swig of beer and noticed that Ernesto, a local who liked to do deals in the plaza, waved him over to his table. Harry walked away from Juan Juan, who was busy counting the money. When he finished putting his money away, Juan Juan saw Harry presenting himself to Ernesto and three men.

Juan Juan casually strolled up to the table where Ernesto was conversing with several men who look liked extras from central casting for every Steven Seagal film.

"Hola, Ernesto," Juan Juan said with a forced smile. "What can Harry do for you tonight?"

"I've got this now," said Ernesto in Spanish. "Harry is my translator."

"No importa." Juan Juan slumped away. Harry looked after him, making sure he was out of earshot.

Wearing a large, white linen, rumpled suit that was bursting at the seams on his large frame, Ernesto had trouble keeping the sweat off his face. Water came down in tiny streams. He simultaneously attempted to dampen his forehead and get up from his rickety seat, but he had trouble balancing the two disparate actions. Harry came to his rescue and pulled up a chair from the table next to Ernesto's.

"Sit down, Harry. Let's do this. Juan Juan wastes my time. These are my American friends, and I need to understand what they want."

Two of the men staring at Harry were in their early thirties. They sported the latest hairstyle – close cropped on the sides, with enough hair left on the top to mold into a long peak, like twins, both wearing clothes that scream expensive. The third American was older by about twenty years. He didn't blink. His face resembled the craggy pockmarked face of a mountain. It never twitched. Perfect for poker. No tells. He bought his clothes from Armani Exchange.

"Hi, I'm Dieter," said one of the twins. Dieter shook Harry's hand. "This is Rudy." Rudy, the other twin, extended his hand to Harry. "And this is Roger," Dieter added without ceremony. There was still no movement on Roger's face and no handshake either.

"We're here to do investing in Cuba, and we need advice on the currency," said Roger. "You use the cucs for tourists, pesos for government workers, and no dollars allowed."

"We call them kooks. That's the way it's done." Harry had seen these simpletons operate before. They were on a fishing expedition. Scrounging for information to make a few bucks. They all sounded alike with flat voices and immovable masked faces.

Roger lit a cigarette, ready for a night of brainstorming.

"We need to find a way to get dollars, so we can move forward in our business ventures on the island. Tourists need to change their money, dollars or euros, into kooks. We want to be the ones to collect the dollars for future investments."

"Tourists can change their currency at the airport or any bank," replied Harry. "Dollars aren't trading instruments in Cuba, so I don't do business in Cuba with dollars. I deal in the tourist industry for translations, transportation, and restaurant recommendations. I'm sure Ernesto can recommend someone else."

"Can't trust just anyone," said Ernesto in Spanish. "I know you and you know me, and we can help these nice Americans."

"I don't have a contact," said Harry. "You know that."

The table went silent. Roger put out his cigarette and stood abruptly. The fashion twins took their cue from him and pushed their chairs away from the table.

Ernesto struggled to get up from his chair and gave up.

"Call me when you've got something," said Roger, avoiding Ernesto's wet hand.

Harry felt no slight as they walked inside the Sonrisa, Roger leading the way in what looked like a religious procession.

"That's not the way we do business," Ernesto lectured. "We give them a yes, even though we know it's a no. You are new at this. You're young, and you don't have the skills to conduct yourself in a business manner. These men want assurances. You need some tutoring, *Señor* Harry."

"Someday we'll do that," said Harry as he respectfully stood to leave the table.

"Sit down, Harry."

He plopped down as an elderly waiter cleaned the table, emptied the ashtray, and collected a few pesos left behind.

Harry knew the only way to trade in dollars outside the Cuban government was to own a business. Maybe those gringos had a good idea for an investment. Maybe it was shipping cargo to Santiago de Cuba's port. But there was nothing to take out of Cuba, not a decent thing to sell but sugar, nickel, cigars, and rum, but other countries made rum. The markup was negligible.

The tones of a soulful guitar filtered through the outside patio and brought a sense of peace to the patrons. Cuban music was like a lullaby that had soothed their souls since childhood. Without the distinct Cuban sound, they wouldn't know how to carry on with their lives.

"*Escúchame.*" Again, Ernesto attempted to get out of his chair. With great effort, he succeeded. "This isn't our business. We are interested in helping businessmen find a leg up in Cuba and receive a commission on trading currencies. The rest is up to them. It's about us getting the percentage."

"*Sí, El Señor.*"

Harry watched Ernesto navigate back to the Sonrisa. He had a soft spot for the big man. He was like a white whale that circled the tank, then retreated to observe. When Harry came back from Newark a punk kid with dreams, Ernesto listened and tempered his anger. *Take a back seat, kid* he used to say.

As usual, Harry wasn't offered a peso for sitting down with those idiots. No conversation of substance. That was not a back-seat he liked to take.

At the bottom of the hill, he saw Juan Juan arguing with Uncle Ray, who shouldn't have to be accosted by that lowlife on his customary one-hour break. The conversation wasn't going well. Juan Juan shilled for his restaurant, and most of the time he was a complete hard-ass, telling Ray he took tourists to his restaurant. Ray knew better.

Harry knew a loser when he saw one. He had an uncanny ability to spot the weakness. *You got the eye, his cousin Mario said. You're a natural spotter. A gift, my man.* Maybe he did and maybe he didn't, but Harry knew he wasn't a loser. Born into poverty like most Cubans, he was saved by luck, good looks, smarts, and a mother who accidently gave him the gift of three years in the States due to her inability to watch over her rebellious teenage son. He was a hustler, but soon, he was going to make a success. He was going to have a better future off the island. Harry may have nothing but a lemon of a bicycle to ride, but there was no way he would turn into Juan Juan.

This wasn't the first time Harry has been confronted with Cuban currency issues. Ernesto told him it was Fidel's monetary blundering that Cuba had two currencies. Cuban pesos were worthless because they weren't backed by an economy that amounted to anything. So, Fidel created a second currency for the tourists, the cucs, for the purpose of compatibility with dollars and euros. Rumors were that the puppet Raúl wanted to trade with only the peso to give economic stability to Cuba. Ernesto didn't believe it would ever happen. Neither did Harry. Money wouldn't trickle down to farmers to increase crops and animal production, to repair rundown dwellings, or to buy machinery, or to keep replenishing what was taken to market.

Ernesto told him it was no better in Havana for Cubans. They couldn't afford to fix up their two hundred and fifty square feet of squalor and stink in Habana Vieja. It was better to be a tourist in Cuba. They received the best food and accommodations. They saw glimpses of fifties glamour and drove around in cool, old cars that once signified prosperity. Forget those glitzy old cars. Cubans would rather drive a new Toyota.

Duty called. An American woman he knew well approached him. She was always good for business. He greeted her with a polite handshake. At fifty-five, Renata looked good despite a lopsided facelift she got in Buenos Aires. She left Argentina because she was humiliated by the outcome of her unfortunate surgery and fled to the island in despair. No one in Cuba noticed.

Renata was one of the lucky ones in Cienfuegos: she came with enough money from the States to buy a flat with two extra rooms. When Airbnb was allowed on the island, she seized the opportunity to make extra money. Harry recommended her place around the plaza. He got a kickback, but he'd do it anyway for her.

Without a word, Renata dug into her large, black leather purse and pulled out a crumpled letter. As Harry smoothed the paper out, she cast her eyes down, expecting the worst. Harry had been through this many times before with Renata. The news was never good. He stopped translating as she began to cry. She motioned to continue. He finished the letter and handed it back to her. She crumbled the letter, stuffed it back into her purse, and handed him a stack of kooks for his services.

"I can't take the money. Your *amor* left you without explaining. He was cruel to you. You deserve better than this *singao*. I can't take money for your sadness."

"*Por favor*, Harry, *por favor*," said Renata. "You are a good boy and you need this."

"Trades must be equal," said Harry. "This is a one-sided transaction, *mi amiga*. Next time be more careful with the man you keep. Everyone is looking for something."

A gang of young kids headed toward the outside patio. As they came closer to Harry and Renata, it was obvious they were drunk or on drugs, laughing, high-fiving, and cursing. Renata's body tightened. Harry stood to face off with them. They looked at him like he wasn't there and jostled each other with childish playfulness.

"Consiga joder de aquí. No tienes los cojones para pelearte conmigo."

Harry watched Renata walk away from the table, tentative steps, still carrying residual fear from the encounter with the menacing teenagers. They were harmless until they were drunk. A gang of drunks could upset the pecking order in the plaza. Hustlers told them to fuck off because they couldn't do business efficiently with gangs drumming loudly around the periphery of their territory. Hustlers worked fast, got what they could, and stuck it in their pockets. They paid the percentage to the couriers, barkeeps, and middlemen who fed their habit. It was a mafia aboveground or underground, covert, dishonest work, angling for opportunities that brought profit.

Cousin Mario explained the Mafia playbook. *You join a posse you got a piece of the action, like the low-life crawlers on the streets of Newark and New York who prey on the weak.*

Harry's playbook. He hustled for money and paid off his middlemen, but preying on the weak, taking advantage of bad circumstances, or representing yourself as someone you were not comes back to bite you in the ass.

Newark's playbook. Harry learned from his Uncle Reynaldo that greed and dishonesty were lodged in human nature, and ethical behavior was never going to be part of doing business in barrios, or on the gritty, crime-ridden streets of Newark, or in Cuba's free-for-all underground. Reynaldo was a better man than his brother, Harry's long-gone father. He waited ten years after the revolution to leave Cuba on a sturdy boat. He was an imposing figure who had the strength to read the future of Cuba.

The story of how Reynaldo went from Miami to Newark was vague. Even though he spoke minimal English, he sold his minor skills as a carpenter to a builder he met in Miami, and along with other Cubans, ended up in Newark. He married, raised a family in a barrio surrounded by crime, and worked his ass off to better their lives. His street smarts, fast-talking energy made him a natural for upward mobility. Harry admired his vision and focus, his ability to get what he wanted in life, to watch, wait, observe the opportunity to leave. Reynaldo said: *Have hope and believe in yourself. If you have courage and direction, your dreams will be fulfilled.*

CHAPTER 2
Trapped

Harry crossed in front of the Sonrisa and almost ran into Ernesto coming out, twins and Roger following dutifully. He dodged out of their way. Ernesto was their meal ticket, and the lemmings never strayed from their leader.

Up ahead, he saw a few young kids circling his bike. They were out too late. Most nights kids didn't have parents that supervised them. Street kids were on their own in Cuba, like he was before he left for Newark, roaming the streets of Cienfuegos, trying to hang with the boys who had cell phones or alcohol. What else was there to do?

The truth in Cuba was that an education didn't get a kid a job that earned him enough to fill his belly. There was no possibility but to hustle or work in a cigar factory. That summed up Harry's life. He wondered how many people his age felt detached from Cuba's fate – how many others planned to leave.

As Harry pulled his bike off the side wall of the building, Juan Juan headed toward him carrying two beers.

"Are we cool?"

"I don't like it when I can't deliver the goods for a potential client. And I don't like it when you harass my Uncle Ray. Stay the hell away from him."

Without waiting for a reply, Harry jogged over to his uncle where Paula and Silas were attempting to make themselves understood. He gave him a bear hug. Ray let him have his fun.

"That's the way I like it, *Tio*, with that big smile plastered across your face."

Uncle Ray told Harry he looked like he was the king around the plaza.

"I met your new friends."

Harry inferred an undertone of caution in Ray's voice. He didn't like Harry to get a big head in the plaza. He directed him to be more cautious with people.

"Hey, you two, how did you like the food?"

"Delicious," Silas said. "Tell your uncle I still couldn't see where he hid the kitchen. It's a mystery where the food was cooked."

"And Alma," said Paula. *"Me encanta."*

"Me voy, chico," said Uncle Ray as he hugged Harry.

Harry took the group to a nearby table, and a waiter immediately came over. He shook hands with the elderly waiter who paid his respects like a loyal serf to his landowner. They joked around for a few minutes, the waiter twirled his dark mustache for Harry's amusement, and Harry pretended to shadowbox with him. He ordered beers for everyone at the table.

Silas said, "Let us pay, Harry."

"No need. I get my beers free. It's all part of doing business around the plaza. How long will you be in Cienfuegos?"

"We're leaving tomorrow, which is too bad, because we like it here."

There was a commotion in the center of the plaza. One of the young boys climbed on the center statue to get a better look at a cell phone, and fell off the edge. He screamed in pain. Blood stained his jeans. The boys lifted him up on to the concrete bench.

Paula stood, trying to decide if she should help.

The waiter brought the beers and everyone drank as the waiter winked at Harry with a smile.

"Our Airbnb host is a doctor who stopped practicing medicine," said Paula as she sat back down. "What about all those other doctors who walk away from medicine?"

"There are still doctors committed to the old way," Harry responded. "But some people want a better life for themselves and their family. Airbnb came to Cuba, and the smart ones took advantage."

Harry knew the U.S. well enough to understand its economy. To keep it strong, you needed entrepreneurs. It was difficult for Americans to grasp a communist system that kept its citizens deprived of opportunities for business growth. But he couldn't say anything out in the open. No political talk, his Uncle Ray cautioned. It's not good for you because people are listening.

Harry asked, "What do you do, Silas?"

Silas responded that he was just another tech guy in the States trying to conquer the world.

Harry told him that Cuba could use a smart tech guy.

"What do you do, Paula?" asked Harry.

"I'm a wedding planner," said Paula.

He nodded with a polite smile and gave her a *thumbs up.*

The usual, *where are you going next, small chitchat.*

Trinidad, Camagüey, Santiago, back to Santa Clara, and then another two days in Havana. Silas pulled out an itinerary and studied it to check for accuracy.

"You're a pretty smart guy, Harry," said Paula. "You could be doing anything you want, including a tour leader."

"Let's not talk too much about how smart I am," Harry whispered. "If I was smart, I would have found a way off the island instead of going in circles in Cienfuegos."

Paula looked out over the plaza and saw that the boy who got injured was better.

"It's funny, but the young men all look similar – same hairstyles, shaved close on the sides and longer on the top, tight skinny jeans, and Nike tennis shoes."

"That's all they've got," said Harry. "It's their tribe, their cell, their counterfeit fashion. They get these ideas from the news."

"Where do they get news?" asked Silas. "I thought it was restricted."

"The hottest product is selling the news," said Harry. "It's part of the underground black market, along with movies, music, television shows, you name it."

Juan Juan leaned into the table and chimed in with a sense of authority. "There are Cubans with Wi-Fi connections that bootleg news from the U.S. and British information services."

Silas was intrigued. "Is this what rebellion looks like in Cuba?"

Juan Juan told them that he used to have a friend who moved to La Habana and picked up news tapes every day on his bike from a safe house. He distributed El Paquete to people who paid five pesos a month to listen to clips of global news. The tapes were the best way to say fuck you to the government.

While Harry found Paula and Silas to be a pleasant couple – maybe not the most compatible, because Paula seemed to be bored by Silas's presence – they were like most inquisitive tourists, eager to label the island a small child who wouldn't grow up.

The youth were the go-nowhere generation of Cuba. Kids clustered in every plaza in every city in Cuba, and they didn't give a damn about politics. A cell phone made the kids happy. Access to cheap alcohol, and life was better. The government didn't allow them to have smartphones. The only way to get one was to steal it off a tourist and that was certain jail. There were no prospects for a job, except maybe as a driver for tourists, or taking tickets at a museum desk. How many cigar factory jobs existed in a crumbling economy? If you wanted to survive, you joined the hustle.

"There's hardly enough juice for them to phone the States though, right?" asked Silas. "What's the government afraid of? Cuba needs a broadband infrastructure. Free Wi-Fi access. That's where you can make some money."

"Forever the entrepreneur," Paula cut in.

"Easy for you to say," said Harry. "The military wants no free speech or discussion of political issues. They take the lion's share of the people's money, and they'll do anything to keep it that way."

"I could figure out how to create an Internet structure," said Silas. "I need to see what's up with the grid."

"This is what Silas does," said Paula. "He figures out tech stuff out. Problem is there is no place to implement his creative ideas in the States. He won't move to a big city so we're stuck in a go-no-where suburb of Chicago. Not exactly Silicon Valley, is it, Silas?"

Harry noted Paula's slight to Silas and pivoted by asking if anyone wanted another beer. He waved to the waiter and indicated a round for the table.

"Hey, do you know who can change kooks for dollars in Cienfuegos?" Silas asked and jumped in to relate his experience in Havana with their driver who had a primitive but amazing exchange system going on. He told them not to change their dollars in the airport, and he could give them a better rate. He made a call and drove us to his apartment building. Silas assumed he called his wife, because she dropped a small bundle from the third floor. He caught it, took their dollars, and made the exchange. Sure enough. The rate was better than the airport.

"Do you remember the name of your driver?" asked Juan Juan. Harry shot him a look to push back.

"Ishmael," said Paula. "He worked for the owner of the Airbnb we stayed in while we were in Havana. He speaks English pretty well, too."

Juan Juan's got radar for guys stepping over the line. Harry knew he was going to ask him to keep an eye on Silas and Paula, get their number, find out how to get to Ishmael, push this driver for his contacts, and find out where he gets his kooks. Harry was already ahead of him. The currency exchange business was a long shot, but life was a long shot. That's what Uncle Reynaldo told him.

Harry was sure Silas knew more than he's telling because he was smart, a techie, and possibly had another agenda envisioning a bigger role for himself in Cuba. Techies talked about growing an empire. Maybe he wanted to find a way to build a tech infrastructure. If the U.S. kept its doors open with Cuba, maybe that would soon be possible.

Harry decided to walk Paula and Silas back to their Airbnb. Maybe he could meet the host. Another good connection.

Juan Juan watched them go, dropped his head, and took a deep breath. He didn't have to look up to know Ernesto was near. He heard the waddle and he smelled the stench. "Nice guys never win," Ernesto once told Juan Juan when a deal fell through.

Ernesto and his lame friends were trying to smuggle cargo out of the naval station near Punta Barloventó, and it was a fiasco. Hiding ammo in chicken feed was not the smartest way to get the contraband out. Chicken feed was porous. You could see the bullets right through it. At the last minute, he squashed the deal and escaped jail. The stench of that fuckup will never leave him.

"Get your boy on this," grumbled Ernesto. "There's more about this money exchange deal."

✳

After the visit with the Airbnb doctor, Harry jogged back to his bike ready to conquer the world. He considered the doctor's choices in his life as honorable and practical. Dr. Fernandez saw an opportunity to create a business that gave him more money and success than practicing medicine. That was his future.

Harry smelled the familiar odor of laundry soap as he entered his small, quiet, uncluttered apartment. He noticed a few pieces of his daughter's clothing drying on a chair pushed in to the living room table. He checked on Katrina, angelically sleeping on the sofa. He pulled a thin baby blue blanket over her shoulders. She stirred and stretched.

He didn't turn on a lamp, but instead undressed by the reflection of a high moon that peeked through the sliding glass door and reflected the grayness of the interior walls. He stripped down to his boxers and walked into the tiny galley kitchen. His gentle mood changed to petulance as he took a beer from the cream-colored, vintage seventies, pockmarked refrigerator. When open, the fridge door skimmed the counter on the opposite side. He slammed the door shut and drank greedily, almost finishing the bottle.

Kobe Cisneros watched her husband. She rubbed her thin hands together, bringing them to her nose, and taking a deep inhale. Harry stopped drinking and watched her. She looked like a thin reed in her white nightgown. She could topple over in a mild breeze blowing on the shore off a river. Her eyes were as dark as the circles under them, but he knew his wife was strong and smart. Too smart for a life that bound her to struggle.

"Did I wake you?" asked Harry. "I'm sorry."

"I heard the fridge door. You're later than usual."

"It was busy tonight, *mi amor*." He kissed her lightly on the cheek, and then impulsively embraced her. He released Kobe gently as if she might crack in half. He took another beer from the refrigerator and closed the door quietly.

"I hate it when you smell your hands."

"Even if I bleach or soak them in lye, the smell is in my nose."

Harry loved Kobe as passionately as he did when he met her at seventeen. She made his world right when he returned to Cuba, soothing his disappointment and anger that his dreams were not fulfilled. They made a comfortable home, living in their humble apartment sufficient for their needs, with a bedroom for them, a sofa that Katrina called her own at night, and a balcony facing the colonial Catedral de la Purísima Concepción.

Moonlight engulfed Harry as he opened the slider and walked onto the balcony. There were no stars, only a void inside the inky heavens. He drifted to a darker place in his soul. He was afraid he would not be free.

The touch of warm hands around his waist interrupted Harry's thoughts. Kobe led him into the bedroom, slid his boxers down to his ankles, and kissed him where he loved to be kissed. He picked her up and laid her on the bed. She rolled him over on his back, climbed on him, and continued to caress and massage his body. He wanted to let go, he wanted to release the emotional anxiety, but he didn't know where to hide the unrelenting hammer that pounded in his head. He knew one thing. Harry couldn't possibly leave without Kobe and Katrina.

"What are you going to do now, my sweet?" Kobe asked. "Are you going to conquer the world? Slay the dragon?"

"I need to find a dragon to slay, because I can't live here forever."

Kobe slid off his back and cuddled in the warmth of his body.

"We have ten years, *mi amor*. We have a happy life. *Es suficiente*."

"But it's not enough."

"Are we coming with you?"

"You are always coming with me in my dreams."

"Where are you going this time?"

"I'm thinking of getting into another business. I'm thinking about taking a risk as the only way to get us off the island."

"But if you can't find a way, what then?"

Harry told her he'd work to make life easier, get a bigger apartment where Katrina could have her own room. They might have a room big enough to walk around their bed. And Kobe wouldn't have to work at the cigar factory. Then he'd make enough money so they could leave.

Kobe heard this story every night. She went to sleep withHarry's dreams, woke up with his mumbling about getting in a boat and leaving the island. But, lately, Harry was changing, more verbal about his needs, more of a restless soul, a tormented man who rarely slept through the night. And Kobe felt a separation from her husband, because she had been learning to be more self-reflective and self-sufficient.

She also had dreams. The circumstances of her life gave her no rest. She was not going to work in the cigar factory for the rest of her life. And escaping to a foreign land was not something that would make her happy. What would make her happy was to be a teacher. That was her dream.

"And I'm hoping I don't go down a rabbit hole, hoping that I can climb up to ground level."

Kobe wanted to stop his thoughts, to silence the dreams, and bring him back to her. She caressed his chest, moved her hands toward his belly. He kissed her deeply, with hope and love. He found the inside of her thigh and stroked it gently. Overcome with emotion, Harry entered Kobe. He felt blissful as they exchanged their sexual energy, their passion, and promise.

Harry rolled onto his back sometime in the night. He heard the sweet sound of Kobe breathing and drifted off in thought. He remembered telling his Uncle Reynaldo in Newark that he never felt any attachment to Cuban culture or Cuban people. Reynaldo told him he was born an accidental Cuban. Harry begged to stay in the States, but his uncle had to comply with U.S. law. He was sent back to Cuba, to his mother, and to a life of acting out, getting into trouble, and getting a girl pregnant.

His mother asked him how could he be so careless? Getting a girl pregnant. *How could you? I raised you better.* But he knewRegina wanted him to stay in Cuba, to work in the cigar factory alongside her. He had to honor his mother with all her faults and failings, with all her strengths and mental keenness.

His father left Regina one day, took up with another woman who had been a revolutionary alongside Fidel before he entered La Habana, and stranded his wife without means. He was a bastard. A good-for-nothing. Good riddance. Harry met him once when he was four but didn't remember the encounter. He came to his mother's small apartment and wanted money. She told him to go to hell and never come back. She went to church again to pray for his death, and when he died, she stopped going to church. She hated politics and revolutions, paid no attention to government restrictions and rules, nor pontifical announcements. Harry thought she spit fire, carrying anger in her heart. It was a heavy burden.

During the night, Kobe woke up after a disturbing dream in which she overheard a conversation between Harry and Regina about how Kobe was a throw-away mutt produced by her crazy Chinese mother, Ping, who came to Cuba in the late eighties to live the communist dream. Regina said that Ping came to Cuba too late. The Soviet Union was gone and the Cuban people had to fend for themselves during "The Special Period." Everyone was living off sugar water and bumming cigarettes. Kobe remembers Regina saying that people were cutting off tags on clothing to patch up their shoes. The streets smelled of shit and garbage overflowed so that you couldn't walk a straight line down the street.

Harry stirred and embraced Kobe's body.

"Are you awake?" Harry whispered.

Kobe wrapped her arms around his body. "I had a dream."

"What dream?"

"About your mother talking bad about me to you." Kobe rested her head on Harry's chest. "Do you know the story about my father?"

"I thought he worked for the government in a low-level job, and you said he was a good man."

"Your mother was right," said Kobe. "I was a mutt. Before I was born, there was a knock on our door and a man from the water district asked my mother to fill out a survey about how much water she used because there was going to be water rationing. Ping asked the man inside and seduced him. He got her pregnant. That was my mother's plan. There was no love between them, but there was an agreement to raise me and help support my mother."

Harry kissed Kobe, brushing her lips with his tongue.

"Tell me the rest, *mi amor*."

"His name was César, and he barely scraped up enough food to feed us. He lived in a world of despair, sacrificing his food rations for us. He got thinner, losing almost a third of his body weight. His teeth fell out, and so did his hair. He finally died of starvation, along with thousands of others who could find no way to sustain life."

Harry sat up and pushed back against the wall.

Kobe remembered Ping holding her when she cried because she was hungry and cold and unable to walk to school. Ping worked day and night. She ate the rotten food and saved the better morsels for Kobe, so she could keep her strength up. Ping had shelter because César forged papers and left the house to her mother. That act of kindness saved their lives.

Kobe walked into the small bathroom and splashed water on her face. She stared at her reflection in the mirror, a blotchy face with loose skin. Chilled, she climbed back into bed.

"You remember I told you a letter addressed to my mother came one day, and the letter was written in bad Chinese, almost unreadable."

"It had Japanese words in the letter, but you skipped to the end and saw Satomi had signed it."

"My mother came into the kitchen and ripped the letter out of my hands, and told me I had no right to read her mail. She stomped around the tiny kitchen and screamed for a long time. She spread the letter out on a round table no bigger than an oil drum and read it. When she finished, she began to shake."

Later, Kobe learned Satomi was a friend she met on the boat from Colombia.

Harry reached for his wife and brought her close.

Kobe had to keep reminding herself that Satomi saved their lives. She wanted Ping to get out of La Habana and come to Cienfuegos and work. Kobe told her mother she didn't want to move to be near Satomi. She was jealous of her. It had always been just the two of them.

"Satomi was an angel sent from the heavens to save you and give life to you and your mother," Harry reminded her.

But Satomi couldn't help Ping with her pain because she insisted on it. While carrying a too heavy bundle of laundry up a steep hill, Ping fell backward and collapsed. Her thin spine broke in half, and she died instantly. Satomi told Kobe she thought Ping died on purpose. Ping's heart had broken decades before, maybe even on the boat to Cuba.

He kissed Kobe lightly and went to the living room to check on Katrina. He was proud she carried her mother's beauty. He returned to bed, put his arms around his wife's thin waist, and laid his head on her chest. He smelled her orange blossom skin.

"What rabbit hole are you going down?" she asked. "I'm frightened this time. I don't know if I have your courage."

Harry's breath deepened, and his body went limp.

She whispered, "Please don't risk us, mi amor." She curled up into the soft curve of his spine.

✣

Harry got up before sunrise, dressed, and gathered a few articles of clothing from the hall closet. He stuffed them in a backpack, as he watched Katrina sleeping on the couch, knees curled into her chest. Her stillness was a reminder that everything would work out for their family. Harry would come back from the rabbit hole with a plan to get to America. He bent down to listen to Katrina's breath. He closed the front door and slipped away into the crisp early morning air.

As he headed toward the bus station across the plaza and into the city streets at the end of town, the decision to leave Cienfuegos for La Habana and find this person named Ishmael was like a rocket shooting into the sky. The conversation with Dr. Fernandez the night before reinvigorated his resolve to leave. He and the Airbnb host talked about Cuba and its problems, its lack of answers to questions that have been endemic since the revolution. For some reason, Dr. Fernandez felt safe to express his opinions because Harry was young, of another generation, and not a communist.

"Who will succeed Raúl?" asked Harry.

"One of his military men, someone close to Raúl who will be his puppet," said Dr. Fernandez. "You see how nothing will improve in Cuba?"

In Dr. Fernandez's presence, Harry made his decision to go to La Habana in search of a solution that would change his life. The decision became a race, and the race became a mission.

Kobe watched Harry from the front window. She never questioned his love. She never doubted his actions. But this time, her fear was real, and Kobe understood her fear. She didn't want to take a journey to a foreign country to start over, and she didn't want to lose her husband. Harry missed his opportunity to go to the U.S. because she was pregnant with Katrina. She didn't trap him, but sometimes she wondered if he thought she did.

She had to resolve, as always, to make faith and trust her constant companion. And she needed distance to think about her future.

CHAPTER 3
The Beginning

arry walked up to the small, cramped bus station in Cien-fuegos before sunrise. He hadn't taken a bus in more than a year, when he accompanied Kobe and Katrina to Santiago de Cuba to visit Satomi and William. It was a happy time. They were off on a seaside vacation, laughing and feeling the lightness of life. It was a different kind of happiness that morning he took the bus to La Habana. It was the happiness of hope.

The station looked the same, run-down, but clean and appearing like it was open and ready for business. He bought a ticket from the unpleasant woman inside the ticket office. Dressed in a clean brown uniform, she barely looked up, but he sensed she hadn't left her seat since he saw her last. She would die in that beat-up seat. Three people lined up behind him. Irritable Cubans, half asleep, half committed to the ride to La Habana. As he waited for the bus to arrive, the stillness of the early morning air was refreshing. In an hour, the humidity would rise and take his breath away.

He settled in a window seat, ready to think about his pitch to Ishmael, trying not to get ahead of himself, staying present. Fatigue finally overtook him, and he was lulled to sleep by the motion of the bus. After a few hours, he awakened and felt some relief from the guilt of leaving Kobe and Katrina. He had a mission, a small opportunity, one phone call, to get a hearing with Ishmael in an urban city filled with people who suspect each other of trying to get the upper hand. He overheard conversations in the plaza, especially from Ernesto, about black-market crime in La Habana. State police were complicit, hiding in plain sight. The tourists didn't recognize the fear, but Cubans knew the island had another face.

✳

The bus station in La Habana was crowded like all bus stations in Cuba, and looked like it hadn't been cleaned since the end of the revolution. The smells of body odor and rank musk hung in the air. Harry smoothed out his shirt and made sure it was tucked into his pants. He noticed that most people, especially the women, were dressed in bright reds and greens, which gave off a festive air, but in contrast to Harry's gray shirt and black pants, the colors made him feel invisible.

With trepidation, Harry approached the bathrooms and imagined that they would be worse than toilets in India. He checked the men's room, but turned around as fast as a ballet dancer's pivot.

The bus station was a place of contact, connection, and even social interaction. While locals were swirling around trying to get in or out of La Habana, tourists were trying to figure out how the system worked. The young hustlers were everywhere trying to entice anyone standing to take a taxi, a bus, or a Cocotaxi. It was a three-ring circus. Harry heard of these Cocotaxi contraptions in Cienfuegos – they looked like auto rickshaws. A friendly driver approached him, and Harry decided to take the ride. A policeman stopped the transaction because the driver had no license. Annoyed, Harry jumped out of the cab. Someone grabbed his arm.

"*Oye, hombre,* where are you going so fast? Don't you have time for your friends?"

Harry turned around ready to face off with the voice, and saw Norm, Juan Juan's buddy in Cienfuegos. He was supposed to be a bartender at the Sonrisa, but he was rarely on the premises. Harry didn't know much about him, but he didn't trust him. Juan Juan's friends were always suspect.

Harry pulled his arm off Norm. "What the hell are you doing here? I haven't seen you forever."

"Don't get your boxers in knots," said Norm. "Just asking if you need a ride?" Norm twitched, sniffed, blinked, and straightened his dirty clothes on his tall, skinny body.

"You surprised me," Harry said. "Aren't you supposed to be pouring drinks at the Sonrisa? You're now independently wealthy and don't need money?"

"Funny," he said without expression. "No, I'm here for Juan Juan. We've got business in the big city."

"What kind of business? Following me kind of business?"

"You might call it that." Norm lit a cigarette and blew the smoke out of the side of his mouth.

"You can tell Juan Juan I don't need a bodyguard, and you can leave me the fuck alone."

Harry ditched Norm and hopped into the nearest taxi and told the driver to stop at the edge of the bus station. He didn't want to waste money taking a cab, besides he wanted to get the feel of the city on his own.

Outside the boundary of the station, the only entertainment in La Habana was watching a bus turning a corner, or counting the number of ubiquitous Che Guevara images that plaster the town. Only the tourists wore Che tee shirts because it was the cool thing to do. Che and his pretentious black beret were iconic. But tourists knew nothing about the history of Che and his relationship with Fidel. They saw the image of a handsome revolutionary, romanticizing his exploits. *Viva Cuba Libre!*

Visitors to Cuba didn't know that Che was only a stepping-stone to Fidel's geopolitical game with the Soviet Union. Harry could recite Che's story in his sleep. Every year, in every grade, he heard Che was the real revolutionary, as Fidel became more and more a politician after his pitiful ragtag army entered La Habana in 1959. Che was probably a better guerrilla fighter than a doctor, but he ended up doing Fidel's bidding as the president of the Cuban bank.

Harry never knew how Che talked his way out of being a banker, probably appealing to Fidel that his real passion was exporting communism to Zaire and the Congo, and Fidel went with that because Che was beginning to be a pain in the ass. In 1966, Che returned to Cuba and gathered a revolutionary army to replace the Bolivian government with Marxism. Che must have felt betrayed by Fidel when El Jefe didn't adequately supply him with men and materials in the mountains of Bolivia. Even so, Che never looked back. He was the real revolutionary.

As Harry began to wander through the plazas and streets on his way to the seawall, he saw potholed streets lined with depressing gray concrete, sterile buildings, and dilapidated structures that pass for homes. He felt a pull to return home to Kobe. Their beautiful little apartment, the opposite of the squalor he saw in the doorways of Habana Vieja. Most people were jobless, with no money to fix up their homes, no way to get out of squalor. Eight to ten people lived in three hundred square foot crumbling boxy houses that crammed narrow alleys. These places reeked of hopelessness. He was overwhelmed by Cuban acceptance of poverty and lack of food.

The military government knew damn well what failures they heaped upon the Cuban people over the last thirty years – a diet of rice and beans, a lack of decent infrastructure, empty shelves in stores. The government showed no sign that it would restore Cuba's former dignity anytime soon.

Harry was energized as he walked into the Plaza de la Revolution. Vintage cars were lined up in a carved-out center section of the boulevards with easy access for the tourists to gaze at the fifties classic cars. He spotted dozens of men polishing hubcaps and cleaning the interior of these prized automobiles, once owned by their fathers. This legacy turned out to be a way for their sons to make money off the tourist trade by giving customers an orgasmic car ride along Cuba's five-mile walled coastline, known as the Malecón.

The vintage car business was a startling juxtaposition of sights and sounds after seeing the poverty of Habana Vieja. The city was full of contradictions since Fidel let tourists come to the city at the end of the nineties. The best restaurants and food were for the tourists. Luxury foreign-owned hotels catered to the Europeans, Canadians, Australians, and Americans who traveled to Cuba on special visas.

Despite the glitzy bars and parks, all was not perfect in El Centro. Tree-lined boulevards jutted up against government buildings encased in black soot. Every building seemed to be under construction, and exhaust fumes could send a person to an early grave. Outside the plazas sprinkled throughout the city, La Habana's flat, dry landscape was monotonous until you got closer to the ocean and smelled the salty sea air.

Ernesto told Harry that in 2007 Raúl Castro established new employment rules that allowed more Cubans to own their own business. Ernesto was excited because business would flourish, and more money could be made. Harry hadn't fully understood what that would mean to Cuba's future economy, because he was too busy working in the cigar factory. When he began to hustle and wander the streets in Cienfuegos, Harry learned that Cuba had an underground economy. Maybe there would be hope for the Cubans.

The following year Ernesto was full of anger when he told Harry that Raúl was going to introduce another Cuban currency. *Idiota! Pendejo!* The new currency was for tourists and called cucs, but everyone started calling them kooks or chavitos. They were supposed to stabilize the tourist industry, but Ernesto said only the government would profit. Regular Cubans felt no change in their daily lives. Regular Cubans still had to marginally subsist.

The sun hadn't yet kissed the horizon before Harry reached the Malecón in the Central Habana neighborhood. Uncle Ray said the sea wall holding the Caribbean coastline at bay was beautiful. *¡Que linda!* But he was not prepared to see the magnificent sight of the Cuban diaspora. The incandescent energy of light reflecting on the water's edge was breathtaking. The sea was calm – flat as piss on a plate – as his Uncle Ray always said. Every now and then the stillness of the night was penetrated by the roaring exhaust sounds that came from vintage cars driving along the Malecón. Further down the wall, Harry heard faint squeals of drunken laughter coming from a group of boys and girls sitting along the wall. A few couples came out of a bar across the road singing *Guantanamera* with lyrics from a poem by José Martí. It was Cuba's most patriotic song, but Harry's feelings for Cuba left him long ago. He stoically looked out over the calm ocean waters and knew he must call Ishmael. He had no idea what came after.

The enslavement of human beings
Is the great shame of the world!

❋

The moment Harry left, Kobe felt the need for family comfort, a soft touch of friendship and warm hugs. She had been tired for months, feeling nauseous after her shift at the cigar factory. Harry's quick and surprising departure had shaken her. She called Satomi and asked if she could visit her in Santiago de Cuba. The sound of Satomi's warm voice was music to her ears as she encouraged Kobe to visit with Katrina. It would be a good time because there would not be any guests for several days. Kobe never thought to tell Satomi how long she would stay. She didn't think she would be staying more than four days, yet she was not completely confident of that decision. Yet, she already made the decision never to return to the cigar factory.

The cigar factory was an odious place to work. Poisonous. The unending smell of death. Hands dry and withering. Crooked spine. Falling neck. Headaches. Stomach and leg cramps from sitting too long. Eyes blurring. Nose running. No social discourse. No music. Mind-numbing repetition. This was Kobe's rabbit hole. Harry might go down his rabbit hole, but Kobe had been living inside her rabbit hole for ten years. It was time to emerge into the sunlight.

After she finished packing and getting Katrina ready for the journey, they walked along the same city streets that Harry took that very morning. But she and Katrina were taking another bus, another path to Santiago de Cuba. Her second home. She longed to see the beauty of Santiago's harbor, the colorful boats bobbing and weaving in the waters a half mile from the shore, tankers moving like turtles from miles away ebbing toward the commercial side of the port.

It was more than a daylong bus ride from Cienfuegos to Santiago, but Kobe didn't mind, because she needed to rest and think, hoping to find work that she enjoyed doing. She knew that ten hours, six days a week, being engulfed by tobacco smells, had adversely affected her health. She worried about long-term illness. No statistics bore that out, but Cuba was never forthcoming with data when it came to tobacco workers. She pushed future thoughts of poor health out of her mind and felt blessed that Katrina was an independent, resourceful, and creative ten-year-old.

❊

Harry sat on the Malecón wall until the sun fully set into the sea. He remembered seeing Norm pass by in a slick 1959 red Pontiac convertible earlier in the day. That's Juan Juan's dirty work. Putting a tail on him. Norm at the bus station aggressively grabbing his arm.

Harry called Kobe after he got off the bus to assure her everything was fine, but there was no answer. He had a hunch she went to visit Satomi and called her when he arrived at the Malecón. Her voice was calm and measured. Harry told her he loved her more than anything, from the beginning to the end of their journey. The sun was setting and the sounds of the waves were peaceful, and he wished they were together.

Kobe did not respond to his affectionate words. She seemed distant and hesitant in her speech. What happened on the way to Santiago? Something was wrong, but he would figure it out later. He had more pressing issues.

Several times he tried to call Ishmael, but he was unsure of how to approach him. He wasn't familiar enough with the money changing business to ask good questions. He knew he needed to be backed by a steady stream of money, details about how it worked, percentages, payoffs. There was much he didn't know.

Harry's mind was speeding as he tried to make sense of what was going on in La Habana. After wandering the city, it was clear that the Cuban government depended on the underground economy to provide the essentials for subsistence to the general population – eggs, sugar, toilet paper – because state-owned markets and ration shops had little on their shelves. Cubans didn't get a ration of meat in a year. The best of everything – food, lodgings, luxuries – went to the military and tourists.

And then there were drugs, bootleg, DVDs, and prostitution running through the underground black market. It was laughable that the government advertised that the island had no criminal activities. Every Cuban knew it was a lie. If you had a good eye and were curious, you could see transactions happening in the outskirts of the city, or on the beach, or in Habana Vieja, but tourists weren't aware that La Habana was as dirty as any big city in the U.S. They only saw the obvious charm of an iconic island city.

In Newark, the gangs ran black markets in drugs, prostitution, and extortion. All you needed were a few good friends to direct you to the right places, or give you the right phone numbers. In Cuba, it was ordinary people who found ways and means to supply what Cubans wanted. It was a racket, but a necessary one for an unstable government with no discernible economic plan, for governments that were not connected to capitalism, for a technologically challenged economy.

Harry dialed Ishmael.

The female voice on the phone identified herself as Ishmael's wife, and she would give Ishmael his message. Harry gave out his phone number, and indicated he didn't care how late her husband called. Before he hung up, he heard children laughing on the sidewalks behind him.

The moon was going behind the clouds, but Harry could still see men in mesh tank tops catching fish from almost invisible lines that stretched from coils firmly hinged on the sidewalk.

✳

Satomi and William's house was on a hill about a half mile inland from the Santiago port. Kobe and Katrina trudged up the hill as the sun was setting. Humidity engulfed them as they climbed the steep steps to the front door. Before Kobe knocked, she turned to gaze at the port, past the docked boats, to the calmness of the Caribbean.

At the door, Satomi embraced Kobe and Katrina with overly tight hugs. The three of them – travelers and hostess – giggled gleefully. Kobe thought Satomi looked better than she had in years. She used to be thin and wan, but her partner, William, full of energy and life, gave her a deeper sense of personal happiness. Her dark hair was piled up on her head in a topknot, and she looked like a Japanese doll that had come alive.

"My, Katrina, you have grown so tall," said Satomi.

The new construction in the front living room didn't exist the last time Kobe visited, but it was taking shape, creating a setting of comfort for the Airbnb guests.

"I'm sorry about mess. Guille is doing remodeling himself and takes forever. Front room will be good when finished. When our guests leave, you will take room off upstairs balcony so you can see beautiful ocean views while you stay in Santiago."

"Guests? I thought you said it was good to come."

"After I talked to you, the guests come too early, and I didn't call you with disappointment. You were on bus, and there was no turn-around, and I want you here, because it's important for you to come here to rest. You sounded tired on the phone. Don't worry. Guille is getting you room for two or three nights, and you can come back after they leave. Let me pour you tea."

Kobe was worried. "I hope I'm not causing trouble."

"Oh, my darling, you are not. You will come back here."

"I'm worried about Harry."

"How is he?"

Kobe told her he was in La Habana working on something new. She doesn't know what, but everything he does is for getting us off the island.

Satomi took Kobe's hands, turned them over, studied the lines, and smelled them.

"How long will you stay with us?"

"I don't know," said Kobe. "Nothing is the same for me and Harry, I think."

"You cannot do this anymore, precious one," said Satomi. "It's not just smell. It's color. Yellow brown. It's deep lines. They are old hands already. How is breathing?"

Kobe started to cry softly.

"Mamma, mamma," Katrina said with alarm hugging her mother. "Don't cry. Everything will be all right. Daddy will be home soon."

Kobe recovered her composure. "I'm fine, little one. Go out to see the ocean and come back with some beautiful shells."

Katrina reluctantly opened the door, but instinctively looked back to her mother, then to Satomi who smiled with assurance that all would be well.

"Harry is always going off for a few days, and I think he works for clients, but this time I'm not sure because it happened fast. And he's never been to La Habana before."

Satomi prepared tea in the small, freshly painted kitchen. It had little counter space, so food and drinks were prepared on the eating table. Tofu and vegetables, potato peels, and a kettle full of hot water were cooking on the stove.

As she steeped the tea, Satomi was worried because she suspected Harry's work might be illegal, because most business in Cuba went through the black market. If you wanted to make profit on the island, you went against laws. Guille told her they would have no house without finding a way around city rules. And she remembered clearly that Harry told Guille he once bribed a city official for Uncle Ray, and Guille did the same for their building permits.

William stopped on the staircase.

"Harry was different this time when he left," said Kobe. "He said things I never heard before. About a rabbit hole. I imagine it is dangerous because he didn't say when he would be back."

William's infectious smile preceded his entrance into the kitchen and lightened the mood. Although, William was a powerfully built man, his face was soft and yielding. He pulled a towel from a kitchen drawer and wiped the sweat off his muscular, black body.

"It's good to see you, Guille," said Kobe. "You look good. I guess it's all that physical work Satomi has you doing."

"She keeps me busy every day," he told Kobe. "Please forgive me, but our guests were confused on dates and showed up early. We just found out, but don't worry because I found a place for you to stay until they leave."

"Gracias, mi amigo."

"I tell you not to worry about this," said William. "We're having an all veggie dinner tonight for you. Your favorite."

"Guille, let's have some wine to celebrate Kobe being here with us tonight."

"Good idea, *mi amor.*"

Kobe leaving in the middle of the week made no sense to Satomi unless she planned to stay with them while Harry was in La Habana. Or unless she wasn't going back to Cienfuegos at all. Kobe would find her own mind soon enough.

❄

Dizzy and dehydrated, Harry hopped off the wall, walked a half-mile down the strand, and crossed the street to a small café so hidden he almost missed the entrance. He slipped inside into the dim light, and saw the outer edges of poverty. The place had three tables, each dotted with water spots and streaks of red salsa, three rickety chairs around each table, and a small bar in a space the size of a queen-size bed. Inside this hovel, the proprietor eked out a meager existence. He needed only basic food and a roof. Healthy food, nutritious food that filled the stomach, was only for the tourists in Cuba.

"Cotado?" asked Harry.

The owner put a chipped cup and saucer on the table in front of Harry and poured dark, thick coffee from a dented steel pot from decades ago. It smelled like the bottom of an oilcan.

The old man's hands were gnarled with deep veins. As he shuffled back to the kitchen, Harry noticed his hunched back and bad hips. The filthy apron that hung on his bony frame was threadbare. He was the proprietor, running the small restaurant on his own, working himself to death for a government that took sixty percent of what he made. If he did business in the black market, he could get caught, go to jail, and he'd never work again.

This was the face of communism attempting to collaborate with capitalism in Cuba. Everyone with a job robbed something or someone. The hombre who worked in the sugar industry stole sugar so he could resell it. The lady who worked with textiles stole thread so that she could make her own clothes. But this viejo had nothing to rob.

Harry's phone rang. He put a few kooks on the table and walked out into the muggy night.

"Me llamo Harry Cisneros. Eres Ishmael?" There was silence on the other end. "I'm a friend of Silas, one of your customers."

"Silas, you say?" asked Ishmael. There was an awkward pause. The voice on the other end of the phone was deep and rough. "You are interested in changing money, *hombre*, right?"

"Exactamente. Can you meet me either tonight or tomorrow at a cafe of your choice?"

Harry's phone call threw Ishmael off because he rarely heard from strangers asking about his money exchanging business. He kept his activities under the radar. He was a cautious, secretive man. But for some reason, instinct maybe, he agreed to meet Harry the next morning at the Hotel Sevilla at eight o'clock sharp. The meeting would be short. He was on the move.

Harry jogged to the wall with a sense of relief. The cloud moved swiftly in the wind and revealed a sky splashed with bright stars. He paid no attention to what was around him until he smelled marijuana. *Norm.* Appearing like a ghost in the night.

"I hardly recognized you," Harry said. "You blend perfectly into the darkness of the night."

"Singao." Norm spit out the words with venom. "What did I ever do to you?"

"Nothing," said Harry. "That's the point. We have no history. What does Juan Juan expect you to find? That I'm pimping for someone, that I'm being taken care of by a rich woman? There's nothing here."

Norm was tired and being high didn't help him focus. He'd been up for twenty-four hours and recoiled at being drilled down by Harry. Harry thought he was so smart because he spoke English and strutted around like he owned the plaza. Juan Juan thought he was a hotshot because he got him jobs, but the joke was on Juan Juan because Harry owned his ass. He was smarter, quicker, and he was *The Leo*. That fat pig burned through money like he was flush, but he was just another hustler.

"I don't know," said Norm, slurring his speech. "I don't know what he's up to. I'm just following you and reporting."

"What have you got so far then? *Nada*. Don't waste my time."

"I'm sticking to you like shit on a blanket," mumbled Norm.

"Before you do, take a shower. You stink."

Harry walked away from Norm, disgusted that he even got into a pissing contest with him. He needed a place to sleep. Maybe on the beach, under the stars, with the sound of lapping waves rolling up on the sand.

Sleeping on the beach at the Malecón didn't provide the comfort Harry expected. After he dragged his feet through the sand, he found a spot near a boulder where he spread out his jacket and laid down his head. During the night, he was awakened by city noises – horns honking, cars revving on the boulevard, planes roaring in the sky. As soon as he fell asleep, a drunk tried to pick his pocket. He wrestled him to the ground and the vagrant passed out. Not having a knife for protection in a big city was an occupational hazard. Why would La Habana be any different from Newark?

CHAPTER 4
Follow the Money

Ishmael clicked off his cell. His baby son crying in the bedroom intruded on his thoughts about the stranger's call. Anna, weary from the long day of washing laundry for neighbors, came into the small living room, held the baby and swayed her body to keep him calm.

He sunk deep into the shabby, brown sofa, set his head back, and closed his eyes. He often slept on the couch when the baby cried. He traded off with his daughter for the sofa. Ariana loved to sleep in the living room because the night lights shined through the slider window, and she imagined the fairies were surrounding her and watching over her when she slept. Her father saw no fantastical visions. Ishmael would never entertain a fantasy. He was a hard-wired realist.

Anna made sure her husband was sleeping, then returned to their bedroom and carefully laid her weightless body on the bed-spread next to her daughter, eyes open, staring at the ceiling, listening to the sounds of young Cuban men laughing and drinking in the streets outside their apartment, resigned to her fate. She tried to will herself to sleep, but sleep was elusive.

Ishmael awakened before sunrise, walked into the small rectangular kitchen, and opened the refrigerator. It started to hum, breaking the stillness of the room. The refrigerator was a constant reminder of his substandard living.

He smiled to himself, remembering how he stole the fridge more than two years ago from a fifth-floor apartment he was remodeling located at the end of Calle Prado near the Malecón. Stealing the refrigerator was on his mind as he was about to pick up an Airbnb customer and drive her to the airport for his boss. She was a pissed-off Colombian woman who rented the apartment next door to the apartment he was remodeling and complained about the loud noise he was making.

"I heard your footsteps," said the Colombian woman as she opened the door to her apartment and dropped her bags next to Ishmael for him to carry.

He picked up the bags and followed her down the hallway. She was pretty for a middle-aged woman, but her resting bitch face erased any beauty she might possess.

"Next time Paco puts me in a dump like this, I'm going to call the narcos on him," she said angrily. "The apartment stinks."

"He has other buildings in good locations," countered Ishmael in a fake accommodating voice.

"Just take me to the airport. I'm not in the mood for excuses. And the elevator doesn't work either. *Mierda*."

"I hope his other buildings look better than this dump," she said opening her purse. "Can you exchange kooks for dollars?"

"I'm better at changing dollars for kooks."

"Do you have enough to change, say, 200 kooks?" she asked.

"I can manage that," replied Ishmael as he called his wife.

On the ride to his apartment, the *Señora* talked shit on the phone to someone about Cuba. Some of what she said was true. Habana Vieja was falling down, smelly, not much use to the Cuban government except to house its poorest. But the good news was that a tourist could find an upscale bar or restaurant tucked away on the penthouse floor in a well-preserved building from the mid-fifties. The eateries served the the newest Cuban cuisine with the best chefs. A few tourist books pointed out the name of these hidden gems; otherwise, tourists had to get the name from hotel porters. *You can't find any damn sign outside the buildings, but there is great action in the upscale bars.* She was still seething mad, as he pulled up to the curb in front of his apartment building. She gave him a stack of kooks. He stood on the sidewalk, and seconds later, a bundle dropped down.

"Nice work," said the *Señora*, with razor-like observation. "You've got business talent. Don't let it go to waste."

Several days later, Ishmael went back with two friends to help him move the piece of shit refrigerator to his apartment. He was in luck. The elevator was working.

Ishmael was pissed that he had to give up his dollars for cucs to the demanding Colombian woman. He was in the dollar business, but he had to placate that sullen, unpleasant woman. She might return one day.

He started to make coffee and decided against it since he was meeting this friend of Silas. He didn't figure Silas was the kind of guy who easily gave up information, but nothing surprised him. He called for the early morning meeting at the Sevilla so that he could be available to Paco for extra work.

He'd been changing money for about a year, but he still needed Paco to pay him for his driving, expediting his work details, running crews, and keeping his name in circulation. His boss wasn't the richest real estate owner, but neither was he on the bottom rung of slum landlords in Centro Habana. Slums didn't interest him. Nobody paid on time. The building on Prado was the most upscale of his properties, closest to the Malecón, but the apartments needed repairs. If Paco wanted to get the highest rate for rooms in that building, he had to do a better, faster job of remodeling.

From the outside, the Hotel Sevilla needed a facelift, and the interior should have been remodeled ten years before. The once pristine Moroccan design had long since faded, and the hotel's reputation for being the jewel of Centro Habana had long since evaporated as European and Asian developers brought money into the city and rich foreign tourists demanded a classier, more luxurious hotel. Preferably, one that had Internet service.

Ishmael was casually dressed in shades of blue, a crisply ironed shirt, dark hair slicked back with pomade. His body was still in good shape for his age. Thirty-five was still young, but he wished he could work out at a gym. He was always as professional as possible with everyone he met, especially with American tourists. He was aware that making a good impression, speaking good English, and using American idioms and slang when appropriate translates to better tips and more driving jobs. Word of mouth counts in the tourist business, and he gave out his cards with a telephone number, hoping to enlarge his connections. Every tourist who looked at his card asked about his email address. They didn't know yet that Cuba had no reliable broadband service, except in upscale hotels.

Blonde, blue eyed, nervous. Damn! Ishmael's breakfast date looked like Leonard DiCaprio. *It was a mind fuck.*

Harry was sitting at a table in the open-air dining room designated for morning coffee or afternoon drinks. The tables and chairs were well-worn and the cushions needed replacing, but tourists didn't mind its shabby, vintage look because the Sevilla had Cuban history in its bones. The idea of the hotel and its dramatic past was more appealing than the decorative plants that lined both sides of the entrance. Although at eye level the room was unpretentious verging on boring, Harry felt the warm morning light through the apex of the cathedral ceiling window arch that cast a golden patina across the ochre tile floor.

"Thanks for meeting me," said Harry as he shook Ishmael's hand.

"Let me get a cortado before we begin." Ishmael waved to the waiter and pointed to Harry's cup, indicating a refill. "Now I can focus on you and Silas."

Ishmael was in charge of this meeting.

"I met him in Cienfuegos with Paula and that's where he told me about how you met in La Habana."

"They stayed in the apartment of my employer on Calle Prado. Nice couple. I hung out with them when they were here."

The waiter put down a cup and saucer in front of Ishmael and poured a cortado. He took his time refilling Harry's cup, listening and waiting for a bit of gossip. Ishmael waved him away. Harry told Ishmael that he met a Cuban names Ernesto in Plaza Martí who asked him if he could change money. He was with some Americans who were interested in exchanging kooks for dollars. That wasn't his business. He's a translator, worked in a cigar factory.

"You shouldn't talk in front of anyone about business, *hombre*," Ishmael said with authority as his eyes indicated the waiter. "The walls have ears. Let's get to it. What kind of information are you looking to learn from me?"

"You work with tourists and they need kooks, so they give you dollars or euros."

"And I gave Silas kooks for those dollars. What's your point?"

"I'm interested in that business. My question is, how do I get kooks so I can do that kind of exchange? Dollars have to come from somewhere."

"Where have you been?" asked Ishmael.

He told Harry that everybody wanted dollars in today's economy. This was the year that kooks were supposed to go out of business, only pesos from now on. Or at least, that's what the puppet Raúl said. But he needed to convince the military that it was to their advantage. Greedy bastards. If that happened, pesos would be the only currency exchange for Cubans and for tourists.

"When is this happening?" asked Harry, thinking Ishmael's English is darn good, despite the obvious slight Cuban accent.

"Chico, wake up. Are you kidding? You don't get news in Cienfuegos? You definitely need an education in the Cuban economy."

Ishmael stood in anticipation of leaving abruptly.

"*Espera,*" said Harry. "Por favor. *Digame.* Why does everyone want dollars? I don't get it."

Ishmael sat back down. "Look, you are a real pain in the ass."

He told Harry that everyone, every hustler on the street knew more than he did about what's going on in La Habana. The currency crisis started about seventy-five feet into Cuba. He picked up an Airbnb renter for his boss a few months ago, and the tourist told him that he got off the plane and asked a woman dressed like the military how to change money. Dollars for kooks. She walked him past the cadeca, but the tourist stopped and got in a long cue at the money exchange kiosk. The airport lady took his arm and pulled him out of the line. At the top of the escalator, she told him that the government exchange rate was seventy kooks for a hundred. She offered him ninety kooks for a hundred and that was a good deal for him. The customer told her he wanted to change five hundred dollars, and she didn't bat an eye. She told him to go into the men's room and count out his money. She would do the same in the ladies' room.

The waiter returned, wide-eyed and hovering over the table, coffeepot in hand, listening to the story Ishmael was telling. He obsequiously topped off Ishmael's coffee, and again he dismissed him with a dirty look. Some of the patrons in the room were distracted by two birds in the apex of the ceiling having a loud fight for territorial space. Either that or they were mating. The waiter joined the gawking group and watched the birds.

"Go on," said Harry. "This is just getting interesting."

"The guy told me the men's bathroom was crawling with people, including staff, doing deals. He went into a stall, without light or toilet paper, and he laid out the money in twenties on his knees. He heard a knock on the stall and the lady was ready to make the exchange. He was still counting. She left, but after two minutes she barged in. They made an exchange. He was freaking out."

"What does she do with the dollars?" Harry asked.

Ishmael said she took a few bucks off the top of the transaction, her percentage, and she gave the rest of the dollars to her boss, and her boss gave her back a stack of kooks equal to the dollars she gave him. She then went back to the airport and repeated the same transactions. It was a whole underground system of money exchange. In the future, puppet Raúl wanted all transactions to be in pesos, and it would be a fairer system for Cubans – a higher standard of living and a cure for what ails the Cuban economy.

"Maybe it will and maybe it won't," said Harry. "But using two currencies is inefficient and confusing to tourists."

For a decade, Ishmael had known that tourism was the gold standard in Cuba, and dealing in two currencies was a loser's game for Raul and the gang. The only winners were the money changers. He wanted Cuba to look good to the outside world and not like the third world country it was. Cuba's history didn't have anything to show for itself, except its eternal hangover from the revolution.

Ishmael asked, "Where do you come by that accent? New York?"

"New Jersey."

"Yeah, yeah, you could be used for better purposes than a translator for pathetic, lonely women in Cienfuegos."

"Did you just think of that, or have you read my resume?" Harry smiled and realized that he liked Ishmael, despite his gruff manner. He reminded him of a cousin in Newark, always with a sweet smile on his tanned face, despite his muscular bearing and casual body language. One of the popular guys in the gang. Harry could learn the ropes from him.

"I'm thinking that's why you're here, *hombre*. You want to follow the money."

"I want to leave Cuba. Get back to the States. If that means following the money, shit, yes. I never should have come back after Jersey."

"Let me guess: your *mamacita* was pulling those strings." Ishmael abruptly stood up. "These chairs are ass killers. Come on. I've got some place to go, and you're coming with me."

✳

They drove through the well-kept neighborhood in Vedado, inIshmael's 1988 Moskvitch 2141. The avenues were broad with an architectural mix of fifties high-rises and crumbling neoclassical mansions. They drove around Calle 23, La Habana's most well-known street, through the first few blocks of the most famous, wealthiest section – La Rampa.

Ishmael lit a cigarette, inhaled, and exhaled a bomb of smoke out the driver's side window.

"Do you know how the black market works?" Ishmael asked.

"I know what the black market is, but I don't know the ins and outs. I came back from Jersey and right away got a job in a cigar factory to please my mother."

"Yeah, yeah, that was your story, but let it go. That's not who you are anymore." Ishmael took another hit on his cigarette. "Do you ever get the smell of tobacco out of your hands?"

"I smell it mostly at night. Wakes me up. Sometimes during the day, I get a whiff and almost vomit. My wife smells tobacco on her hands all the time. Maybe the smell is there. Maybe it isn't. Does it matter?

"*Mira*, the orderly transition from kooks to pesos won't be easy," said Ishmael. "But anyone who can hoard dollars, make deals within the black market, or private business, or government contracts will make money. And because no one is a communist anymore, it's easier than ever. You should know that, because you're on the streets, even if it's the streets of go-nowhere Cienfuegos."

Ishmael was right about his go-nowhere situation in Cienfuegos. From what he was observing in La Rampa and elsewhere, he needed a change of scenery. His city was beautiful and charming, but there was little opportunity and excitement for making something of himself. Rolling through in the tidy tree-lined streets, he admired the well-groomed, single-family medium-size homes complete with green lawns. Traffic was light and the streets were quiet – a must in an area where there was a modicum of wealth. Harry wanted to be in this money game, and he hoped Ishmael could hook him up.

"You need volume," said Harry. "I don't have a large base to work with."

"You ain't got no Rolodex, *mon*."

Ishmael told Harry that the Cuban government wasn't concerned about what goes on in the black market. The police didn't bother them. Plus, Raul didn't want to see the Cubans go on a starvation diet again. El Jefe let the military police take their cut when the government issued a license to a number of private businesses and taxed them. That's about a fifth of the workers, about five million, who were moving into private businesses. Underground capitalism made the government money.

"That's some powerful shit."

"What are you smoking, Ishmael?" asked Harry. "I don't want to bust your dreams, but Cuba isn't going to change. They're never going to a one-currency economy."

"Maybe it will and maybe it won't, but this is all I got for now. I need a cup of coffee. We're in La Rampa now. These rich barrios have some damn rich coffee."

Ishmael pulled up to a corner store that needed a paint job. The red color had faded to orange. From the street, Harry saw the dumpsters at the corner. The stray cats were having a field day fighting over scraps of food. Several skateboarders crossed in front of the coffee shop on their way to a park at the end of the block.

"So much for what rich looks like in Cuba."

"Don't get smart. I'll buy you a cup."

Harry sat down at a corner table and watched Ishmael buy two cups of coffee. He liked Ishmael's confidence, energy, and hard edge. They were about the same age, and he was a hell of a cut above his Cienfuegos crew.

A few well-dressed customers noticed the two men confidently walk through the door. The young lady sitting behind Harry nervously giggled. He heard "Leonardo" and more laughter. An older man got up and shuffled to the cash register.

Ishmael placed the cups on the wobbly table and flirtatiously smiled at the women behind Harry. He told Harry he found the money exchange business when he was traveling around town and met a man who owned a restaurant in Centro Habana. This was his first contact. Both he and his partner provided a steady source of kooks for him, and he delivered dollars to them. He made five percent on the exchange, but he kept his job with Paco because of the tourist connections.

"How many years have you been doing this?"

"Damn, I can't remember how many years I've been hustling for a decent job, but working for Paco is the closest I've come. I used to fix cars. Hell, everyone in La Habana is a mechanic. The repairs I do in Paco's buildings pay the rent, along with Anna's job. She takes in laundry. Paco saved my ass when he offered me a job as a part-time manager for his ten properties, then as a permanent driver for his growing Airbnb business. That's when Anna quit cleaning houses and washing dishes for a bootleg restaurant. Get this. It serves food on a neighbor's driveway. Three-course meals. I shit you not."

Ishmael pulled up to the curb in front of his modest apartment building on the fringes of the Vedado neighborhood. He looked up at the third floor and remembered he didn't call Anna ahead of time to tell her he was coming home.

"You seem like a good kid, *hombre*. You're naïve, and I like that. You don't bullshit. You want to get off the island, and I want to make good money to support my family and have a better life. We both want what's best for us."

"Come upstairs. I want you to meet my wife and kids."

They entered the small apartment. The smell of cooking oil was stronger than the smell of laundry soap.

"*Mi amor,* I've brought Harry home," Ishmael called out. Ishmael picked up a few toys off the couch and indicated that Harry should sit. "I'm working on getting a new sofa."

Harry was impressed with the freshly painted walls, although a few sofa springs were stabbing him in the butt.

"Your place is in good shape."

Ishmael proudly told Harry he paid a few kooks to two of Paco's workers to paint his place, so the apartment looked clean.

The photos of children on the wall made the living room feel personal and lived in. A vase of flowers made an old coffee table look new.

"About how many exchanges do you have to do to make decent money with five percent commission? Do you skim off the top?"

"We've got time for that later," bristled Ishmael. "The restaurant guys are always looking for smart kids who know how to work the dollar market."

Anna entered the living room and extended her hand to Harry. "*Con mucho gusto,* Harry," she said. "I'm sorry but my little one is asleep. The oldest one is at school."

"Igualmente." Harry noticed how tired Anna looked. "I've got a daughter who is ten years old. They grow up fast."

"Take a look at my fridge," said Ishmael. "Piece of shit."

The faded white refrigerator took up too much room. Harry had the same problem. The door almost hit the counter.

"I have a love-hate relationship with this white elephant," he said. "Do you know anything about refrigerators? Does your mother own one?"

Harry couldn't imagine that his mother ever saw a refrigerator this size. She had an icebox she plugged into the wall that barely cooled food. The only good thing about that piece of shit was that it didn't make a grinding noise.

"The point is the fifties fridges are crap, but buying a full-size model means coming up with 910.65 kooks or 22,675 pesos. You know how long it takes a guy like us – the average Cuban grunt – to earn that much. Shit, four years. If you're going to buy a refrigerator, you can't pay for it with kooks. You have to buy with pesos, and that means carrying it in a truck."

"What if a year from now, the peso still isn't stabilized?" asked Harry. "If there's inflation, the purchasing power of the peso isn't what it should be."

"Then it's going to be all about hoarding dollars to hedge against the economy taking another nosedive."

"No one to save Cuba but Cuba," Harry mumbled.

"Cuba should start by making deals with the U.S. in technology. Get an Internet grid up. Cuba's ninety miles away from the U.S. and they can't make that happen. But Obama's coming today. It's 2016, and this is our definition of progress."

"It smells of desperation," said Harry.

"I'll tell you about desperations. Would you believe that there is a business on the streets of La Habana for selling dead light bulbs?"

"You're shitting me," laughed Harry.

Ishmael explained that it started with one *hombre* and a light bulb. He took his good light bulb from his living room and screwed a dead one in. He told his landlord he needed a new bulb. Bingo. The landlord came by and he gave him a new light bulb for free. Now he had two good light bulbs. He sold one of the good light bulbs. It was a daisy chain.

But Ishmael pointed out that when Anna dropped down kooks for him when he needed to exchange them for dollars, it wasn't much different. For a little more money, Ishmael was doing the same crazy shit.

"She never missed a drop. I couldn't do it without her."

�֍

Ishmael pulled up to the corner of Calle Industria and Calle Barcelona in the Habana Vieja district. They walked to a faded black door, barely visible from the street. No identifiable name.

Harry entered Kirpan, a stylish, chic restaurant that existed for the tourists and for wealthy Cubans. The decor was a combination of Singapore kitsch and Indonesian panache. Banquet seating with faded flowered coverlets hugged the walls on two sides. High-quality metal tables and chairs were neatly set in the middle of the restaurant filling out the dining area. The modern service bar stood against the wall opposite the front door. The effect was minimalist. No mirrors or glitzy lighting.

Harry admired the slightly raised balcony, four steps above the main dining room, that expanded the architectural space. There were a few tables on the upstairs balcony scattered in front of a colorful wall with Asian art and saris. About a hundred old and colorful ties hung over the balcony railing. Harry couldn't take his eyes off the ties. They dazzled him and brought the restaurant to life.

Ishmael motioned Harry to come over to the bar. He shook hands with a tall, lean, and elegant man. His beige and brown linen clothes from Neiman Marcus fit perfectly on his frame. He looked like a 21st century male model, but with a devastating smile instead of a pout. Green eyes and wavy brown hair gave him his Ronald Colman movie-star looks, right out of the forties.

"Greetings and salutations," said the man with a slight French accent.

"Charles Duran, I'd like you to meet Harry Cisneros." The men shook hands. "Where can we talk?"

"Let's go up to the balcony. The cleaning crew has left." Charles led the way upstairs, his French cologne and charm floating behind him.

"What's the story behind the ties?" asked Harry.

Charles explained that the co-owner, his partner, collected ties. He lived in the States, but he thought they looked better withKirpan's decor rather than in his home in Silicon Valley.

Harry was expressionless and Ishmael was pleased. He felt in charge because he didn't bring just any man around Kirpan to work the money exchange business. He saw that Harry was all business, focused, and that made him a winner.

"How much did Ishmael tell you, Harry?" asked Charles.

"The bare skeleton of the business. Changing dollars for kooks with tourists."

"In this establishment, dollars are the game, and it's a hustle like everything else," said Charles. "What kind of background do you have in the money exchange business?"

Harry told him he had no experience, but he was a quick study. And he was motivated.

Charles motioned to a worker behind the bar to bring over three bottles of beer.

"What motivates you, Harry?" asked Charles. "You don't strike me as someone who would go the distance with this line of work."

"Probably not. I want to get off the island, but I need money to set it up. I'm not hanging around some immigration center in the Keys or Little Habana in Miami eating shit food. When I land, I want to land with money."

"Anger is good, but anger is not my business model. My partner is a tech entrepreneur, but he likes Havana and sees opportunity. You might change your mind once you see how the business works. But you made a good start when you got out of Cienfuegos."

"Why did you come to Cuba?" asked Harry.

"New investments. The power of the underground economy is the real power in Cuba, even though Fidel and the military want you to think differently."

"What kinds of investments? Private or government?"

The waiter set down three bottles of beer and obsequiously returned behind the bar.

Charles knew this kid was smart from the moment he saw him. Intelligent eyes. Mentally focused. Ishmael found a twin, but maybe better. He had stamina, a devastating appearance, and a compelling reason to change course. He was no Hamlet. He wouldn't dither. He had killer focus.

Charles told Harry that many Cuban business people have to look around, watch their backs, and find the spots to do business confidently. The scramble for dollars was a race. They recruited and developed a very close-knit group of Cubans to operate an outside ground game. All runners spoke English, worked on commission, and kept a low profile when working the plazas or with tourists. If you have a problem, report to Ishmael and stay away from Kirpan.

Ishmael clarified. "We collect dollars. We don't have to know what Charles and Justin do with them."

Harry sensed the lecture was not over. Charles aimed to put him in the right frame of mind for his work with Kirpan. Charles was a cool figure with piercing eyes and laser focus.

"Why do you want dollars?" asked Harry.

"For the time, we need dollars for future investment in infrastructure, broadband, cellular systems."

Harry nodded and took a sip of beer. Guitar music filtered into the restaurant from a speaker.

"Do you ever have live music at Kirpan?" asked Harry.

Charles took a breath and looked around the restaurant.

"We tried it once or twice, but people didn't pay much attention."

Harry walked around the upper balcony and peered out into the restaurant several steps below.

"Just don't bullshit me and keep a low profile," encouraged Charles. "Do something else as a cover, like Ishmael does. Be a driver or a ticket taker at a museum."

Ishmael interrupted. "I got a better idea. I'll ask my boss to put him on maintenance and cleanup at his buildings. That way, I can keep an eye out for him, help him along until he gets a better understanding of handling the details of the money."

Don't discuss commissions. No negotiations. If Ishmael knew more, he wasn't telling.

CHAPTER 5
On the Ground

Kobe and Katrina settled into a quiet room above a cozy restaurant called Los Lobos. It was located in the most attractive section in Santiago de Cuba, a beauty shop on one side and a laundry on the other side. The neighborhood was located high on a hill that had a splendid view of the harbor. The plaza was called Parque Céspedes and locals and tourists flocked to its lively environs to get the gossip or to sit in contemplation on benches under shortleaf fig trees.

Guille knew the owner of the restaurant, a man named Ezra, who was gentle and welcoming. He told Guille that they could stay for as long as they needed. In fact, he needed a waitress to help out, and Kobe was welcome to take the job. In the blink of an eye, Kobe and Katrina settled in and took to the neighborhood in a few days. Kobe even found a school to put Katrina in thanks to Ezra knowing everyone in the area. They made friends, helped out Ezra, and Kobe began to smile.

It was only at night that Kobe thought of her life, how she ended up in a room above a restaurant. It felt as if she had started her life from the beginning. She was waking up.

Before he left for La Habana, Kobe never worried about Harry leaving for several days at a time. She never asked him where he goes, what he did, or if there was going to be a change in their lives. Belief and trust were everything in a marriage. Harry's steadfastness, how he stood by her when she told him she was pregnant, and how they worked overtime at the cigar factory to make a home before the baby arrived – all of it gave her hope and confidence that their lives would be happy.

Kobe wasn't bitter when Harry's mother was disappointed that her son got a Chinese-Cuban mutt pregnant. Regina put her feelings aside and offered to take care of Katrina while Harry and Kobe worked.

When Regina got too frail to take care of Katrina, Satomi stepped in and raised her until she entered school. Dear Satomi, always ready with a smile, even though her life hadn't been easy. She adopted everyone: Ping, Regina, Harry, Katrina, Kobe. She was the energy around their lives for years. Satomi was a mother figure for Kobe. When Satomi felt she needed to move on, she courageously went on another journey.

Kobe was happy when Satomi moved from Cienfuegos to Santiago de Cuba and met William, a man with many life skills, among them the ability to love Satomi. They were ready for life together, ready to piece together a spiritual covenant that involved trust, love, and commitment. Satomi loved William, her Guille, like she loved no other. They worked together every day to make their house an Airbnb treasure and everyone said they were the most wonderful hosts in Santiago.

Kobe missed Satomi's guidance and strength. Growing up, she had little nurturing from her mother. Ping didn't have a belief system or spiritual insight. Her mother was like a leaf blown by the wind, running toward a populist culture without a sense of self, she embraced communism without knowing why and was disappointed that it ever had a chance to impact her life the way she dreamt it would. Kobe did not want her life to be an imitation of what her mother experienced. She needed Satomi to guide her gently on a new path. She had no desire to live on dreams. *Like her husband.*

Charles Duran rarely left his restaurant. Kirpan was his base of operations. Located on Calle Industria, it was difficult to find because its obscure front door flattened against the dark building's façade, effectively making it invisible. That began Kirpan's mystery. The reputation of this trendy and popular restaurant was built on word of mouth with the locals and the tourists. The clever owners knew that Cubans would never suspect that their jewel of an eatery was a cover for a lucrative business operation.

Charles remembered vividly when he met his partner, Justin Levitt, in 2007, at the end of his first year as head chef at Paladar Los Amigos. Cuban cuisine was not distinctive or trendy, but Charles wanted to make a statement with his menus and build a reputation. He was trying to combine some of his own French recipes with the traditional Cuban fare of rice and beans. Justin came into the restaurant and was so impressed with the twisting and blending of flavors that he asked to talk to the chef. It didn't take long for Charles and Justin to develop a friendship. Justin changed the direction of his life.

He remembered Justin talking about the ever-growing waistlines of the Cubans, as well as the ever-growing want for things. With kiosks on the corners rapidly multiplying, Charles envisioned that a more successful Cuban economy was underway. Justin told Charles that if he kept his eyes open and paid attention to logistics, they could open a restaurant in Havana and make money. Charles bragged to Justin that he ran three restaurants in Paris. He didn't tell him they all failed. *Too much competition. Paris was crowded with restaurants. Costs too high. No money to advertise.* After the third restaurant closed, his brother made him an offer he couldn't refuse. Paul came back from a vacation in Cuba, and saw tourism was vigorous and restaurants were proliferating. He told Charles to go to Havana and open a restaurant, then bet him one thousand dollars that he would also fail. He gave Charles money to try his hand as chef and wished him luck. No strings attached.

Both men shared their dream of designing a trendy establishment that served a unique blend of Indonesian and Cuban dishes. Charles understood that this successful man from Silicon Valley, this flashy and manicured dresser, was a man with a mission. They needed each other – the artist and the financier – and together they launched Kirpan, a modern, chic restaurant in Centro Habana. It was an instant hit.

In the convening years, Justin and Charles made plans for another, more lucrative business venture that had nothing to do with food. Again, Justin needed Charles. He was French and that made the difference.

✛

Harry worked long hours for Ishmael, or rather, for Paco Canto. To his credit, Paco owned some good real estate in La Habana. His Airbnbs were located in popular districts in the city and apartments were usually rented. Ishmael tried to teach him the trades when he was not driving Paco's customers, but Harry had little aptitude for skilled labor.

The best part of Harry's job was that he had free shelter in a cubbyhole of an apartment behind the Prado building where he worked. The place was so small, he could barely turn around. The kitchen was the size of a bathtub. The toilet was in the corner of the living room. It was a janitor's hideaway. The worst of his situation was that he missed Kobe and Katrina, the warmth shared, the way they took care to raise Katrina, a special little girl with bright brown eyes and straight, black, silky hair.

Before he took the job at the Prado apartment building, he called Kobe again at Satomi's, and she explained to him that there was a mix-up with the Airbnb reservation. Guille found her a place to stay in the meantime. Satomi explained that Kobe liked her new living arrangements and planned to spend more time in Santiago. Harry pleaded with her to ask Kobe to call him the next time she visited.

"Did she quit her job?" asked Harry.

"She will let you know."

Jazz played over the speakers in Kirpan as Harry entered. Louis Armstrong was crooning. The atmosphere was calming, like the music. He was getting used to the Kirpan vibe. Charles was busy cleaning up behind the bar.

"How are you doing, Harry?" Charles asked without looking up at Harry.

"I'm not a carpenter or a plumber or an electrician, so I guess it's not going well," Harry said, trying to hide the dirt under his fingernails. "I'm not suited for working in the trades." And not used to feeling embarrassed by my appearance.

Charles looked at him with an air of ingenuous concern and told him not to be ashamed of his lack of trade skills. Patience in everything.

"I want to go out into the streets and plazas where the tourists are."

"You can do it on your own time," Charles responded. "You need to have a job that pays until you are ready to put your sales skills to work. Suck it up for now."

Harry picked up the bundle of kooks without regarding Charles. Singao. Charles pulled out an accounting book behind the bar and buried his head into the numbers.

Three percent, even five percent commission was never going to get Harry to the States. It would take him years to build up enough capital. He decided to work the plazas at night and up his game, do some translating, and get to be known as someone who changes money.

Harry discovered he wasn't going to be successful getting translation gigs without a Juan Juan as a go-between. The little weasel did have his place in his world. But Cienfuegos was a small town, and he didn't need much to cover the bills. Harry had to be patient or get lucky.

He was distracted by missing Kobe, and he was disturbed about her silence. He called Satomi again, and she told him Kobe and Katrina would be over for dinner the following evening. Three days later, Kobe called. She didn't sound like herself. She was more distant than the last conversation. She quit her job, put Katrina in a local school, and wasn't returning to Cienfuegos until Harry found his way back to her. It was to be expected. He left and he resolved to make it right.

✛

A few days later, on balmy spring evening, Harry took off work early, stole a bike, and rode to the Plaza de la Catedral in Habana Vieja. The bike was in the back of one of Paco's buildings for weeks. It was a piece of shit, but Harry built bikes from parts faster than he could fix an overflowing toilet. Everyone in Cuba repaired bikes, cars, and motorbikes. It was the national pastime. With lightning speed, he fixed the stray bike with spare parts he found in Ishmael's auto repair shop, including a rearview mirror. The bike rode like new. What he needed most was a heavy-duty lock, and Ishmael picked up one in his friend's chop shop. Ask, and Ishmael found it.

As usual, the plaza was packed with tourists. A trio was playing Cuban music in the corner of the restaurant entrance. Yet another version of *Guantanamera*. Tourists and locals couldn't get enough of this song as they swayed to the music. Most tables had tall funnels of beer in the center. He listened for English being spoken.

A table of Americans were boisterously drinking from double-size glass funnels of beer. The Canadians were quiet and reserved. A few Germans were hanging around, mutely observing the scene. He heard one of them butchering English as he spoke to a waiter. Russian accents were so thick they gave themselves away with a broad distortion of vowels. Uncle Ray was right. His ability at language might be his best talent.

"Hey, you! Leo! Leonardo DiCaprio! You look like him. Do you speak English?" asked a fat man chewing through a Cohiba cigar. Harry never saw a man so fat. He was wearing a food stained purple shirt and baggy sweatpants. Massive sweat rings covered his armpits. Repulsed, he shuffled to the table.

Harry answered the Fat Man in his finest New Jersey accent. "Of course, I speak English," he told the foul-smelling Russian.

The Russian broke out into loud laughter, got up with effort and hugged him. Harry reeled back, wanting to vomit.

"Well, I'll be damned. It's Leonardo DiCaprio as I live and breathe. Sit down, kid. I got a proposition for you. I'm Victor with a V. Kostroff is my last name."

The Fat Man was Russian but doing a fair good job trying to sound like an American born in Brooklyn. He wanted Harry to exchange one thousand dollars for kooks. He didn't care about the exchange rate. He also wanted him to sit at the table and translate for him.

Harry noticed a Cuban man wearing a dark suit and an executive tie sitting at the table. It looked like a business meeting. Three weeks in La Habana and he found a mark. He excused himself from the table and made a call to Ishmael.

"Can you change a thousand dollars into kooks?" asked Harry. "Do you have that much?"

"I'll get it," Ishmael whispered into the phone. "See you in about an hour in the vestibule of San Cristobal de la Habana Catedral. Stall. Do some fancy translations."

Harry did more than some fancy translation. He was in on Victor's deal by the end of the hour. He knew chapter and verse about how this crazy New York Russian émigré was going to invest in the Cuban water and sanitation system. Next up, he wanted to build an Internet network around the island. Victor was excited, sometimes agitated when he talked business. He gave up any pretense of being a native English speaker every third sentence.

The Russian émigré from New York wanted to keep Harry on as a translator. Bingo. He was finally certain that he was not going down the rabbit hole yet, despite the Fat Man's appearance as the evil twin of the devil. Best of all, he knew he could stop doing building maintenance and get Paco off his ass. Victor was Harry's way back to clean fingernails.

"What you got, Leo? Ants in your pants?" Victor laughed at his own joke and choked on the cigar smoke engulfing his face. "Is there a problem?"

Harry waved the cigar smoke away from his face. It was the smell of poverty.

"Time to collect your cucs." As Harry excused himself from the table, he noticed a huge fake gold Rolex watch on Victor's fat wrist. Skateboard size. He turned too fast and knocked Victor's white ivory cane off the back of his chair.

Harry apologized, carefully picked up the expensive walking stick, set it straight on the side of the chair, and jogged to the far end of the plaza. He entered the dimness of the vestibule in the Cristobal de la Habana Catedral. It took him time to adjust his eyes. Evening light shone through the dull color of the stainglass windows to reveal Ishmael dipping his fingers in the holy water and making the sign of the cross. He reverently genuflected on the cold marble floor, bowed his head, lips moving, and made another sign of the cross. Harry never figured Ishmael for someone who had religious beliefs. Most Cubans left the church decades ago. Fidel and communism stripped the light out of Catholicism. All that was left were the beautiful Spanish cathedrals and their towering gold-leaf baroque altars, posing eminently in the apse of the church.

"It's a fitting meeting place," said Ishmael. "Means God is watching over us."

"The church must be blessing the transaction," added Harry, feeling like he was baptized in by Victor.

"What's going on?" asked Ishmael.

Harry told Ishmael about the offer to interpret for the New York businessman, Victor Kostroff.

"He's in water and sanitation," said Harry. "He wants to get the Internet up and running."

"You mean hacking. Russian technology is good for weaponizing information. It's a good cover for something else."

"What does it matter? I don't want to work for Paco anymore."

"That's fine, but when this Russian asshole rides his high horse out of La Habana, you're on your own for work. These guys come and go and have a million ideas to con the Cubans, but the Cubans are just as smart as the New York Jews or the Russian mafia. We can smell double deals before they happen."

"Yeah, okay, but maybe you get me my own stash of kooks. Wouldn't that be easier?"

"I'll look into it. I have to run it by Charles."

Over the next few weeks, Harry was schooled into the business of water and sanitation with Victor Kostroff. He was privy to a few elementary plans for developing broadband connection, either through towers or underground, boring Harry to distraction. And the translations were punishing. Night and day, Harry was at Victor's side in his apartment on the Prado. The lawyers spoke English, but their Russian accents and bad sentence structure exposed their lack of English competency. Victor was pleased by Harry's position and patted him on the back for correcting the lawyers and keeping important conversations flowing.

"I love this kid!" Victor yelled. "I love my Leo."

To keep up with Victor's money demands, Harry decided to go to Charles directly for his kooks. Ishmael didn't check back with him on his request to have his own stash. Maybe Ishmael was reluctant to let Harry fly on his own, because he controlled the money operation in the plazas and insisted that everyone report to him. But Harry considered Victor a job, and he wanted his commissions without interference.

❋

Late one evening, after customers left and waiters were cleaning up, Harry entered Kirpan. There was no sign of Charles, but there was another exquisitely dressed man in his forties counting receipts behind the bar.

"May I help you?" Harry couldn't pin down his regional accent. His tone was flat. Maybe he came from California or the Mid-West. It felt perfectly articulated.

The man's presence was stronger, more intelligent than Charles. Harry was about to meet the brains behind Kirpan.

"I'm looking for Charles Duran."

"You have business with him?"

"Yes," responded Harry. "I'm Harry Cisneros."

"I'm Justin Levitt. What can I do for you?"

Justin, the partner in the shadows with eyes that could cut an apple in half. He knew everything that went on with Charles and Kirpan, and he already knew Harry. It was a surreal moment. Justin seemed to be graced with unnatural stillness.

"I came to talk to Charles about getting my own line of kooks. I'm working for a guy who's doing business with some Cubans, and he changes money every other day. Ishmael is sometimes hard to find."

"Nice get. How'd you land it?"

"I'm doing full-time translations for this guy until his business is up and running. His Cuban lawyers can't put an English sentence together."

The man wore a poker face. He reminded Harry of a sniper hunting his enemy.

Justin straightened the bottles behind the bar with limited motion and complete attention and intensity before he poured Harry a Cristal beer. And then he poured a measured shot for himself out of an eleven-year-old Ron Santiago de Cuba rum.

"I suppose you might want to know what he's up to," said Harry.

"Go on."

"He tells me he's into water and sanitation in La Habana," confided Harry. "His next move is to develop a cellular system."

"Are they Russians?"

"What makes you say that?"

"Keep tabs on him."

"Huge man. Huge appetite."

"Everything in La Habana takes years to accomplish," said Justin. His eyes turned to slits. "Infrastructure is shabby. Too many government layers. Your Victor might have a good investment in the long run, but everything turns to shit when a Russian does business with Cuba. Don't tell him that. Watch with patience."

Harry met the boss. Justin Levitt, commander in chief.

"I suppose everyone tells you that your looks and brains can take you places."

Silence. Was he dismissed?

Justin was in a different league. The man was impressive. Not just his intelligence, but the leanness of his speech, how he questioned and phrased his thought. He was a cut above Charles. And Harry could learn much from this man of substance.

He heard a banging noise on the balcony and saw that a workman dropped a speaker that was supposed to be secured to the wall. Justin poured a beer, took it over to the workman. His boss reminded him of his uncle in New Jersey – the way he reached out and took care of people.

When Justin returned to the bar, Harry asked him if he would invest in other businesses in Cuba.

"It's a sinkhole."

Justin knew Harry was no pushover because Charles briefed him – smart, aggressive, curious, someone they could use. Time to throw out a compelling story.

"Anything else?"

"Charles said you worked in Silicon Valley."

"People ask me if I'm in love with Cuba, and I tell them I was in love with Cuba in the old days, but now I'm simply compulsively interested in its opportunities."

"What did you do in Silicon Valley?" asked Harry.

"Software engineer for Intel, but more money could be made in start-ups. I created a merchant app for small businesses, got it funded, then sold it for more money than I could ever spend. Charles came along and the rest is Kirpan."

"I don't get the Cuban appeal," said Harry. He understood the appeal very well, but wanted to continue the conversation.

Justin filled in his relationship with Cuba. When he was twenty-two, he fell in love with everything Cuban, because he believed in the mythology of the past, believed in its magic. On his first trip to Cuba, he explored every city on the island, talked to hundreds of people, learned all things pertaining to the revolution, and, most importantly, gathered information about the Cuban underground economy. He saw the potential of an economic boom over the next ten years. Cubans were exhausted from decades of not having enough to eat and living in a failed infrastructure. They felt betrayed and adrift without a plan for the future.

"Do you believe in alchemy?" asked Justin.

"I'm not sure what you mean."

Justin poured himself another shot of rum. Harry waited for him to add more to his trip down memory lane, but further details were not forthcoming – what transpired during the years in the States, other travels, family ties, education. Justin's memoir was predictable and rehearsed.

"Charles will let Ishmael know about the change."

He stood outside in the bright sunlight and held his face toward the sky. Harry met the big man and he was impressed. Justin gave him his version of Cuban economic history, and he wasn't interested in Harry's opinion. He was the boss. Charles worked for him.

Before he started his evening's business, Harry wanted to check out Justin Levitt on the Internet. Not having a smartphone was a problem. He biked to Hotel Parque Central in the rich touristy section of town, swerving through the busy streets, almost getting hit by a 1952 black Buick.

He spotted an American sitting on a bench at the edge of the plaza. The man was frantically conducting business on his phone, running his hands through his spikey salt and pepper hair. Harry could spot an über-cool, Silicon Valley techie a mile away. Navy cargo shorts, Bob Marley tee shirt, beige leather clogs, scruffy beard, and the obligatory two-hundred-dollar Peaky Blinders haircut. He waited for a pause in the man's manic movements on his smartphone before striding confidently toward him. The man intuitively looked up at Harry and smiled. He was ready for shock and awe.

"Jeez, kid, you look like Leonardo."

"I know. I get that all the time," said Harry in his with a disarming smile and his New Jersey accent. "I kind of give it up to DiCaprio for my luck."

"Are you Cuban or what?"

"I live here, but I studied in the States," responded Harry. "I noticed you have a smartphone. Cubans aren't allowed to have them. We can get an old flip phone if we're lucky."

"That's terrible. Either Cuba has no Internet or it's sporadic, like in Hotel Parque Central. Why the hell the government won't talk to the U.S. to get this service operating is a mystery to me."

"Old enemies die hard."

"Hey, Leo, sit down and I'll teach you how to use one. It may come in handy one day."

There was a lineup of cars, taxis, busses, and guides waiting for tourists in the front entrance of the hotel. The one valet frantically listened to the shouts and calls from the wealthy patrons who thought they were entitled to have their needs met first. Traffic was getting crazy as cars tried to jockey for a proper parking space. It looked like a video game.

"Thanks, I know the basics. I just want to Google something fast."

"Have at it," said the American good-naturedly. "I'm Michael Shamen, by the way."

"Nice to meet you." Harry was having fun perfecting his Leo voice and manner. "I bet you work in tech."

"Yeah, this Cuba trip was the brainchild of my company. We all had to come to Cuba to check it out to see if we can come up with a super cheap, super effective cellular grid. Five thousand dollars for five days. It's a ripoff."

"I could have showed you around for half of that," said Harry. "And you would have seen more of Cuba than Parque Central."

Harry was not finding Justin Levitt on Google. He searched Silicon Valley. Nothing. Intel. Nothing. Maybe Justin's information was fake, a cover for something he did that was criminal. Or maybe Justin was not a big deal. Or maybe Justin goes by multiple identities.

Anything was possible. Multiple scenarios. People go underground in Cuba and hide for decades.

Harry clicked off Michael Shamen's iPhone.

"Find anything good?"

"I appreciate your lending me the phone."

"You know anything about technology?" asked Michael.

"Practically nothing. We don't have access to computers."

Harry was almost ashamed to tell this man how he lacked technology information. He knew he had smarts, but limited education and resources stifled the brightest.

"I know this might be forward, but could I have your card? You never know what might happen in life."

Michael handed Harry his business card and shook his hand.

"Good luck, Leo." Michael Shamen walked back to the entrances of Hotel Parque Central.

Harry was walking a tightrope. His instincts were to run back to Cienfuegos and talk to Uncle Ray. Time was getting the better of him – away from Kobe too long, missing Katrina. What was she learning? What books was she reading?

He made a call to Victor telling him he needed to source more kooks for the upcoming weeks.

"Don't be gone too long," said Victor. "I need you here."

Harry decided to come clean about his other life.

"Victor, I've got a wife and a daughter in Cienfuegos. I need to check in. Give me a few days."

"Maybe that's a good idea," Victor replied. "I want you to check out the water and sanitation situation in Cienfuegos. My company applied for partnership in that city. See if there are other contracts, what's the competition? Any wiggle room with the government on percentages depending on how much is put up? Do the same with any technology applications. Santiago, too. I need a front man to do some research. There's a bonus in this."

"What's the name of your company, Victor?"

"Caspian Corp. Come to my apartment on the Prado and give me that information when you get it. I gave you the address, right? Do you still have it?"

Victor's address was indelibly imprinted in his brain. The Fat Man was his lucky charm.

CHAPTER 6

Unbearable Burdens

The four-and-a half hour bus ride to Cienfuegos from La Habana was a quiet time to think and to get distance from the city. His journey was taking him to freedom, but what did that mean for his family. Harry imagined the sweetness of setting up a new life with Kobe and Katrina. They had been through struggles and joys, and there was always hope for an easier life. His family resided in a safe place and that brought him comfort.

His mother was old and frail and wouldn't understand why he and his family must leave Cuba. She had neighbors to watch over her, but that was a bittersweet consolation for a life of struggle and heartache. He regretted that his mother was not open to telling him the story of his uncle and his father, how they fell out over the revolution, had differences about Fidel in the later days of the resistance.

Instead, Reynaldo told him about their struggles. His uncle saw El Jefe as a flawed, power-hungry man. Not good for Cuba. As bad or worse than Batista. He didn't marry so he could plan his escape freely. When Russia propped up Cuba's government with an iron hand, Roberto and Reynaldo stopped speaking. In the late sixties, Reynaldo and three cousins built a boat, crossed the Caribbean and put his wet foot on dry American soil.

Harry watched the island's flat brownish landscape pass by. Small, unkempt farms dotted the landscape. Fruit and vegetables grew on patches of sparse land. Some farms had a few cows that produced milk and some were fed enough to provide beef for the tourists or for the wealthy. Along the road, pickup trucks filled with farmworkers and their tools passed by; other trucks carried fruits and vegetables on their way to markets in the city. They faced only backbreaking work in the fields, while their stomachs went hungry.

The bus stopped at a small casita where food and drink could be purchased. Harry needed to stretch his legs and get water. Most of the people in the bus cued up for the restrooms and walked around the grounds talking and laughing. One of the men, a father with two children, resembled Victor. The man with a big picture, the man who strategized partnering with the Cuban government and made big money along the way. He cared nothing for the poor, the agricultural workers who barely subsisted. The opportunity to work with private companies might result in better crops and healthier cows, cleaner water and more efficient sanitation. But Victor wasn't concerned with the greater good of Cuba.

Victor's got to have an angle. Russians didn't do anything unless they had an advantage. They lived to get the upper hand, like the gangs in Newark. Harry witnessed the evil twins of money and influence. His cousin Mauro used to point out the mafia guys to Harry on the streets. He called them all Tony Soprano. "Yo, Harry, there's a Tony," he'd say. Mauro enlisted Harry in his game, and the two cousins checked out the Tony Sopranos in the neighborhood to see if they were mafia guys. They would go into bars and stores and clubs to see if they were accurately identified. Mauro was dead-on right every time.

❋

Harry found no one home at his apartment in Cienfuegos. It was clean and smelled of Kobe's sweet scent. Their apartment meant everything to Harry. He and Kobe worked hard to get it. To keep it in perfect condition was an honor. In his heart, he thought Kobe would be home by now, but he must have been dreaming.

He showered and changed his clothes, and selected a few clean shirts from the closet, holding them to his nose to inhale the familiar odor of laundry soap. He headed out to Uncle Ray's place in hope of finding information.

Ray was sitting in the restaurant drinking coffee and reading a newspaper.

"*Hola, Tio! Qué pasa?*"

Ray looked at him as if he saw a ghost.

"Where have you been?"

"Working in La Habana."

"You leave your family and go off for weeks? You're being careless."

"*Tio*, I've got a job and a chance to leave the island. Kobe understands."

"I'm not so sure about that. She left about the same time to see Satomi in Santiago."

"I know that. Maybe she needed some rest."

"You've been dreaming this for years," said Uncle Ray. "If you wanted to leave Cuba, you would have left already. You would have gone on a boat to the Keys or Miami. You're not desperate enough. You don't have the guts, no fire in your belly. That doesn't make you a bad man, but it does make you a man who lives with illusion and wasted dreams."

Uncle Ray talked straight to him, but Harry heard something else in his voice. It was the voice of a shaman, a holy man who saw and heard more than a mere being, and that made Harry ashamed of what he was trying to accomplish.

"I'll get off this island. You'll see, and you'll know I haven't lost my soul. I won't lose my soul."

"You parked your soul in the lost and found, *chico*. You may get it out, but you may lose it many times over."

Ray turned back to his paper.

"Do you remember when I was growing up, and one night you came up to me in the plaza and asked me what I was doing out so late. I told you I couldn't stand the baby crying all night. I was eighteen and full of anger and guilt for my stupid mistake. I felt ashamed. It was all self-pity shit, and you told me to grow up and accept responsibility. That if I didn't, I'd end up in the gutter. You told me to show up at the restaurant and work at night for extra money, and be grateful that I had gifts."

"I told you that you looked like goddamn Leonardo DiCaprio. And you're smart."

"You're a proud man," Harry said. "And I'm proud, too, like you, *Tio. Gracias.* Don't give up on me."

Harry's mother still lived in a fifties three-hundred square foot, one-bedroom apartment on a side-street three blocks from the main plaza. He hadn't checked in with her for weeks and felt guilty, even though the neighbors took care of her. He felt relief to know that she could get a ride to the health clinic when she wasn't feeling well. A neighbor, an old, withered, dark-skinned man about sixty, stood outside her door smoking a foul cigarette butt.

"Hola viejo. Dónde esta mamacita?" asked Harry politely. The old man didn't respond, so Harry entered the ground floor apartment, passed through the living room and entered the bedroom. There was a foul-smelling odor, left over from burnt cooking oils.

"Clinica," responded the old man dispassionately as Harry left his mother's modest dwelling.

"¿Qué pasa?" Harry asked in a panic.

"Dolor. Dolor aquí. Consuela es con ella. Elle necesita pastillas."

"Regreso en unos días," said Harry.

Harry gave the old man twenty kooks. He finally smiled.

Harry raced to a government building and located the offices of the Water and Sanitation Department on the second floor. The building had been in decay before Fidel's Revolution. The walls in the hallway were stripped of paint, the doorknobs were falling off their hinges, and the smell of stale cigarettes seeped out under the offices. Inside the water and sanitation office, the brown leather sofa was cracked and the chairs were unstable, far worse than in the DMV in Newark. This administration building should have been condemned decades ago.

He flirted with the cute receptionist to soften her up and get the information Victor wanted from the files. The beautiful young woman flirted back and asked his name. Harry told her it was Leo. The more she flirted, the more he became Leo. He asked to see all the files applying for water and sanitation partnerships in Cienfuegos. She happily granted him the favor. Maybe they would go out for drinks after work.

He remained calm as he read through the applications. He noted that Victor's Caspian Corp was not the only foreign company interested in applying for partnership with Cuba in the water and sanitation sector. Many foreign agents shared Victor's brilliant idea. But one name stood out. It was a French company, and they applied to partner with Cienfuegos Water and Sanitation Department at least half a year before Victor did. The bid was lower than Caspian Corp.

He gave the receptionist a quick kiss on the cheek and left the building. Harry didn't realize how crushed she would be by his lack of interest in her.

On his way to the bus station, Harry saw Juan Juan and Norm in the plaza. He took a quick pivot and jogged around the wide commercial sidewalk that led out of Plaza Martí. Business was brisk in the stores. The main boulevard was an anthill of people. Tourists and local were sitting on the stone benches, conversing or reading. At the end of the long stretch of shops, he saw the two domes in the distance – the Government Palace and the Ferre Palace, and hailed the first vacant cab.

It had been three years since Harry entered the cigar factory where he worked. He never returned, not even to visit Kobe. Memories were vivid. Before Katrina was born, his mother worked next to him. Regina was slowing down and working the nine-hour shifts took a toll on her body – painful handwork, aching back and hips, and the stink of cigar on clothing, skin, and hair that wouldn't come out with soap. Katrina's birth was Regina's savior. But Kobe had to endure.

The factory was housed in a large, old warehouse about fifteen minutes out of town. He skipped two steps at a time, and entered the second floor, 2,500 square feet where almost a hundred workers, men and women, sat at small, cramped tables with tobacco leaves spread out in three separate piles stacked on the front shelf of their tables – from the least expensive to the most expensive leaves. The air was stifling. The work was grinding. If backs weren't literally broken, spines were compromised, sometimes for life. Floor supervisors made sure the tobacco stacks were replenished.

When tourists came into the factory, they were surprised to know that the manual labor skills of the workers belied their intelligence and verbal acuity, especially Harry and his movie star looks, who could converse with any tourist.

Harry walked around the room and inhaled the nauseous tobacco fumes, he didn't recognize anyone. A worker sat behind every table. There were no empty seats. Kobe's station was occupied. As he choked back the feeling that he was going to vomit, coupled with the fear of not finding Kobe, a man approached him from behind.

"Harry," said a short, mid-fifties man whose skin had blotches of brown and yellow stains.

"Morgan, good to see you."

"What can I help you with?"

"I'm embarrassed to say I am looking for Kobe. Did she quit or call you? Do you think she is coming back?"

"Both. She quit and she's not coming back," Morgan said. "She was getting sick. It was no good for her anymore in this place."

"*Gracias, mi amigo.* I appreciate this."

"*Cuidado, amigo.*"

Juan Juan was, as usual, overdressed for the heat. He mopped his forehead with a handkerchief. Norm hid a marijuana cigarette in his palm and inhaled the smoke when no one was looking. There was no easy way to get to the bus station without passing them. They had nothing to do but wait for Harry to appear.

"Don't you have time for your old friends?" Juan Juan asked Harry as he walked through the plaza. "Too good for us? Think because you work in La Habana, your shit doesn't stink?"

"I'm just doing a job, Juan Juan, get off my back."

Juan Juan wanted his commission for giving him the idea to change money. He deserved something for that meeting with Ernesto and the Americans.

"You don't deserve shit because I didn't do business with Ernesto."

"I gave you the idea, *singao.*"

"Don't bother me with your garbage," said Harry. "Money changing is booming all over the island, and you don't have a monopoly on it, so don't waste my time. Besides, you should have thought of it years ago."

"No one is wasting time on you anymore, Harry. Not even your wife."

Harry had to step back, view the scene at a distance. Take control like Justin took control of his business. It was not worth laying hands on the creep. He was triggered by the remark but couldn't help thinking the little fucker might be right.

The bus ride to Santiago was long and agonizing. Harry slept and dreamed about the ocean, living underwater with the fish, eating plankton and gliding with the ease of freedom around coral and sand drifts. He encountered a white shark with penetrating white eyes who was determined to discover why this strange water creature was swimming around his territory. Harry paddled away from the shark and kept his distance. The shark moved away, seemingly uninterested, and staked out new territory while protecting the waters around him. But curiosity got the better of the shark, and he kept returning to the human creature.

Harry woke up to an empty bus and the driver gone.

It was late afternoon. Another day had passed. The sun was torturing his eyes, and he couldn't see clearly for the first five minutes. His mouth was dry, his throat burning. Somewhere along the thirteen-and-a half-hour bus trip, he lost his sunglasses. His beard was rough and he smelled like the inside of a garbage bag. A gaggle of men loitered in front of the bus station, ready to pounce on tourists, or anyone walking and breathing. Everyone needed a ride somewhere. He fended off a few seedy-looking young men in brightly flowered shirts with the wave of a hand, keeping his arm out low and unassuming.

He could see the hills in front of him. Satomi and William lived a half mile from the stunning Santiago de Cuba harbor. He knew the route well. At one point in time, he and Kobe used to be regular visitors. But he hadn't been back since he went to work as a translator in the Plaza Martí. As he walked up the hill, he turned around to take in the breathtaking view of the Caribbean Sea in the southeastern part of the island.

Santiago had always been Harry's favorite city for its charm, friendliness, and Afro-Cuban cultural influences. The original and well-worn cobblestone streets added to the city's charming history. The hills surrounding the city were deeply green with fruit trees and flowers that gave the landscape the feeling of postcard vistas. Music played on every street corner, in every restaurant and bar, cautiously uplifting his spirit.

Harry was the last person Satomi expected to see, especially looking defeated and tired. She had always seen him as a serious young man. Secure in his choices. But not today.

Harry wanted to make a conscious effort to enter the house carefully in order to avoid appearing agitated. He examined the living room that was under construction. It wasn't there the last time he visited. Plastic sheets hung loosely around the room, masking particles of dust floating in the air.

"It's good to see you, Satomi."

She embraced Harry and assessed his mood. "Guille went to get groceries."

There was a palpable awkwardness as they moved into the galley kitchen.

"Your kitchen always smells of spices and fried oil," said Harry. "You two should open a restaurant."

She knew why Harry was visiting. He should not worry about Kobe. She was safe and peaceful. Harry should stay away.

"I think Kobe didn't want no more yellow tobacco hands. No more red eyes and dry hair. No more round back and cracked spine. Maybe she was afraid you would be mad."

William entered the house and gave Harry a bear hug.

"*Compay*. Good to see you," he exclaimed in his deep resonant voice. "You will stay for dinner. I'm making an Asian Fusion Cuban concoction. I'm in a creative mood!"

As William reached into the refrigerator to pull out a couple of beers, Harry noticed the stain of sweat running down his muscular back through his tee shirt. At almost six feet, William was an imposing man. But his physical strength was not his only attribute. He was kind and gentle, so Harry was sure it must be difficult for him to be in the middle of Harry's sadness and Kobe's needs. William took his time pouring the beer into two glasses.

William understood how difficult this situation was for Harry. He was locked in a trunk with no way out.

Harry grew tired of placating them, and his anger was rising. He demanded to know where Kobe was staying.

"She doesn't want us to tell you," said Satomi. "This time when you left her, she said it was different. You must give her time to think and find her life. Not your life."

He should have seen the signs. Listened to her more closely. Asked her more questions. The dream she told him about the night before he left for La Habana. What did it mean? Why did she tell him about Satomi rescuing her mother? Is this why she is in Santiago, to be rescued by her mother's best friend, by her second mother, following Satomi for security and peace? He has to find her, but he didn't know where to begin.

William put his arm around Harry's shoulder and gave him a strong embrace.

"Do you mind if I go upstairs, Guille?" asked Harry. "I need some air."

"Go ahead, please."

William returned to methodically cutting the vegetables as Harry climbed the stairs. Satomi reached into the refrigerator for greens and tomatoes. As she chopped, she felt Guille's eyes on her. Together, they held Kobe's secret.

Harry looked through the window of the upstairs bedroom and hopefully expected to find something that reminded him of Kobe and Katrina. A bottle of perfume to take away the tobacco smell from her hands and arms, a notebook that Katrina wrote in every day. There was no trace of his family. He walked to the edge of the rooftop. It was growing dark.

In the years since he left the tobacco factory, Kobe listened to his dream of going back to America, and she gave him her blessing. Did she lie or had the dream gone on too long? He wasn't aware of her feelings, didn't see any change in attitude or conviction. How could she tell him what she wanted when their life together was all about his dream and not about what Kobe wanted.

"Amigo," said Guille as Harry came downstairs. "Drink your beer and relax.

"What you do in La Habana Kobe found scary?" asked Satomi. "She was afraid for you."

"I exchange money. Collect dollars for some business people for a commission."

"What else?" asked William.

"I work as a translator for a guy who's doing business in Cuba. I'm doing research for him in other cities."

"What business? I'm asking for the whole picture. Not bits and pieces."

"The group is interested in partnering with the government for a better delivery system for water and sanitation."

"Who's collecting dollars?" asked Satomi.

"It's a partnership between a couple of guys who own a restaurant in Centro Habana. Dollars are a hedge against Cuba's idea of someday adapting a one currency policy."

William knew that Harry was a smart guy. But he didn't have street smarts. He lived in Newark for three years. Big deal. He didn't know about mafia deals and Russian deals. Guille knew something about those things. He never told anyone about what he did for the Russian mob fifteen years ago. Extortion and fraud. That's how he ended up in Santiago. Running and hiding. Time passed, and they forgot about him. He was safe.

"Stay out of it. Go home and wait."

"It's time to eat," said Satomi. "I hope you're hungry."

"Starving."

The next day, Harry wandered the narrow and colorful streets of Santiago looking for favorite places where he and Kobe went on their visits around the city. He looked for her in restaurants, bars, travel agencies along the steep, narrow steps of Padre Pico. Maybe

he would find her along the mixed quarter of Tivoli, a packed neighborhood of mixed generations and cultures. He strolled east around Parque Céspedes, the archetype of Cuban street life and the

highest point in the city, and he marveled at the 180 degree vistas of the Caribbean Sea.

Every city dweller, every tourist flocked to this mecca. It was the heart and soul of Santiago de Cuba, a throbbing kaleidoscope of walking, talking, hustling, flirting, guitar-strumming humanity. Surrounded by colonial architecture, this most ebullient of city squares still took Harry's breath away. Children were playing at the foot of the bronze bust of Carlos Manuel de Céspedes in the center of the square, the leader of Cuban independence in 1868. He remembered the date. Indelible on his brain. It was all too familiar and all too painful to be there without Kobe.

The sun was prickly hot and he was hungry. He slipped into a bar on a hilltop, door open, ordered a beer, and listened to the Cuban music by a trio of musicians playing *Chan Chan*. Snap Snap. There was no turning back. Kobe doesn't want to be found.

He slept badly in a rented room in the Tivoli section. Nine o'clock sharp, he entered an empty government building. The lobby smelled like the inside of an old shoe. The guard was napping, so he wandered the hallways until he found the application office.

Government buildings opened at nine, but workers showed up on their own time. He flipped through the files looking for applications to partner with the Cuban government for a water and sanitation contract. *There it was again.* A French company, Institut Français des Aquatiques, the company's whose application he first saw in Cienfuegos. In both cities, the French underbid Caspian Corp. In both cities, the name signed on the French application was Charles Duval. Duran. *Doing business as* a French company. Justin's signature was nowhere on any application.

Charles the Frenchman was the perfect front for Justin. American investment wasn't welcomed in Cuba. That was the attraction for Justin at the beginning of their restaurant relationship. He didn't give a rat's ass about restaurants. It was just a cover. How could he not make the connection? It was time to play a smarter game. He won't tell the Fat Man any names on the filings. Information was as good as money.

The afternoon sun rose high and hot as Harry was drawn back to Parque Céspedes. The young kids were out of bed and into the plaza with their flip phones trying to get an Internet signal.

Three large sailboats two miles out to sea provided a distraction for Harry as they raised their wide, flowing white sails. Their speed increased with the wind at their backs and the sails looked as if they were floating like angels through the blue sky. A group of tourists gathered around a blue balcony where Fidel Castro made a speech before his revolutionary band began their march to liberate La Habana.

Harry sat on the base of the statue of Céspedes and felt a tap on his right shoulder. He turned, hopeful it was Kobe.

"Harry! How the hell are you?" said Silas. "I never thought I'd see you again."

"Good to see you," Harry said. "Where's Paula?"

"We had a big blowup and she left. I don't blame her. I'm not the easiest person to get along with. Anyway, I don't have my shit together. But it's no joke that Cuba is ripe for tech development. Hell, you can't get a fucking Wi-Fi connection unless you go to a five-star hotel in Havana. It's pathetic."

"I have a feeling you probably have an idea how to implement cellular service in La Habana, right?"

"I'm working on it. Hey, maybe you can change dollars for me. Paula took most of my money, and I'm running low on kooks."

"Sure thing," Harry responded. "You hooked me up with Ishmael, so I owe you a few favors. Are you headed back to La Habana?"

"In a few days. It's going to be a madhouse. Obama is coming to town today."

Harry forgot about Obama's visit. He reached in his pocket and gave Silas a business card. "Give me a call on my cell in a day. It has my number on it. Gotta run. See you in La Habana."

Harry didn't have the stamina to ride another bus and the traffic would be punishing after Obama left. He rushed back to Satomi's house to get William's friend to drive him back to Cienfuegos to see his mother.

Ibrahim wanted an arm and a leg for the drive, but Harry didn't care about money at this point. He needed to get back to work.

His phone rang. "You're in trouble," shouted Ishmael. "Where have you been, *singao*?"

"I was on business for the Russian. Just back off."

Ishmael's anger seemed too big for the situation. Like he was putting on a show for someone. He closed his flip phone, took a deep breath, and felt the calming energy of Ibrahim, a man of impeccable grace.

Ibrahim used to teach English in a high school, but the money was insufficient to pay for his own apartment. This forty-five-year-old man still lived at home with seven siblings, all educated, all professional, all making a piss-poor living. He struggled to make a decent living because tourist work was sporadic. But he was never bitter. He took pride in everything he did, no matter how small. He was a professional. Satomi and William hired him when their customers needed a tour or car service, but his dream was bigger – to open a travel agency with a couple of friends. He was smart, focused, and an asset to any business. Someone needed to discover this man of many talents and few words.

"Everything okay?" asked Ibrahim.

The phone rang again. Silas hired a car back to La Habana. He didn't want to deal with the leftover Obama traffic in town. He heard from a friend that the city was a madhouse, people screaming and shouting and cheering for Obama, waving flags and acting like he was the second coming. The festivities should be over by the time he got there early in the morning, but he wished he had been there to see the great man.

"Where can I meet you to do the exchange?" asked Silas.

"Tomorrow morning at eight. Hotel Sevilla."

"Sounds great. I haven't been there yet. I guess you know the history."

Harry looked at his watch. He didn't want to listen to the rest of the story Silas was dying to tell. He had to be polite.

"Graham Greene used room 501 as a setting for his novel *Our Man in Havana* and the mafia used the hotel as its operations center for their North American drug racket. Is it myth or real?"

Harry wrestled with the idea of bypassing Cienfuegos. He needed to get back to La Habana and make a quick connection with Silas to exchange money. He felt like he was on a skateboard going downhill. No stops allowed. Every day out of the big city was a day he couldn't move his agenda forward. His heart told him one thing and his mind another.

"You're not going to Cienfuegos?" Ibrahim asked.

"I don't have time to make the stop. As it is, we'll get there early tomorrow morning, and then I need you to take me to my apartment so I can get a stash of kooks for my customers. I'll pay you well for this, Ibrahim."

"I'm not worried," Ibrahim said quietly.

CHAPTER 7

Hints and Hindrances

Harry entered the Hotel Sevilla cafe. Silas was talking on the phone, pen in hand, writing without a stop. Silas motioned Harry over. He sat and put his backpack under the table, and took out a package wrapped in newspaper.

"There's a thousand kooks in here. That'll buy you a shitload of Ernest Hemingway daiquiris."

They make the transaction under the table.

"Let me know if you need anything else before you leave."

"Please sit down, Harry. I'll get us more coffee."

Harry felt like he was living on another planet. He was spaced out and listless, his mind fading, and his body stiff. He needed more coffee, but food would be better. He had never been so hungry.

"Hey, buddy, what's going on?" asked Silas as he sat down.

Harry told Silas about his missing wife and daughter in Santiago. They were supposed to be staying with friends who lived in the city, and they knew where they were staying, but wouldn't tell him.

"Do your friends run an Airbnb?" asked Silas.

"Yes. Why?"

"I got my booking screwed up in Santiago. Paula and I arrived early, and there was some confusion because other guests were expected the same time we came."

"An Asian lady and her daughter?" Harry asked.

"I didn't see them at first because we settled into the upstairs room then went out to dinner. We came back early because we had a fight. Paula wanted to go home, but I convinced her to wait until we got back to Havana."

"When you got back, did you see my wife and daughter?"

Silas hesitated to tell the story. It would upset Harry. But Harry pushed, needing answers. After introductions were made, it was awkward. They went upstairs, and then heard a child's voice scream-ing. Paula grabbed her duffle to go, and they went downstairs and his daughter was crying. William calmed the situation and told them not to leave – it was a contract, and they would honor it. His wife and daughter had another place to stay.

"What did Katrina say?" asked Harry.

"She was crying and calling for you. She wanted to go back to school. It was heartbreaking. We ended up by staying one more night. Then, Paula left to go back to the States."

Katrina in tears. And it was painful to think of Kobe starting to unravel, losing hope, planning another life. Why not talk to me, why not tell me how she was feeling? He knows why. No talk would make any difference.

Choices and decisions were already in progress.

"I don't mean to be curious, but why do you need all that money?" asked Harry. "Are you planning to stay in Cuba?"

"I don't have to get back to the States. I'm a tech programmer and I'm looking for opportunities. What's this business you're in, Harry? Exchanging currency can't make you big bucks."

"I'm helping out some people with government contracts. Cuba is opening up to private partnerships."

"Not with the U.S.," said Silas. "It's Russia. Or China, or Canada. So long as there's a big enough piece of the pie, everyone wants in. Especially high tech."

"You and everyone else are greedy at the prospect of investing. Only the cunning will survive."

City streets were spattered with signs and papers left over from Obama's visit. Workers were cleaning up as groups of Cubans continued to celebrate the President's visit, milling around the promenades, talking in groups on corners, complaining about the hot, muggy morning. Harry's hunger gnawed him to distraction. On his way to Victor's apartment on Calle Prado, Harry would have been happy to eat the rotten fruit hanging on the carts tucked into side streets off the boulevard.

"What's up, Leo?" Victor inquired, his purple shirt already stained with grease. "What'd ya got for me? I hope it's good, because you were away a long time."

The last time Harry was inside the Fat Man's apartment it smelled of garlic. That morning it smelled of onions. His eyes started to tear up.

"Hold on to those horses, Victor," said Harry. "It was only a few days. I had things to do."

He checked records in Cienfuegos and Santiago and there were several foreign companies that had put in a request to partner with the government in water and sanitation in both cities. He thought if he visited every city on the island, he'd find the same applications.

"Did you check La Habana's water and sanitation department to see who has already applied?" asked Harry.

"Fuck! That's the job of my lawyers!" yelled Victor. "Do that for me today, will ya, kid? And help me figure out who's stealing my idea."

As Harry greedily buttered toast and grabbed fruit off a full platter, stuffing his mouth and washing it down with coffee, he glanced around the room. He thought Victor's apartment would look like the lap of luxury. Russians were supposed to be rich. The definition of *rich* was relative because money was no substitute for good taste. Victor was a slob and lived like a pig. The two rooms barely accommodated one man, let alone a man the size of Victor. The Russians were more interested in food than good furniture. The platters spread out on a vintage fifties dining room table were fit for a Roman orgy.

Victor lit up a Cohiba, inhaled with satisfaction, and watched Harry chew like a hungry lion.

"I wish I could eat like that," observed Victor. Harry almost lost all the food in his mouth as the smoke slithered up his nostrils.

To keep him from throwing up, Harry tried to address the question of why Victor kept his Cuban businessmen with him all the time. He told him they were useless. Even Harry knew Victor needed to do business on a higher level. He was sure they sold him a bill of goods.

"How do you know this shit?" asked Victor. "You been holding out on me? Don't answer that. Snoop around the Havana application office and see what you can find."

Victor gave Harry a stack of dollars. "And clean yourself up before you go. Get a haircut and some decent clothes. You look like shit."

❋

Harry felt comforted by the ties hanging on the balcony rail at Kirpan. They hung straight and strong and bright in the stillness of the darkened room. They were Kirpan's anchor. Steady as she goes.

Charles stood behind the bar working on menus. He glanced up, saw Harry, and returned back to his work.

Harry sat on a barstool and waited patiently.

"What's on your mind, kid?" asked Charles.

"Why did you come to Cuba?"

Charles knew that Harry was unusually intelligent. Strong, sturdy, with the right kind of boldness. He wasn't interested in money for money's sake. The money was freedom, the right to choose his destiny. The kid could never imagine becoming involved in Cuban business. He was cynical about the government. That was his usefulness. Harry lost his Cuban soul a long time ago. He was born in the wrong country. He was an American at heart.

"France was boring," said Charles as he put two beers on the bar. "The country lacks imagination. It was probably more fun to live in France when it was governed by Louis XIV. Now, it is stuck in outdated thinking, as opposed to Cuba, which isn't about communism anymore. Cuba is about finding opportunitis to live a good life."

"You think Cuba is an adventure?"

"Why not? Besides, Paris was crowded with restaurants. It was competitive in a nasty way, like the French are snobby about cuisine. Havana is wide open. No preconceived opinions."

He laid out the stack of dollars on the bar. "All yours."

"You've been gone for a few days," said Charles. "You worried us a little."

Harry grabbed his beer and took the stairs two at a time to the raised balcony and studied the hanging ties. He didn't want to touch them because they were arranged perfectly by color.

"Don't worry about me, Charles. I won't let you down. And you'll be the first to know when it's time for me to leave your business and get off the island."

"How's the Russian situation?" asked Charles.

"Gets more interesting. I'm sure Justin told you about this Russian guy, Victor Kostroff. He applied to partner with the Cuban government in the water supply and sanitation department. He told me to find out what his competition was in Cienfuegos, then in Santiago while I was there. I'm going to check out La Habana next."

"What did you find on your hunt?"

Harry jumped down skipping the four stairs and climbed on a stool in the center of the bar.

"A French company got there first. I should say you and Justin submitted your applications first, so I believe you both haven't been completely honest with me."

"We don't have to be anything with you. It's none of your business."

"Justin couldn't do business as a U.S. citizen in Cuba. Some fairly educated guy could put that together in a New Jersey minute."

"Mon cher," said Charles. "I'm the front."

"Charles Duval. Silent partner. Justin Levitt."

"You think you're a smart kid, but you don't know shit. The Cuban monetary economy rests on a strong peso. Then we can get out of the kook business."

"Then it's a win-win for you both."

Harry went behind the bar and poured himself a cup of coffee. He took it to a table on the edge of the dining room and sipped it slowly.

"Don't worry, Charles. You, Ishmael, and Justin have been good to me. I told Victor that he has competition, but that didn't mean he has lost the bid."

"And what's the bid?"

When Charles asked a question, his tone implied a threat. Harry was put off by his manipulative manner. Facing Charles on his own turf, without backup, wasn't a warm and fuzzy experience, so he was brief. He told Charles that the Institut Français des Aquatiques underbid the Russians.

Charles took his cell from the bar and walked to the back room. Harry hadn't been dismissed. The more he knew about the Institut Français des Aquatiques, about Justin and Charles and what they were up to, the more complicated his life would become. Too late to make a U-turn. The waters were muddy.

Charles came back into the room. "The Russians always have the edge in Cuba, no matter what any other country bids. We are in the process of fixing that situation."

❖

Victor was on the phone waving his expensive cigar in the air, when Harry entered the smoky room. His agitation was obvious as he talked to someone about the water supply and sanitation deal.

"How come you didn't make sure our bid was exclusive? I'm fucked and so are you unless we can get someone in the government to give us the contract," Victor shouted. "What about the Russian attaché? He should be able to get us the deal."

Harry needed to give up something to Victor so that he could get out of the Russian spy business. He would rather not tell Victor a French company was his major competition. The easiest way was for Victor to bribe a Cuban bureaucrat in upper management and get information from the application office. That was the way everyone did business in Cuba.

Victor took a puff on the Cohiba and stared at Harry. "Find me a guy in the water and sanitation department who can be my agent or whatever the hell it's called. And that agent guy will give me information about my competition."

Bingo. Harry stayed in the game for another day.

"I'm on it," said Harry. "Meanwhile, maybe you should consider that Russian attaché idea."

"I heard you before," Victor snapped. "You get what I'm doing, right? And you will do this in a day or two, right?"

"*Sí, Señor.*"

Harry knew he'd never be able to find an inside guy in the Cuban Embassy, unless he got lucky. Or better yet, maybe Ishmael had a friend somewhere in the government system who wanted to make money spying for the Russians. The spying business was dangerous shit. Harry had to get out.

Ishmael was working on the slider door to the balcony when he was interrupted by a knock at the front door. His hand slipped and his fingers caught in the slider.

"Come in," he yelled, holding a handkerchief around his hand so it didn't bleed.

"This damn door doesn't square up with the wall. Sorry for the heat. Would you like something to drink?"

Ishmael took a bottle of soda water and poured two glasses.

"This ought to cool you off."

"*Vamos*. It's cooler outside."

"How did you figure to drop the money from the balcony?" asked Harry. "It's ingenious."

"Anna figured it out. She's got a good eye for the drop."

"Why is she still working like a dog. You've made plenty of money with Paco and the Kirpan guys and probably fixing up cars for friends. What's up?"

"You're a curious *hombre*," quipped Ishmael. "I guess it's good you're a fast learner. Maybe too fast."

"Let's talk and walk," said Harry.

It's a beautiful day in La Habana. The sun shined with flirty signs that autumn was in the offing. Last week's oppressive humidity blew away with a mild, cooler breeze. But it was only temporary. Humidity returned in the blink of an eye. Ishmael took out a handkerchief to wipe his face, then realized that it was more out of habit than need. Harry told Ishmael about Victor's water and sanitation plans and how he discovered another company competing for the same government partnership – a French company.

"It wasn't hard to put it all together. Charles signed off on the applications, but he used a different last name. I guess the government doesn't care, as long as it's any foreign company other than American."

"What's your plan? You're in the middle of this Russian war, and it could get sticky."

Harry asked him to suggest someone in the government as an agent for Victor to help him with his applications. This agent would be a plant that he controls.

"No can do. I don't have that kind of access. Charles has an agent that helps him, and getting another one would complicate Kirpan's position."

"How much trouble am I in?" asked Harry.

"No trouble yet," countered Ishmael. "I mean, the Russians might draw you in deeper. But for now, you're simply a double agent trying to cover your bases."

"Do they really own our asses?"

"Charles and Justin don't own our asses, but they have leverage with us. If they want to continue to get a larger share of government business in Cuba, they need your help on the inside. You provided a lucky break for the jefes."

Ishmael's phone rang. He had no response to the caller on the other end. He closed his phone and shook his head. "Hold on. It's just beginning."

�֍

Harry remembered that the Capitol was being repaired and all government offices moved to a building on Calle Dragones. It was an unassuming building in a well-kept block in the Prado district in Centro Habana. It took Harry thirty minutes walking down corridors and peeking into offices to find the government application department. The sign was small. He walked past it three times.

With his usual personable manner delivered to the attractive female government official, Harry was once again able to gain access to foreign application. He was now more focused on the monetary value of the bids from foreign countries.

He entered a large file room. It had no windows and little ventilation. Sweat ran down the sides of his face as he roamed around the claustrophobic room until he found the large, yellow plastic bin for the Institut Français des Aquatiques. The bin had more applications than any other foreign country. The water and sanitation application was only one of many French bids. Other applications included partnering with the Cuban government in building water towers, drainage projects, sanitation, garbage, and supplying trucks and trailers to support all their proposed projects. Just as in New York and New Jersey, the garbage business was the biggest prize of all.

Charles and Justin had more knowledge of the inner workings of the Cuban way of doing business than Victor who looked like small potatoes in comparison, the preverbal low- hanging fruit. It was an easy guess that the Institut Français des Aquatiques had underbid everyone, and was offering to provide more services than any applications on file. There was also a minimal application for cellular service. It was not complete, designed as a basic, broadband service.

The lovely lady who allowed Harry to visit the file room waited patiently for him to leave the file room.

"Find anything interesting?" she asked.

"Not really. Just checking some things for my boss. But you were really kind to let me inside." Harry gave her a kiss on the cheek and smiled seductively. The young lady was happy, probably happier than she had ever been in her life. Being kissed by Leo.

"Will you be back?" she asked, demure and hopeful.

"Most probably, beauty."

Harry needed to clear his head. He rode his bike along the Malecón, where he found solace for the first time in days. He had a strange idea that life sprang up from the sea. He liked the idea that humans came from fish rather than apes or gorillas. He learned that evolution from fish was a possibility from his science teacher at Barringer High School in Newark. He often returned to his dreams about water and fish, trying to figure out what the symbols meant in his unconscious state.

During three years at Barringer High School, teachers didn't push any political ideology, no brainwashing techniques like they did in Cuba. Nobody was trying to convert or exploit people. They didn't get involved in party politics, except to teach students about the three branches of government, how the checks and balance system worked, and how lobbyists pushed to get favored legislation passed. After some history courses and newspaper reading, Harry thought that the American way of governing moved slowly, like a turtle, and was probably as corrupt as the Cuban government. Not all laws were about the greater good. Democracy provided space to fulfill dreams, and the government didn't send a person to jail for thinking differently. America had its perks.

Harry knew time spent in Newark's North Ward with his cousins was as educational as time spent in the classroom and library. His cousins taught him about how to negotiate around the fringes of gangs if you didn't want to be sucked in. And Harry didn't want to be involved in crime. Neither did his cousins. His urban experience in the States taught him that loyalty was prized and no one ratted out a friend. Secrets were kept and elders were respected. Trust was everything.

CHAPTER 8
Keeping Secrets

alfway to Victor's, Harry impulsively turned his bike around and headed back to Cuba's application department to find the beauty who let him inside the file room. Something was not right about the French files. Not actually the French applications, but their basic, simple application to provide cellular service to La Habana, building out a fully functioning network and providing computers. This was Justin's area of expertise, and the application was too rudimentary to be taken seriously.

Asking the charming lady to go back into the file room was risky. The lady expected something in return. Harry didn't have time to worry about that. He realized, after reviewing three government offices in three cities, that he didn't know enough history and operational strategies to be conversant about how private partnerships work with the government apparatus.

His intention was to investigate pending applications from all countries so he might learn what information was required to win government contracts – the ins and outs of filing partnership applications. At the same time, Harry might discover how money was made by the private sector.

Harry peeked around the door and saw the lovely lady at her desk. She smiled and motioned him inside. Harry studied the knickknacks on her desk, a few pictures of her family, a dog, and a friend. He looked around at the peeling walls and the cheap furniture.

"What brought you back?"

"Your name."

"Felicity."

"I'm Leo. We weren't formally introduced."

He also didn't notice her bright red fingernails, her fine features, long aquiline nose, green eyes and skin that shines like a light pink rose.

"Nice to know you, Felicity," said Harry, appreciating her long waist and slim razor-straight back. Her shiny, blonde hair was back-lit by the light of a small window behind her.

"What do you need, Leo?" she asked. "I thought you finished your research."

"I need to go back inside the file room." Harry rushed his words because he was afraid she wouldn't say yes.

"And what do I get out of this?" Felicity lowered her head and blushed.

"Whatever you want." Harry sat on the edge of her desk. He was uncomfortable with flirting and putting on a fake sexual vibe. He was married. It was wrong.

"Lunch, dinner, a drink?" Harry suggested.

"All of it," she said, her blush now gone. "Go in and find what you want. Keep one ear on the office. If anyone comes in, my voice will get louder and I'll laugh. Then, I'll get rid of the person."

Harry investigated as many applications from foreign countries and private businesses applying to partner with the Cuban government as he could get through in the lucky window of opportunity. He hoped to find something he didn't see before. Russians applied in early 2000. China came later to Cuba to make investments in the Latin markets. Colombia, Brazil, then France and Spain, followed by Canadians and some Dutch companies. Most applications were directed at fixing Cuba's infrastructure in La Habana, other applications were directed to a variety of industries, the oil and gas industry, food, goods, water management, sanitation, garbage, recycling, and bids providing distribution of tractors and trucks.

Water interested Harry. It was one example of how to game the system. He read recently that water was cheap – a good investment and easy profit. And private ownership of water companies meant opportunities for price gouging. The poor got screwed, like in Bolivia. Those big corporations charged consumers exorbitant fees for water everywhere in the world. Water was the new oil.

After two hours, he found nothing new on his second application review. The only way to spin it with Victor was to give him the truth and a caution to deliver better systems.

He leaned against the wall, closed his eyes, and took a few deep breaths to get clarity. *Run through what you have seen.* Brazil's application file was bulging. It was a huge country with important resources. He studied Brazil in a geography unit in high school and was impressed. Maybe he missed something.

A half hour later, he was still poring over a large bin from Brazil, which had the most comprehensive application file of all the countries who submitted contracts to construct and implement a broadband infrastructure, complete with computer programmers. He couldn't gauge if the bid was cost-efficient. He didn't read techspeak, but, as he looked through the file, he understood that Brazil laid out to set up a complete cellular structure for the entire island. He read to the bottom of the page and didn't recognize the signature for the proposal. The name of the corporate executive was unimportant because this plan had Justin's name all over it.

Although GlobalNet was a small technology company, its assets were in the billions. Not hard to believe that Justin could jump ship in the near future.

Harry reentered the office carrying the Brazil bin.

"How many people came in while I was doing my research? I didn't hear a noise."

"I locked the door," said Felicity. Her smile looked like a warning as she walked seductively over to Harry and kissed him on the lips. Harry responded with some interest, still trying to guard his guilt.

"I'm bad, aren't I?" said Felicity, with a grin that could bring down the sky.

Her way was unfamiliar, but exciting.

"Look, Mr. Leo, you aren't allowed to take out anything from the file room, although we do have these applications on my computer. We're still a bit old-fashioned in Cuba so we back up with paper. As you know, no one else has access to Wi-Fi in the country except hotels and the government."

"I want to ask you a favor."

"Depends," she replied.

"Can you copy everything in this Brazilian application for me?"

Felicity didn't bat an eye. She took the thick file from Harry. "It will take time."

"Meet me at Kirpan Restaurant at eight tonight. Calle Industria. number 502."

He thanked Felicity with all the gratitude he could muster. At least he had information that might be used as leverage. But not with Victor. With Kirpan, with Justin.

Harry smelled garlic in hallway downwind from Victor's apartment. One of his guards opened the door with thuggish intent.

"It's okay, big guy," said Harry. "You can let me in. I have important news for Victor."

Victor took a thousand-dollar stack of dollar bills from his desk drawer. They made the exchange. It took all of ten seconds.

"What'd you have for me, young Leo? It better be good. Talk is cheap, so give me some expensive information."

Harry told Victor the truth about the many foreign governments bidding to partner with Cuba.

Victor lit up a cigar. "Give me something I don't know."

"The name of your major competitor," Harry replied. "Institut Français des Aquatiques."

"What's the bid? Higher or lower?"

"Higher. You're in a better position. And the Cubans like Russians." *First lie.* "Stick to your bid for water and sanitation in all the cities on the island. They won't split up the monopoly." *Second almost lie.* The Cuban government will do whatever the hell they feel like." *Maybe a third lie.*

"You better be right," threatened Victor. "We go after other business after this. Garbage. Supplying trucks and more Russian cars. Keep your eyes open, Leo. You did good for now."

Harry gave Victor a tease telling him he'd have more intel for him next time. He left the apartment and leaned against the wall. There would be no next time.

Kirpan was dark inside, and the air was steamy. Somebody was washing loads of dishes. Harry set a stack of dollars at the end of the bar and told Charles what he discovered.

"What do you think Victor is going to do when he finds out you lied to him about the bid? We underbid everyone because we know what everyone is bidding. The Fat Man is going to lose."

"Who's on the inside for you?" asked Harry.

"Why would you want to know that?"

"Because I've got someone helping me and she's coming here tonight for dinner. It's my payback to her for letting me snoop around the government application office. How good is your source and are you sure your guy is honest, because the facts are inside those applications?"

"How many companies are there?" asked Charles.

"You count them. Russia, China, Canada, Dutch, Brazil – too many to count. Your bids are still lower and more spread out over the island. You guys have a better plan for a legitimate infrastructure with added perks."

"Victor can easily verify what you told him."

"He has to have an agent on the inside snooping around and looking in files, and he has to pay them well. And he doesn't."

"Where'd you learn all these business words, Mr. Leo?" asked a seedy-looking man with a British accent sitting at the end of the bar. "I'm impressed."

The voice surprised Harry. He wasn't aware that someone else was in the bar. He should have been more cautious. Harry's new business vocabulary came from listening to Charles and Justin talk about how to strategize deals, how to define market values, and how the Cuban government functions with dysfunction. Hanging around Victor's lawyers increased Harry's legal knowledge, and besides, he's been reading all those files.

Charles shot a look at the boney man. He wore a crumpled, threadbare herringbone suit.

"Who's this guy?" Harry asked Charles.

"Harry, meet Spencer," said Charles. "He's someone who helps us in diplomatic circles in Havana."

Spencer stands and sways. Once he got his bearings, he walked unsteadily to Harry and shook his hand limply. Close-up, Harry saw that Spencer's hair was gray and thinning and his skin wrinkled and sallow.

"How did you learn the ropes in such a short period of time, Sir Harry?"

"You don't have to be a genius to figure out who's on first as they say in the States. And of course, I've been learning how to follow the money."

Spencer plopped down on a barstool.

"Speaking of money, Charles, when the Fat Man expels me from his inner circle, the dollars dry up and I need a new rich client. That is, if I can stay alive."

"Try to get more information from the girl in the application office."

"I might be able to have her remove Victor's applications from the files, or I can do it."

"Leave the Russian files alone," mumbled Spencer as he bumbled back to his perch. "You'll create more suspicion. When other bids come in, have her tell you. You have to keep that ball in play."

"You're not in the game anymore, old man," said Charles. You've been put out to pasture. Your usefulness is over."

A stark white light streamed in from the front door of Kirpan and Ibrahim entered.

✥

North of the Casco Historic districct, Santiago de Cuba turned residential. Near the Catedral de Nuestra Señora de la Asunción, there was a hostel on Calle Mariano Corona. Several doors down from the Hostal Las Terrazas, on the same side of the street, a friend of William's owned Los Lobos, a small restaurant in the middle of the block. Kobe and Katrina resided in the two empty rooms above the eatery.

Ezra was happy to have Kobe and Katrina as guests. He didn't care how long they stayed. He liked the company. Several blocks away, there was a school that Katrina attended. Kobe volunteered there and was often an assistant teacher in several grades that were overcrowded. She loved the work at the school, and Katrina was happy that her mother was around. Both mother and daughter were quick learners. Within several weeks, Kobe was paid a small stipend to be on staff.

A weary William walked up the hill to Los Lobos. It was midday, hot and dry. He wanted to check in with Ezra, to thank him, and to see what was happening with his guests.

William saw Ezra behind the bar. He was drying a glass with his thick hands, obsessively wiping, studying the glass as if it were a piece of gold newly retrieved from a mine. His face was furrowed and lined, and at fifty, he looked decades older.

"*Hermano,*" said William. "*¿Cómo estás? ¿Todo bien?*"

Ezra lumbered over to William and gave him a big bear hug.

"My hips are bothering me. I'm *gordito* and short of breath. *Que lió!* What an old Jew, I am."

William admired the way Ezra kept his restaurant looking fastidious and sparkling clean. The walls were full of colorful artwork by locals.

"Do not be concerned, Guille. Kobe and Katrina have a comfortable life in this neighborhood."

"I need to talk with Kobe," said William. "When does she come home from work?"

"*A las cuatro,*" he responded.

"I'll wait. In the meantime, *por favor*, make me some of your famous plantains."

Promptly at four, Kobe walked into the restaurant carrying an armful of books. Katrina was not with her, and William was relieved. He took her books, set them on the table, and embraced her happily.

"Your books are heavy. Remember to keep up your strength."

"You worry about me too much, Guille. Believe me when I tell you that I am eating more and smiling more, just like you counseled me to do when we first moved in upstairs at Ezra's."

In the last two months, Kobe was gaining more confidence in herself. She made her own decisions. Depending on Harry for everything in her life, including how she felt about herself, reduced her self-esteem. She wasn't seventeen anymore, lost in her marriage and a dead-end job, without any chance of fulfillment.

Before Harry left for La Habana, Kobe knew she wasn't going to America. She never said it to her husband. She never said it to herself. Watching him walk away from her, through Plaza Martí, gave her courage to take a risk and start a new life. No more sickness. No more crushed spirit. She created distance from Harry, not because she didn't love him, but because she loved him. She wanted him to fulfill his dreams. And she wanted to take her own journey without compromise.

"I've come to tell you that we saw Harry and he misses you," said Guille. "I didn't tell him where you were, but sometime, you might want to talk to him about your plans. It will give you both peace of mind."

"I have peace of mind. I'm making friends, helping Ezra and assisting in Katrina's school. This is what I want. This is what makes me happy. No rabbit hole for me."

Kobe brought two glasses of water to the table.

"Please don't tell me what he is doing. Changing money has nothing to do with me. I want no part of his business."

"Are you planning on staying with Harry no matter what is going on?" asked William.

"I think here is where I belong for now. I like being responsible for Katrina and me."

Ezra was eavesdropping at the food bar, but he didn't feel the need to weigh in because he knew Kobe was filling her days with what matters to her most. He came around the food bar with a dish of limes and two cups of hot tea.

"What's important is that you stay here, do your work, watch over Katrina, and when this is over, let's hope Harry finds his way back to you."

"Don't worry, Guille, you won't have to take care of Katrina and me. I am taking care of us. You and Satomi are different. You came together when you both lived separate lives, and when you met, you both had similar goals. It was a perfect match. I don't have that with Harry. We were too young and we didn't know ourselves or as a couple. Don't you think we should find that out?"

Ezra thought Kobe was wise beyond her years. She had a good mind and she used it well. She needed to get away from her past and find a future.

As he left Los Lobos and walked down the steep steps away from Parque Céspedes, William noticed that the afternoon temperature had cooled. He needed the walk, to breathe the air and clear his head, relieve his worried thoughts about Kobe and Harry. He was grateful that he was a different man because of Satomi.

He was bartending when they met ten years ago, and he was adrift, hiding from the Russians, worried that one of the thugs would give him up for his crimes, and he would end up in a loathsome Cuban prison. He was aggressive by nature, but when Satomi walked into his bar one night, everything changed for both of them. She was waiting for a friend who never arrived, and after several hours, they knew that their lives would never be the same.

They began to see each other regularly, and Satomi brought the light back into his life. She paid no attention to his defensive manner, and in time, she found his true gentle nature, a softness that defied his strong bearing.

Although William was fifteen years younger than Satomi, their minds were equally matched. William continued to work steadily as a bartender, and Satomi did triple duty as a costume designer, seamstress, and shop manager. And, of course, Satomi had to leave the country every six months to renew her Cuban visa. She was happy to do so because she always came back to the man she loved.

Eventually, Satomi and William had enough money to buy a hillside house that was barely livable. Over the years, they fixed it up. William discovered Airbnb by accident when he was requesting a permit on their house and he and Satomi explored their options. They got in on the ground floor of the movement in Santiago, and with Satomi's computer savvy, they started a business.

William rounded the corner that led to his home and knew Harry and Kobe were not fated to be together. He believed that to stay in a loving relationship, it was necessary to have shared goals and beliefs. That was not part of Harry and Kobe's life. It may never be. He had his life in the Cuban underground, and he saw its danger and limited vision. Get money quick and get out fast. Stay in too long and you don't own your life anymore. You become someone else.

CHAPTER 9

Nothing Is as It Seems

Harry was not surprised to see Ibrahim at Kirpan. He looked tired, but he was presentable and professional.

"*Mi amigo,*" said Harry. "You look like you're ready to do business."

"Nothing's as it seems," replied Ibrahim as he walked to the bar. Charles turned around and extended his hand.

"I'm Charles," he said. "And you are?"

"Ibrahim Cruz. I'm pleased to meet you."

Ibrahim had determined before he entered Kirpan to present a plan, to make a pitch to Charles. There was a strategic compatibility between a money exchange business and running a tourist agency. On the drive back to La Habana, when Harry talked to Ishmael on the phone, Ibrahim listened to his conversation, as well as what he was arranging with Silas about changing money. With laser focus, Ibrahim was formulating a plan to get in on the deal. But he needed connections and money. Competition was intense for the tourist business in Santiago. With backing from Kirpan and coupled with his competence and intellectual skills, he thought he could run a successful tourist agency.

"Ibrahim drove me back to La Habana," said Harry.

"He's planning to open a tourist agency with friends in Santiago."

"As well you should," Charles remarked. "Let me get you a beer." Charles placed a couple of bottles on the counter. "Did you study English in the States?"

"I studied English in Cuba and used to teach English in high school, but the salary didn't cover a rented room. I'm tutoring and driving tourists for friends of Harry in Santiago."

"To begin, if you are a friend of Harry's, you are reliable. Let's talk details in my office. By the way, Harry, Justin wants to talk to you."

Harry had a hunch Ibrahim knew where Kobe was living, and he wouldn't allow Ibrahim's business transaction to move forward unless he located Kobe and Katrina. That's the price Ibrahim had to pay for getting in on this deal.

"Before you go into the office, just to be clear, did Satomi and William tell you what I'm doing in La Habana?"

"They knew the basics," he said. "But this pitch is my idea."

Harry took Ibrahim's arm gently and drew him close. "One more thing before you commit to this deal. Either you know, or you find out, where Kobe is living."

"I'll get that done."

Justin sat behind a shiny antique wooden office desk. He was studying a spreadsheet, crossing through line-item numbers with a yellow marker. Harry stood above him and noticed that Justin's hands shook. Not a lot. A mild palsy. But if someone looked long enough, you would notice.

"My Leo, please sit down," said Justin. He pushed his Eames chair back from the desk, adjusted his seating position, and crossed his legs.

"How much do the Russians know?" asked Justin.

Harry told Justin about Caspian Corp and everything he discovered researching the files in La Habana. He didn't reveal the plans for a full broadband system submitted by Brazil's GlobalNet company.

"I told them your company's French name. They can find that out easily, and I couldn't keep stalling. Your company has more than forty low bid contracts with the Cuban government. The Russians applied in every city for water and sanitation contracts, but the bids are higher. I don't know where to go from here."

Justin enjoyed reviewing the details of the Russian's business position as it unfolded in Cuba over the decades. He sounded like a college professor, full of himself. Harry was bored by Justin's details. Russian cars, cargo ships in and out of Santiago bringing in oil and commodities. It was a familiar old story. Uncle Ray told it better.

Harry wanted Justin to tell him something he didn't know.

"The French guarantee a five-year subsidy with no increase in cost to the people. We plan on getting into other businesses, like renewable energies, tourism, urban development, food products, transportation, and a tech infrastructure."

"I don't want to be involved in your business."

"You're already involved," said Justin.

Justin's forceful reply caught Harry off guard. He thought he had Justin's number. There was a directness in his manner, maybe even a ruthlessness that warned Harry to be cautious going forward.

"What about the girl – your dinner guest?" asked Justin. "How much does she know? And will she give up that information to anyone else who snoops around?"

Felicity was complicated. He needed to insure her loyalty to help him, and keep her on his side. She expected more from him than the business relationship. He was a novice and had no idea how he'd handle dinner, trying to look like he was in the boy's club, getting a nod and a wink at Kirpan. He was conflicted by guilt and excitement.

"I can't be sure she'll tell me who comes and goes, or what topics of conversation take place, or who the Russians are talking with or bribing. Or, she could give me up out of fear."

"What will keep your lady friend quiet?" asked Justin.

"Me."

"Show her a good time tonight. Give her what she wants."

And that fast he had formally entered the rabbit hole.

Justin reached into his desk and pulled out a smartphone and a small piece of ordinary paper. "I want you to have this. It's time you came into the 21st century. Keep it somewhere safe and use it only in an emergency."

Harry put the phone in his pocket, the piece of paper in his wallet, and he walked out of Justin's office without another word, somber, almost desolate. Felicity's track ran one way. He conjured the image of Kobe and Katrina and tried to feel the warmth of their bodies. Instead, he felt cold.

Ibrahim waited for Harry at the bar. "Thanks for trusting me," he whispered, shaking his hand.

They walked to a dark corner of the restaurant and sat together like a couple of mafia guys planning a heist.

"I'll let you know where your wife and daughter are staying," offered Ibrahim. "William arranged it. I don't want to be heartless, but Kobe was clear you should not know where she was living."

"Did you meet Silas, the guy who stayed with Satomi?" asked Harry. "I did an exchange with him in La Habana after his girlfriend left. He's a techie interested in the prospects for building Internet service in Cuba. He thinks he can make money."

"Arming Cuba with knowledge is a long shot," said Ibrahim. "An American techie won't get anywhere in Cuba without money. You should bring him in to talk to Justin."

Justin was already doing that from Brazil.

"I don't want to rebuild this island. The Kirpan guys are smart with swinging dicks, and I'm having a case of impotence."

"You can't afford that," said Ibrahim.

�֍

Felicity entered Kirpan looking like a movie star with dark glasses, moving toward him like a fashion model. Harry was waiting nervously for her at the bar. She sauntered up to him like Lauren Bacall meeting Humphrey Bogart, took off her sunglasses, and planted a kiss on his cheek. No doubt this was a sexy lady. Harry thought she was pretty in a California kind of way when he first met her, but she was growing on him. She was New York. Almost Paris. Tonight, he was Leo in the middle of the Atlantic on the Titanic. Harry knew Charles was watching, so he played his role. His right hand went to his blond hair and smoothed out any imperfections. Nothing out of place. Harry was Leo, right down to his dreamy eyes and sexy smile.

Charles escorted the couple to a table on the balcony. A private space. He hovered to make sure the waiter delivered perfect service. He wanted Harry to look more than impressive to Felicity. The dinner was more than foreplay to an evening that gave Harry the final advantage over the Russians.

Harry's flip phone rang. Charles heard it and moved closer to their table. He hovered.

"Did you get the address?" Harry asked.

Harry felt the need to offer Felicity something for the interruption. He stroked her cheek, then closed the phone.

Charles placed menus on the table. He made no suggestions. Harry ordered for her. A delicate cucumber-beet salad, Asian beef stew with Cuban flavors, and a fragrant pinot noir. Harry asked for eggplant and beef stir-fry with a beer.

The phone call changed the intimate dynamic of the dinner. Felicity forced a smile. Her Lauren Bacall sultriness all but gone.

Harry picked up the ball, chatted up the history of the restaurant and the story of Charles as a chef with ideas to fuse Cuban cuisine with a French influence. Talking about types of food cheered Felicity, while he tried to push back the gnawing guilt, losing his appetite in his struggle. The opposite was happening to Felicity. She was eating out of a lustful joy that her evening would consummate her sexual desires.

Charles brought the dessert menu to their attention, moving along the end of their dining experience. He indicated that he wanted to talk to him. Felicity was focusing on the menu and didn't see the exchange. Harry excused himself.

The two men stopped outside a restroom in the hallway.

"Don't blow this, *mon cher*. You've got the perfect conduit to move up in this organization. You're going to have to use her. And whatever news you have of your wife is going to have to be left on the table tonight. You can get to her later. Wives wait. You're not a schoolboy anymore."

The evening with Felicity was like a dream. He had never been on a date. Not in high school in Newark. He was too scared, too insecure. Girls were all over him by the time he was a senior. A beautiful girl asked him to the prom. He didn't go. He didn't have the money to take her to dinner, a car to drive, or a tux to rent. She offered to pay. He politely declined.

Felicity led Harry into her dark apartment.

"Wait here. I'll turn on a light."

The light went on but the apartment still looked dim. Felicity wasn't embarrassed. She passed no judgment on its contents and dullness as she walked toward him. This was a woman who could probably turn on any man, but he wasn't any man.

Time stopped. This was the moment that he feared the most. Having sex with anyone other than Kobe was not right. Felicity was a stranger. Worse. There would be no love, no emotional connection. Only lust.

He put his hand in front of his mouth as she unbuckled his belt and felt his penis. Maybe this was what women do when they didn't want to have sex with a man: They gulped and held their breath. Harry exhaled slowly, so as not to disturb Felicity's passion. He needed her to be loving and attentive. He needed her to be available and giving. She had done this before. But what she was doing wasn't mechanical, and his erection stayed strong and firm.

Harry was taken by surprise when Felicity stood and started to undress. Not with the grace of a stripper or the hardness of a whore, but with patience and grace. She was naked, supple, and warm with all the pride and knowledge a beautiful woman possessed. She took Harry's hands and placed them on her waist. He wondered if she saw his heart pumping through his chest. Without words, she leaned in and asked him to kiss her. The energy she created with her lips drew Harry to her face. The kiss invited more.

The bright morning sun struck through the one small window in Felicity's apartment and hit Harry's face like a flash from a camera. He didn't remember where he was or what he had done. He rolled over on the single bed and almost fell off. Felicity was at her closet, hurriedly dressing. She saw him and smiled like the Mona Lisa. Still innocent.

"I'm late for work," Felicity said. She walked over to Harry and kissed him on the forehead. "It was wonderful. I'll see you again soon, my Leo."

Harry's eyes burned with guilt. Memories of last night returned. It was unthinkable. His breath came in short bursts. He tried to stop the tears from falling from his eyes by noting the details of her room: photos of La Habana city life hung on the walls of Felicity's studio apartment – bed on one wall, kitchen, opposite wall, old wood floors in need of repair and paint, a small closet with no doors, clothes neatly arranged, no dishes on the counter, a well-worn chair in the corner. Felicity's reality.

Felicity barged through the door. She clutched her heart while letting out a mournful cry. "Fidel is dead. Everyone is coming out into the streets. It's chaos. It's madness. It's the end of Cuba."

"No, Felicity. It's not the end. Raúl's been running the government for eight years already. Nothing's changed. Nothing will change because nobody wants to empower Cubans."

"You're wrong. He brought democracy and liberty to our people. He reformed land and gave property to the poor."

Harry knew Fidel's death wouldn't change anything. Cubans never had democracy, never had freedom. If a Cuban owned a piece of land, there was no electricity. Every building needed paint, a functioning refrigerator, a larger space to live in. The streets were clogged with old shark-fin Cadillacs and ragged beggars. The photos on Felicity's walls depicted the fairy-tale La Habana. These were scenes for tourists, not for Cubans who lived and worked in the city under impossible conditions. Every day Cubans got out of bed and struggle.

"Where are you going?" asked Felicity.

He ignores her question. "It might be a sad day for some people, but it's not a sad day for me."

"Wait, Leo. Please. You can't go off crazy into the streets."

"Cuba is purgatory with or without Fidel."

"But he had vision."

"If Fidel had vision, why did he depend on the Soviet Union? Why didn't he see the collapse coming? Cubans suffered after the Soviets left. If it weren't for tourism and some foreign investment, we'd still be starving. So, Obama came for a visit. So, today we can trade rum and cigars. Maybe things will change and maybe not, but it doesn't matter to me because Fidel's lies will forever be a part of Cuba's history."

"When am I going to see you again?"

Harry put his arms around her. He felt painful confusion. *Beware the fury of a patient man.*

Harry plowed his way through the crowded streets. Flags waved, people cried, some were cheering Fidel's death without fear. He tried to weave back to his hovel underneath Paco's building on the Prado, but the crowds were dense and difficult to push through. He headed back to Kirpan and saw Norm trying to shadow him, but he was dazed and confused. Stoned. Not functional. Shit. But he was still on his heels. Harry pushed through the people in the street, used them as shields and raced across the street, out of sight for the time being.

Kirpan was closed. Just as Harry walked away, the phone rang. Ibrahim was on the other end. He knew where Kobe lived.

"How about a celebratory drink, my friend," said Spencer, slurring his words as he walked toward him. "Fidel is dead. Long live Fidel. Charles should open the doors wide. Drinks on the house. A celebration is in order."

"He's probably keeping a low profile for a while."

"Doesn't mean other places aren't open," Spencer proffered.

"I have to keep moving."

"Do you have a plan, my man? Got any ideas as to how to foil the adversary? The Russian Victor, the fat man in the purple shirt."

Harry turned around to Spencer. "You got a line on what happens next?"

Spencer took Harry by the arm and maneuvered him through several groups of raucous Cubans along Calle Industria speaking in excited raised voices about Fidel's death. This was usually a sleepy, quiet street off Calle Barcelona, but today, the energy of their leader's death gave off anguish and despair.

"For you to know, Sir Harry. Find me a drink and I'll debrief you."

As Harry and Spencer moved through the streets, the louder the noise. Harry smelled marijuana and inhaled it into his lungs trying to get a contact high. Spencer was unsteady on his feet, but Harry thought it was worth it to hold on to him for a while. He might learn something. Spencer was agitated when he recognized that every restaurant and bar was boarded up.

Harry locked Spencer's arm into his ribs and forged his way through the neighborhood with tenacity. On Calle Barcelona, Harry knew a bar that never closed, and if it was locked, he knew how to get in through the back door.

"Where the bloody hell are you taking me, Sir Harry? Bitch of a walk."

Several blocks east of Kirpan, he knew of a tavern with no name. It was called The No Name Bar to those who frequented this watering hole. He pushed him through a small wooden door at the back of the bar and into darkness, flipped a switch, and the place lit up like a Christmas tree.

"Jesus! What the fuck!" yelled Spencer. "Like fucking broad daylight in here."

Harry found a bottle of bourbon from behind the bar and poured a thimbleful in a glass. He noticed for the first time how decayed and oily Spencer appeared. He figured him for fifty-five or sixty, but his hunched posture and red, runny eyes made him look eighty. Probably closer to death than he suspected.

"Bless you, my child," Spencer crooned. He sipped the bourbon slowly and breathed deeply. "Now turn off those goddamn lights."

Harry turned off the lights and opened the window slats, which let in sufficient light to see.

"I'll not bore you with the gory details of my past lives," Spencer said. "So that brings us to the present. My last name is Merryman, and please make no jokes about that for I am truly a merry man. I'm also the soon to be ex-husband of a French diplomat stationed in Cuba. She is leaving the island soon, but not with me. Frances is quite the lady. Charles knew that, knew her charms. She works for an inter-governmental program at the French Embassy. It is a humanitarian program that helps distribute food to the poverty-stricken Cubans. And you would know what a thankless job that is. You could live a lifetime on this island and never have enough food or time to accomplish the task of feeding the hungry."

"You and Charles. Nice combination. Two Europeans discuss the Cuban world as they discover its business potential through the eyes of the French Embassy. And since Charles has a bar at Kirpan, you can drink for free and be of service. And how is it you serve Charles?"

"I don't know where you got to be so fucking smart at your tender age. You may be older than I think. Baby face Leonardo DiCaprio." Spencer laughed at his own joke. "I trade inside information at the French Embassy for booze. Like what kinds of contracts and applications come down the pipeline. I'm a one-man show. I flirt with the female government employees, even the men sometimes, and ask to see this and that regarding trade and government partnerships. I've been involved in French trade, so I have a bona fide."

Harry flashed on Felicity and wondered if she ever exposed information to others. Was she for sale, part of the intelligence game?

"Is Charles your only client?"

"He's my main client, but the applications are from Justin, and processed through this quasi French diplomat, Lucien Chabrol, who is thoroughly distasteful."

The electricity came on again without prompting, and the jukebox in the corner of the room played spontaneously. Lights flashing. Fifties rock and roll.

"Crappy wiring. Harry, my love, turn those jukebox flares off."
Harry pulled the plug on the jukebox.

"Did your wife have a clue about how you traded information?"

"I make friends in the embassy at parties and social gatherings, so she has no idea what I do except drink. She's going back to France because she can't stand me any longer. It's going to be more difficult to snoop now that she is leaving and I have no reason to be on the premises."

"What's next?"

"It's all over for me, but you, my dear young man, have given me an idea. You will be the snoop. You will be the man who gathers information for the forces that be."

"It's not as easy to collect information as you suggest," said Harry. "Is this distasteful Lucien Chabrol someone you can trust?"

"I trust no one," countered Spencer. He went to the bar and poured himself another half glass of bourbon. "It is dog eat dog on this island. Everyone wants a piece of the pie, so the game is to eliminate the weak ones and get to the top. Justin is at the top of Cuba's junk heap."

"What do you know about Justin? Charles is pretty much an open book, petty, secretive, and greedy."

Spencer added, "And weak. But Justin is of another breed. He's very rich, a genius I would say, and he is secretive but more Machiavellian. I'd bet my last shekel Justin Levitt is not his real name."

"Who do you consider weak?"

"Victor is small potatoes. You've seen his operation. What's he got? Three or four flunkies around him. We can get rid of him. Get him off the island one way or another. Your job is to set him up so we don't have to worry about him anymore. Until the next Russian lowlife appears. An oligarch sends one Russian businessman at a time with enough money to fund the project, and if things don't work out, the businessman is history."

"You're shitting me, right? That's not my part in this. I don't set up anybody."

"Let me explain how this works. Got any more bourbon back there?"

Harry set the bourbon in front of Spencer. He spilled the bourbon as he poured, then gulped it down.

"There is something you don't know about this Cuba game. A French official, or diplomat if you wish, is an agent, a middleman who gets deals done for us. And that takes money. But the middleman must be a trusted cohort. Any suspicion of double-dealing and the agent is, well, shall we say, dead meat."

"How many agents do the French have?" asked Harry, trying to get chess pieces on the board to give him an advantage.

"Just Lucien. One more French agent would be one too many."

"I'm leaving this island soon like your wife, Mr. Merryman. I don't want or need to know more."

"Not for some time, my man, Leo. You have work to do for Charles, and Charles does work for Justin. It looks like a partnership, but it isn't."

"What does that mean? You talk in riddles." He headed for the door. "When you have a moment of clarity, let me know."

"The phantom Justin Levitt leaves no trace."

CHAPTER 10

The Ties That Bind

Harry left the No Name Bar and walked into the blinding afternoon sunlight. Spencer followed with temerity, putting his arm over his eyes and recoiling from the sun. He had been a bar vampire for too long.

Harry walked ahead without waiting for Spencer to catch up. He was not sure he believed everything Spencer told him. Drunks were liars. And Spencer was a spinner of tales.

"You'll hear from someone, so don't get lost," Spencer yelled, meandering and stumbling down the crowded streets, shoulders slumped, head tipped forward, and yet with a little jaunt in his walk.

Harry's head was throbbing. He put his baseball hat on to shield him from the intense heat. The sun beat down from a cloudless sky and the humidity made it hard to breathe.

Norm jumped out of the shadows of an alley, entered the street, and spotted Harry. He jogged to catch up with him, but he was sluggish. It felt like he was moving through a hot oven.

"Harry!" Norm yelled. *"Espera."*

Harry walked faster. Norm was a cockroach. Step on him and he wouldn't die.

"You're a slippery guy," said Norm? "I got some bad news."

"If it's about Juan Juan, I'm not interested."

"Your mother died," Norm said catching his breath.

Harry felt a wave of nausea and moved into an alcove inside a doorway.

"This is no joke, Norm, right? You got this news from Juan Juan? When did she die?"

There was so much yelling and cheering in the crowded street, Harry had trouble hearing Norm."

"When?" Harry insisted.

"Yesterday," Norm said as Harry stumbled in grief. "Juan Juan told me. Her heart gave out. Uncle Ray was with her."

"I have to go home, Norm. Can you get me back to Cienfuegos?"

"Oh, so, now I'm an important part of your life?" Norm quipped.

"For now you are." Harry was burning up.

Guilt and shame. The evil twins.

✳

Norm drove around Plaza Marti, the main plaza in Cienfuegos. It was crowded with older people in various states of grief. Same story, different day. Some were softly crying and some were facing walls in prayer; others were moving rosary beads through their fingers. These old Cubans believed Fidel gave them a new life, the opportunity to work, and above all, hope. He was *papi*, brother, grandfather. They never understood that Fidel kept Cuba in bondage to the Soviet Union, like Batista, never thinking that promoting economic development and trade might serve the Cuban people better. It didn't matter to Fidel that the Cubans had no voice. They did his bidding at the expense of their happiness.

At the corners of the plaza, groupings of the younger generation gathered. Some were smiling, some had blank looks on their faces. Some kids were only concerned with getting a Wi-Fi signal. Most were dispassionate onlookers to a historic moment that meant nothing to them. Young kids didn't buy into communist ideology. They saw what suffering did to their parents, the years of despair, the years of silent acceptance until the old Cubans became catatonic.

Uncle Ray couldn't figure out why, if the government knew that people lacked food and common necessities, officials looked the other way and offered no help. People could last only so long without filling their bellies. It was as if the government went to sleep and woke up to the same dying economy, an economy they never fixed.

Uncle Ray took matters into his own hands during the special period, when Cubans lost half their weight, had no options to make a living, couldn't feed their families, or scrape together a shred of dignity. He grew every possible vegetable, some he didn't know existed, cooked everything, sometimes in rancid oil, and fed his neighbors. No money was exchanged. Uncle Ray and music inspired the Cuban spirit to survive.

Norm dropped off Harry at his Uncle Ray's.

"I'm sorry for what I said to you before. You've been good to me with this favor, and I won't forget it."

The lingering odor of fried plantains and onions hung in Uncle Ray's restaurant. The absence of noise felt ominous. Alma entered the room dressed in black. Red suited her better, but red wasn't appropriate for mourning.

"Good to see you," said Alma. "Your uncle is getting ready for the funeral."

Her words felt like a slap across the face, but he understood. "I'd like to go with you and Uncle Ray."

"It's up to Ray. Sit down and I'll get him."

Harry felt the need to call Kobe and hear her voice, to be reassured she was still in his life. He needed her love, but he was unfaithful. Unfaithful to himself, to his mother, to Uncle Ray. He let all of them down in his quest to escape Cuba. He had a dream to bring his family with him, but all he left was neglect. Fueled by loss and resentment, he faced the prospect of mourning for his mother and for what his beautiful island could have been.

Uncle Ray was wearing a dark suit that hung on his withering frame. He did not acknowledge Harry as he walked to the door. Alma followed. Then Harry.

Catedral de la Purisma Conceptión in Plaza Martí was bold and graceful in its stark whiteness, lovingly maintained by the older generation of Cienfuegos. Narrow towers seemed to be suspended against the backdrop of a blue sky, encased with puffs of white clouds. Harry waited on the side of the tall, dark brown wood front doors that were spotted by age.

Uncle Ray and Alma walked into the cathedral, heads down in reverence for Regina. He tried to hide his presence from God as he walked behind them. The lacquered wooden pews stretched on either side of the main aisle and covered the stone floor with a brown glaze.

There was a scattering of older people in the first three pews on the left side. It was a poor turnout for his mother's funeral. He sat in the fourth pew, instead of following Uncle Ray to the first row where relatives knelt in prayer, none of whom Harry remembered or even knew.

The priest was a grizzled, wrinkled man in his seventies. His garments were threadbare. The vacuous cavern of the cathedral washed out what the old priest said. The priest didn't know her. His mother was gone.

He suspected his mother hadn't been to church in decades. His poor, dispirited mother. A woman who knew little joy, who worked her fingers to the bone without the support of a husband or a companion. He wasn't a good son, going off wildly and leaving her without help. Despite his lack of care for her, Regina loved her son and sent him to his uncle in Newark. It was partly selfish because she couldn't control him in his teens, but she also knew he would get a good education. She also thought he would stop being angry. He came back angrier.

The priest gave a blessing, and Harry stood as the mourners filed by in procession down the aisle. He nodded to a few he recognized, but he wasn't sure. The old man who took care of Regina passed by without a nod.

"Don't bother me now," Harry said as he walked by Juan Juan at the back of the church.

"I'll go along with you to the cemetery," Juan Juan said. "I'm sorry for your loss."

As Harry walked to the cemetery, clouds drifted over the blazing afternoon sun. Uncle Ray looked behind him to make sure Harry was following. The formal ritual was important to his uncle. He was a blood relation, a cousin of Harry's father. Long gone. Long forgotten. His mother cannot be forgotten.

The cemetery was well-maintained. Most of the flowers were fresh. Weeds did not cover the headstones as they did in most Cuban cemeteries. Even the white marble markers were clean and polished. A deep plot was already prepared for Regina's casket. The priest said prayers before four of the mourners, fragile elderly men who struggled to lower the pine box into the ground. Harry picked up a handful of dirt and threw it on the coffin. Juan Juan did the same. There was no finality for Harry. There was no peace. He wanted to say something to Uncle Ray, but he was deep in mourning, head down, saying the rosary. He didn't know his uncle was religious.

"I have to talk to you," pressed Juan Juan.

"Not a good time." Harry wanted to get to Santiago to talk to Kobe. It felt like Ibrahim gave him the address months ago.

"Remember those Americans I introduced you to in the plaza? They wanted to be in the money exchange business? I went to work for them because they got a money supplier."

Harry walked with Juan Juan into the plaza. "Lots of Americans want to invest in Cuba."

"They want me to get them government contacts. They asked about you."

"If these guys are working an American angle, you can tell them to fuck off. Fidel is dead, and Cuba is still the same. No business with the U.S., especially since the American government might get a new president. I wouldn't put an ounce of effort into what they're thinking of doing. Now, get out of my space. I've got to find Norm."

"No, you've got to help me out," pleaded Juan Juan. "Ernesto thinks I've got contacts."

"If you fed him a line of shit, I can't help you. Didn't you learn anything in school about the last fifty years?"

"Put me down all you want, but you don't know everything. You don't know what Silas is planning."

"What about Silas?" asked Harry.

"So, now I've got something you want."

"There's nothing I want from you, *singao*."

"Big shot. You'll want this. Silas came back through Cienfuegos and met up with Ernesto and his people at the Sonrisa one night. They talked of doing a tech deal with the Cubans."

"No surprise to me," said Harry. "Stay away from this. Everybody's looking for something. Everybody's out for themselves so the best play is to keep your head down and look the other way."

�֍

Harry sprinted up the steps of Padre Pico to Ezra's restaurant. His heart raced. He wasn't sure what to say or how to handle the situation with Kobe. He was the intruder.

It was lunch hour at Los Lobos, a hole-in-the-wall restaurant at the entrance to Tivoli. It was packed with local Haitians, Jamaicans, Puerto Ricans, Arabs, Dominicans, and Chinese. He stumbled over some chairs. A few men looked at him and turned away. Harry spotted a seat against a wall with a good view of the small kitchen in the back. He heard bits and pieces of conversation, about Cuban football, work, and family gossip.

He caught a fleeting view of Kobe preparing food in the kitchen. She didn't see him yet. He watched her, took in her presence until the spell was broken.

Kobe walked out of the kitchen with plates for customers on the other side of the restaurant. When she turned, she saw Harry. He stood. She walked back into the kitchen.

He waited until all of the patrons finished their food, drank their beers, and left.

Kobe returned to the dining room carrying a plate of food and placed it in front of Harry.

Whatever feelings of anger she had a half hour ago subsided. Harry inhaled half his food before he looked up.

"I like your new haircut," said Harry.

"Thank you." She squeezed his hands.

"I miss you," said Harry.

"And I miss you."

"Why are you doing this, staying in Santiago?"

"To discover if I want your journey as badly as you want it. You've gone missing, not me."

"I'm here."

"It was different when you left this time. I realized I need to learn to live my own life."

"I respect that, but you don't have to hide."

"Yes, I do. You went down the rabbit hole. It's probably the black fiery hole of a volcano by now."

Harry went silent.

"What's the matter, Harry? What has happened?"

"My mother died. We buried her yesterday."

"Why didn't you tell me?" she asked. "I could have been with you. I should have been with you."

"I needed to be there alone."

"Katrina misses you."

"Then, wait for me."

"That's what you want," said Kobe, "but that's not what I want. Your dream is too complicated and too dangerous. My dream is to live happily in Santiago and teach school and have a simple life."

The honesty of Kobe's words and the power of her feelings surprised him. She was creating her own life without turning to her husband for permission.

"I learned that I don't want the things that you want. I'm happy here and Katrina is free. I don't want to be in harm's way." Kobe was getting agitated. "Don't put me in harm's way, Harry. I'll never forgive you."

Harry didn't know what he expected from seeing Kobe, but nothing he could say made either one of them feel better or change what was happening.

"I'll be going now," said Harry, "and I won't return until my business is finished. When I come back, I'll ask you to come with me to the States."

Kobe didn't look Harry in the eyes. She loved him, but she wasn't sure love was enough.

"I don't know," she said. "I may never know if I will make the right choice about my life. Sometimes it's out of our hands."

"When can I see Katrina?" he asked.

"She'll be here soon. I'll get you a cup of coffee."

This was Kobe's world, happy and secure. She had no will to return to what was.

"Daddy!" Katrina ran to her father, carrying her journal tablet under her arm, and squeezed her father with all her strength. "Please don't cry, Daddy. Everything will be all right."

Harry ran down the Tivoli steps. He was terrified that everything he loved was going to be taken away from him.

He remembered when he lived in Newark and went to the movies every week, mostly in the afternoon when prices were cheap. He watched the film from the center row, center seat in the movie theater, a place that gave him distance from the action but allowed for a perfect view of the screen.

When Harry thought of his life, it was like watching a movie. His real-life movie was that he got up every morning at six o'clock with Kobe, drank a cup of coffee, ate a piece of bread and a piece of fruit if he was lucky. Kobe got Katrina up, dressed and fed her, then, they took her to day care. And the ten-hour shift in the cigar factory began.

After work they picked up Katrina, ate dinner together, played a game or read a book, tucked Katrina into bed and talked to each other every night until they fell asleep. It was a ritual that went on every day for ten years.

One day, the film stopped. It was the second act, the middle of the movie, and he was suddenly left without an ending. He had a meltdown, fixated on the smell of tobacco sticking to his hands and fingers. He was sick every morning. It was morning sickness without being pregnant. He lost weight. Kobe watched her husband go through his pain with compassion, and she endured. She told him to leave the cigar factory, insisted that he use his skills as a translator in the plaza. But once out of the factory, Harry's dreams got bigger – they grew out of his control – and the drive to leave the island became an obsession.

Harry was still out of breath when William opened the door. He asked William to take him back to La Habana. Harry was grateful for his friend's generosity. William was grateful for the company.

While Harry waited for William to get ready for the trip, Satomi asked, "What if Kobe won't go with you to the States?"

"I won't be much good to Kobe if I stay in Cuba," said Harry. "When I'm settled in the States, I can send for Katrina and show her another life. Kobe always knew I wanted to return to the U.S., and my decision has never changed."

Satomi knew it was settled. Kobe would stay and make a life. Harry would go on his own journey, wherever that would take him.

Harry slept most of the drive. As he came out of his slumber, the streets of La Habana were quiet.

"Same Cuba, different day," said Harry.

After the mourning period ended, the streets would come alive with energy and noise. Life without Fidel.

"You don't have to work for anyone else, you know," said William. "You can get a license to work."

"You think I want to be a wedding photographer, or a manicurist, or drive my car with stinking sausages stuffed under the passenger seat? You think I want to sell women's miniskirts? Everyone steals from where they work, only to resell. That's ghetto shit. I don't want to steal goods from the docks or warehouses or factories and rob Peter to pay Paul."

"What got you all wound up?" asked William. "You put that all together after you just woke up? You're on a kick, *hombre*."

"Everyone in government looks the other way and takes the bribe. That's survival in Cuba."

William told him to do it the right way and stay out of trouble. Get a license to do what you want. Pay taxes and play by the rules and you could still exchange money for tourists.

"Breaking the law is built into the system. Why would anyone prefer this Marxist crap to freedom?"

"You got a lot of anger," said William. "What's happening to you?"

Harry got out of the car in front of Kirpan. "Thanks for the lift. You must be wiped out. Do you have a place to stay?"

"My cousin lives in Habana Vieja. I got a notice from the tax department that they didn't get the money we sent to the government office for taxes on our Airbnb. I don't want any trouble, and it's best to show up in person."

"Let me know if you need help."

Kirpan was dark and cool inside. Delicious smells came from the kitchen. Ishmael was making himself a meal of fried chicken and plantains. He dished out a serving for Harry and pulled two stools up to the cooking counter.

"I suppose you've heard."

"Probably not. My mother died in Cienfuegos and we buried her. Then I found my wife living in the hills of Santiago, and we had a talk that didn't go well. Not a good couple of days."

"Wasn't good here either. The Fat Man took advantage of the of mourning period, and stole the French files in the government's application office. Your girl was working in the office on Saturday, and they tied her up. I don't know if she talked, and I don't know what happened to her. They've got our bids, our strategies, and our contacts."

"I have to see her," said Harry, bolting from his seat.

"Sit back down. We've got else something to do."

"She's important. What if she's hurt?"

"It won't matter if we don't get this done."

"I didn't sign up for another line of work."

"You signed up for anything that brings us success. The Fat Man is in the way. He knows too much." Ishmael throws their dishes in the sink. "Vamos, hombre. Time to grow up."

CHAPTER 11
Down the Rabbit Hole

Night temperatures were cooling the city. Humidity lifting. Three more days of mourning Fidel. Shops and restaurants were still closed, and people were staying home at night. As he passed the corner of Calle Barcelona, Habana Vieja felt menacing.

Harry had a hard time keeping up with Ishmael. His legs felt like Jell-O, acid burned his stomach, his lower back stung with pain. They walked past the Capitolio Nacional, freshly scrubbed for President Obama's visit, but empty inside due to repairs. The Spanish architecture looked as imposing, as imposing, as the U.S. Capitol on which it was modeled. He caught a glimpse of the Museo Nacional de Bellas Artes in the distance. Flashes of the great Cuban artists – Collazo, Blanco, and his favorite, Raúl Martínez, master of sixties Cuban pop art. He remembered his mother took him to the museum. It was the day his father left.

They crisscrossed streets and found themselves on Paseo de Marti, a very long, wide boulevard with trees and benches, scrubbed almost clean of any black smudges left over from past decades. Ishmael sat down on a bench under a large, bright yellow moon. Harry kept walking. Fear made him oblivious to everything outside of himself.

"Harry!" shouted Ishmael. "Get back here."

Ishmael, angry and frustrated, searched for an Internet connection. He stepped into the center of the boulevard and finally connected.

"Is he seated outside or inside?" Ishmael asked. "How many people are around him? Has he been served?" Harry was pacing, rubbing his hands through his hair. "Okay, thanks. We'll get the timing right."

"I'm not doing this, Ish."

"It has to be you. Victor knows you. Ibrahim is at Los Nardos, watching the waiters and customers. Not many people in the restaurant. You'll walk up to him inside the restaurant, and Victor will greet you with a fake smile, or shock because he thinks you've double-crossed him. Be fast when you come around to the back of his chair."

Ishmael took out a slim, four-inch, silver knife. The handle was carved into the image of Che. It looked like a kid's knife. "Cup this into your palm, keep the blade down until you brush past him. No big moves. You want to cut the neck artery and he'll slowly bleed out. No one will know what happened for about thirty seconds. You'll be gone by then."

"This isn't who you are, Ish. It's not Ibrahim. How the fuck did this happen?"

"Ibrahim will walk in front of the table to deflect attention. Victor's got two men with him. It will be too late to notice you've gone, or that Ibrahim is part of it. Listen up, Harry. Ibrahim will look different. He's wearing a scarf, glasses, a dark wig. Victor's guys won't be able to trace him."

"But they'll trace me. I can't do this. I'm not cut out to be a killer."

Out of the darkness, a businessman, briefcase in hand, walked past Harry and Ishmael. Harry turned away from the man, paralyzed with fear and paranoia. Even the trees had ears.

"Justin needs Victor out of the picture. He has our files and knows what our bids are. That's all we need to know."

"What about every other country that has applications on file with the government? Are you going to kill their men, too?"

"You had value to Justin and Charles when Victor put you on the payroll. If you didn't figure that out, you're not as smart as I think you are."

"What about the Russian government? They'll find out, and I'm a dead man. Victor's been sent by some fucking Russian oligarch. They'll be sniffing around when Victor doesn't call."

"The Russians send people to Cuba all the time hoping they'll score some contracts. You throw enough shit on the wall and something will stick. Victor is expendable to his handler. We'll take care of Russian follow-ups if that happens. Charles promised to give you $25,000 for this hit. That should make you feel better."

Charles. $25,000. Doing a hit. This happened to other guys – guys with no brains, no moral compass, no potential. This was a simple inquiry, change money, make money. Killers are other guys, not guys like him – good looks, brains, tiger-by-the-tail kind of guy. But this is a killer's world, a world where money is made and men die.

"I won't do this!" said Harry. "No amount of money will make me do this. Fuck dollars! This is murder."

Ishmael put one hand on Harry's chest and one over his mouth. "You have no choice." Ishmael smoothed out Harry's shirt and fixed his collar, like his personal valet. He locked eyes on him with animal intensity. "You'll do this, Harry. You're in too deep. And Justin will tell you when you can leave the island. In fact, he'll give you a full ride out of La Habana, wife and daughter included. After he is done with you."

Harry pulled at his collar, looked down at his shoes, and whispered, "I don't know where the artery is."

Ishmael placed his finger on Harry's neck and pressed.

The phone rang again. Ibrahim. Ishmael listened, looking directly at Harry while talking into the phone. "Are Victor and the two guys at a table?" Ishmael was still watching Harry intently so he wouldn't lose him. Sweat glistened on his upper lip. "Harry will wait outside until you text him it's good to go in. If the Fat Man goes to the bathroom, Harry will step inside to follow him. Otherwise, he'll walk around the back of the table and get it done. You're the diversion. If Harry doesn't get it right, you finish it off."

Ishmael reached in his backpack and threw Harry a bottle of water and a baseball cap. *New York Yankees*.

Ibrahim, the school teacher? The man with above average intelligence, a classy guy, with an education. How did he turn into a killer? Harry felt like he was going to shit his pants. He gulped down the entire bottle of water.

"Jesus, it sounds like you made this stuff up. The hit is right out of *The Godfather*."

"You'll make it work. Ibrahim will make it work. Hold your mind together. You have Ibrahim's number?" Harry dropped his head. "Now get over there, and keep your adrenaline pumping."

Harry stood outside Los Nardos on Paseo de Martí and waited for a text from Ibrahim. He tried to remember the layout of the restaurant. Victor sent him to get takeout food a few times. He wanted two seafood dishes and their famous Spanish paella. Harry vaguely remembered the inside looking like a movie set with rich reds and mahogany tables and chairs. No waiter was under seventy and they served food as if they were in old-world Europe, hovering over and flattering the diners. Victor liked the restaurant because it was a good bang for the buck. The food smelled of oil and grease and garlic.

He felt the vibration in his right hand. The text told him to come inside. Victor came back from the bathroom and returned to the table.

Harry entered as the Fat Man returned to his table. The dim lighting was straight out of the third Circle of Hell. He got an immediate whiff of cigar smoke: Victor and his Cohiba. The foul smoke pushed his senses into chaos. He gagged. His eyes watered. He tried to get his bearings and adjust his eyes.

Victor looked up and thought he saw a ghost. The ghost of Leo. He continued chewing, mouth open, drooling paella broth onto his bib, worried he spilled food on his beloved purple shirt. He looked down at blotchy stains that missed his white cloth napkin.

"Goddamn grease on my shirt," yelled Victor. "I need more napkins." The ghost was walking toward him. *What's that snitch doing here anyway? He should have killed fucking Leo.* Victor started screaming. His two companions were paralyzed by his reaction.

"Get me another napkin! Can't you see I need help?"

Harry walked deliberately in Victor's direction, but his eyes looked forward toward the red booth behind Victor's table. He slid behind Victor's chair as the Fat Man looked in confusion toward the front door trying to track Harry's movements. One of Victor's companions went to the bar and grabbed a pile of napkins.

Harry and Ibrahim looked at each other with the understanding that Harry's knife would go directly into Victor's neck. Ibrahim would do the same to the Russian standing next to him at the bar. Both knives sliced each man's throat simultaneously with one swift move.

In a split second of conscious control, like a doctor cutting precisely into a human heart with his scalpel, Harry felt the knife sliding into Victor's flabby, moist neck. A thin line of blood seeped down the front right side of Victor's purple shirt. The red and purple colors turned black. In an instant, Harry knew he leaped into a void. There was no reentry into his former life, no magic to turn back what he had done. Harry Cisneros vanished from the planet.

Harry and Ibrahim headed away from Los Nardos and kept their eyes forward. Paseo de Martí was a long boulevard and had few places to hide. Ibrahim noticed blood on Harry's hands. They found a fountain with running water. Harry washed the murder knife and scrubbed the blood off his hands.

"Clean the fountain," said Ibrahim.

The bright moon made it easy for Harry to see the circular fountain. He swished the water and rubbed the bowl clean.

"Go home, Harry, and on your way, get rid of the knife. I'll do the same. My car is parked on Calle Neptuno. We're coming up to the street. Keep walking ahead."

All color drained from Harry's face. White as a virgin's veil.

"You all right?" asked Ibrahim.

"I murdered a man. I'm never going to be right."

"Neither will I. So, spare me the drama. We are both sick of waiting for things to change."

"I don't know how I got to this place of saying yes to killing."

"You had no choice. After it's over and we get back to business, you'll feel better."

"How did you let Ishmael or Charles or anyone talk you into getting into this mess?" asked Harry. "How do you go from being a schoolteacher to a murderer?"

Ibrahim drove off into the quiet night.

We have bartered with the devil and lost our souls.

Harry entered his cubbyhole and heard noise in the kitchen. He dragged his body along the wall, heart racing, still clutching the murder weapon. No blood on the knife. His hands were clean.

Felicity was boiling water and tending to the multiple scratches on her body. She turned and screamed. Harry put his hand over her mouth.

"*Cálmate, mi cariño.*" Harry held her close and felt her heart pumping.

Felicity began a long, painful wail. Her body shook, but there were no tears.

"Calm yourself."

Felicity tried to control the uncontrollable. She hugged her body to stop the pain. He slipped the knife into a refrigerator bin and made her tea.

She sipped from the cracked cup, and the warmth of the tea began to calm her nerves. Harry took her in his arms and carried her over to his bed. He laid her down patiently and delicately and put a blanket over her tired body.

"How did you find my place? Did I tell you where I lived? If I did, I'm glad." He gently stroked her back and shoulders.

"You told me where you lived the first night we were together. You said I should know where you live for my safety. You don't lock your door."

"There is no lock."

"Rest. Then, you'll tell me what happened."

He moved the one chair in the room against the door. Two people to protect now.

Harry watched over her, almost forgetting he killed Victor. Someone else did that. Someone else murdered a Russian man in a restaurant in Cuba. Ibrahim was not Ibrahim. Ishmael was not Ishmael. Harry was not Harry. No one was who he thought he was.

❋

Two more days of mourning for Fidel. Two more days before Kirpan reopened for business. Everyone laid low. Charles was in the kitchen cooking. Norm sat in a corner, head on the table, his lanky arms and legs stretched out. Tired and stoned. Juan Juan called. He was in La Habana. Juan Juan heard about the murder of two Russians. Norm had no idea what he was talking about. He never heard anything. Track down the information. Find Silas because he owed him money. Meet at the Hotel Sevilla, and Norm had to be there, or else.

Juan Juan was a worm. He had spies in La Habana and Cienfuegos, even Santiago. He dreaded meeting up with the little fucker. He would grill him to get information. He also played Ernesto. Norm couldn't figure out who was smarter or dumber, Ernesto or Juan Juan, but it didn't matter. What Norm knew for sure was that when it came to money, all roads tracked to Charles and Kirpan.

Charles came around to the bar and saw Ibrahim enter.

"Coffee?" asked Charles. "Go into the kitchen. I've got breakfast cooking."

Charles stood over Norm like an interrogator ready to pounce.

"Who was on the phone, Norm?" asked Charles.

"A guy I used to run errands for in Cienfuegos," said Norm. "He has a money changing business, thanks to Harry."

"Don't make me ask questions. Tell me the deal."

Norm was high and having trouble focusing.

He told Charles that Juan Juan worked with a Cuban guy named Ernesto. He was with some American gangsters who wanted to change dollars into kooks and Juan Juan thought Harry could help. Harry hated Juan Juan and blew him off.

Charles pulled his hair so that Norm looked directly at him. Norm screamed in pain.

"This is bullshit. Juan Juan's got nothing, no bankroll. He's interested in blackmail." He let go of Norm's hair roughly. "If this Juan Juan found out something, would he run it by Harry to make a deal?"

"I wouldn't put it past him." Norm rubbed his head.

He shoved Norm's head into the table.

"I'm meeting Juan Juan tonight at Hotel Sevilla," offered Norm, trying to get on the good side of Charles.

"Friendship is overrated, Norm. Remember who you work for. I give you money for dope. You play by my rules. Do you hear me? Have I gotten it through your thick skull yet?"

Charles threw Norm a flip phone. "I've got a job for you. Find out the word on the streets about the Russians who got killed. Meet up tonight with Juan Juan. Find out anything new about that low-life. If you see Ernesto hanging around, tell me that, too. Now get some food and get out of here."

�֎

Harry woke up before sunrise. Felicity was sleeping. Beautiful Felicity was a complication he didn't need. With Justin's $25,000 for killing Victor, he's off the island, but only if Charles kept his promise. He wasn't safe in La Habana. It was too dangerous to contact Kobe. He wished he had some faith to hold onto, some belief. Too late for that.

Darkness was a good time to roam the city and gather information. He dressed and heard a knock at the door. Juan Juan pushed his way inside.

Harry pushed Juan Juan back into the street. The humidity engulfed his body like a vise as the sun begins to rise.

"You fuck. You still have Norm tailing me."

They started to wrestle each other, but both pulled back.

Juan Juan shook Harry off him. "You're in danger, idiota. You need to hide. No one knows it's you who slit the Russian's throat. You're playing in the big leagues now."

"You don't know shit," said Harry. This second-rate punk was an asshole and assholes were dangerous.

"I know you or somebody you know killed the Russians."

"Prove it."

"I can't, but you are out of your league."

Harry pushed Juan Juan against the wall. "You're a fucking wannabe and that'll come back to bite you in the ass."

Juan Juan shook off Harry and straightened his clothes. "Don't you want to know how I know this?"

Harry backed off realizing he was walking a fine line between stress and collapse, between a long-ago friendship and two plaza hustlers in over their heads.

Juan Juan told him there is a snitch in the organization.

"This angle won't work. You don't have proof."

"You're right, I don't know all the details, but I was just with Silas and Norm, and Norm knows more than he's telling. He's heard some things around Kirpan."

He was guessing. He knows nothing. He's a pothead. Juan Juan might be right about a snitch, but it wasn't Norm.

Everything was a hustle, a game, a killing. Harry had no stomach for it. When he was in Newark, the street gangs ruled the ghettos with ironclad fists. The system was about status, who's on top, who's on the bottom. It was a layered infrastructure, like the military, like the mafia, and it was highly disciplined. It was loyalty to an ideal. Easy to follow if you believed in the party line. In Cuba, the cues were different. If he went back to the U.S., he wouldn't deal with the gangs. He wasn't up to speed on the tics and feints of the business culture either. He had to recalibrate his position. Think like a captain, move like a foot soldier.

Felicity was brewing tea when he entered. Her face still blotched from crying. She seemed smaller than before. He always thought of her as strong and confident. But torture and fear, intimidation and defenselessness fed vulnerability. He was responsible for her situation.

"Please tell me exactly what happened. It's for your protection."

Felicity drank her tea in measured sips. The burglars were Russians. They must have snuck past the guard. They tied her up and threatened to kill her if she didn't tell them who came into her office to look at the files. They asked her about "Leo." She told them someone had been to the office, but she didn't know his name nor what he was looking for. They asked her to describe Harry. She lied about what he looked like.

Harry held her in his arms. "It's going to be over soon."

After they left, the phone rang. Felicity couldn't answer it. She thought it might be her supervisor, so she rolled over, and with her head pushed the phone off the desk. She didn't know how long it was before *Señor* Paz untied her. He told her to go home. He'd take care of it. She was going to lose her job.

Harry knew her job was safe. She knew too much, had the knowledge to run the application office, and was valuable to her boss. But why did Alberto call her office a few minutes after the burglary?

"What happened to the night guard?"

"I don't know. *Señor* Paz took me out the back of the building, and I got here on my own."

There was a noise at the door. Shuffling feet.

"I'm Harry, not Leo. I let you think my name was Leo."

"I don't care what your name is. I care about you. That's all I know."

Harry embraced her frail body.

"Please tell me if you remember anything else."

Felicity didn't hear much because they were in the file room and they spoke Russian. She knew some Russian because she had to learn it in school. They said this Leo person lied to them and everyone was going to pay.

"That's good, very good. This is what I want you to do when you feel up to it. Go back to your office, clean up the mess, and try to find out what's missing. It's been less than twenty-four hours, and it's a weekend, so everything should be in order."

"Nothing is missing. I made copies of all the French files. I thought they might be important to you. I already made copies of the Brazilian files like you asked. You misfiled everything. You're not a very good clerk."

"Where are these copies now?"

"In my office," replied Felicity. "Where would you like them to be?"

"Where would you suggest?"

"I planned to put the copies of the French applications back in the system, but I have a secret place to put the Brazilian files. I will give you the key in case some day you need that information. It will be our secret."

CHAPTER 12
Threading the Needle

Felicity fumbled for the key to the temporary government building on Calle Dragones. The street in front of the entrance was eerily quiet.

The morning guard was not behind the front desk and not behind the reception area. One of the doors was ajar in the hallway. Felicity peeked into the room and saw the feet of a man lying on the floor. She pushed against the door. The night guard was tied up and gagged. His uniform was clean and pressed. He looked like a mummy.

She forced herself up the stairs to the third floor. The door to her office was closed, but not locked. Papers and files were strewn on the floor. The office was always ugly, but the men who were killers and thieves sullied it forever.

Felicity suspected the Russians bound and gagged the night guard and killed him. She pushed the thought away because there was work to do. Her mind ran through what applications go into particular files based on a color system that identified countries. She decided to put the copies of the French applications into blue folders instead of red. Chinese applications would go into red folders.

All will be well in time. She made Harry happy.

Somebody was a snitch for the Russians. Harry knew it wasn't Juan Juan, but he was a good source to follow because his reason for existing was money.

Time to find Charles and collect his money before he went deeper down the rabbit hole. Charles had to open Kirpan for business the next day. In the meantime, Harry had no dollars for him, no commissions for himself.

Where the hell was Ishmael?

Harry dialed Ishmael on his cell. No answer. He dialed his home phone. Anna answered.

Anna was upset. He heard her crying. She told Harry that Ishmael came in late the night before, or maybe it was early morning, and he looked like he got into a fight. Clothes were torn. Face bloody. He showered, cleaned up, and left without telling her anything, except to lock the door.

"Don't panic, Anna," said Harry. "Just listen. Get out of your apartment and go to relatives. Don't stay around because you think he's coming home. Do you have my cell?"

"Ishmael wrote it down. I know where it is."

"Copy it and then tear it up," said Harry. "Take the copy with you. Call me with any news and I'll do the same."

The conversation with Anna seemed too pat. The part about being in a fight the night before doesn't seem plausible. Ishmael would be more cautious in his movements.

The streets were beginning to get crowded with Sunday strollers. He picked up the pace and jogged to Kirpan.

Harry entered the familiar darkened restaurant and took a few moments to adjust to the shadows in the room. Two waiters were putting new bulbs in the wall lights. Charles was behind the bar counting dollars.

"What are you doing here, Harry? You need to be out of sight."

"Is that my payment you're counting out now?" asked Harry.

Charles motioned Harry to follow him into Justin's office. He sat behind Justin's desk, taking his place and playing the role of his partner.

"Surely, you don't think I have that much on hand."

"I think you have it somewhere. And I think you'll pay up. Aren't we on the same team? Let's play fair."

"You'll get paid and so will the others. Ibrahim is already back in Santiago opening up his tour agency as we speak."

"Where is Ishmael?"

"Ishmael takes care of Ishmael," responded Charles.

"And I take care of me."

"That's why you are walking around today. Your brain. Your nerve. All intact. What else do you want besides $25,000?"

"I want to fly off this island on Justin's plane. I want Ishmael to be alive, and I want Ibrahim to come to no harm and be protected until this has passed. And I want to find the snitch in your organization."

"Why do you think there might be a traitor?"

"A hunch. I haven't seen Spencer around lately. Did he go back to England?"

"Think he's the traitor?" asked Charles.

"Doesn't he feed you information from his French connections at the embassy?"

"He's got no information, and he's not the snitch. Spencer couldn't get near the Russians in his condition. Besides, our Cuban agent knows more than he does."

This was the first time Harry heard about a Cuban agent. Kirpan's business model had more layers than an onion.

Times were changing. If Charles could play big shot in Justin's office, Harry felt emboldened to flip him off. He poured a drink from Justin's private bar. Scotch neat. He didn't care what Charles thought. He took a sip and the ceiling lights flickered. The room went dark. Three seconds later, lights came on again.

"Shit wiring still doesn't work," said Charles.

"Maybe you should be in the electrical business instead of water and sanitation. Ever hear the story about the light bulb scam? Have Ishmael tell you."

"We're working on the wiring."

"Sorry, I don't know your Cuban agent," said Harry. "I haven't had the pleasure."

"Then maybe you need to meet Alberto Paz," Charles said.

Harry wasn't surprised by anything anymore. He chose to say nothing about Felicity's connection to Alberto.

"I want assurances from Justin that I'll get off this island," he said.

"Leo, my Leo. Spoken like a true soldier. I'll confirm this with Justin."

Harry left the office. On his way to the entrance, an outline of a figure walked toward him and escorted him out of the restaurant.

Charles opened the front door and saw Justin and Harry walking together down Calle Industria.

The familiarity of Calle Industria comforted Harry. How many times had he walked past familiar storefronts, small shops selling auto parts or fruit or textiles? Even though some shops changed the items that were sold, the signs above the shop never changed.

Harry knew there was no specific destination. Justin liked to walk and talk. Walking induced an informal dialogue on topics Justin wanted to discuss. The listener was easily drawn into his orbit.

"You'll get off the island, my Leo, but not until we tidy up the Russian burglary. You told Victor about the Institut Français des Aquatiques applications. But to get inside Felicity's office, to know how to get to our files, the Russians needed a contact in the Cuban Embassy. There was a traitor."

"I don't have an answer," said Harry, understanding that he was not going to leave Cuba anytime soon, not tomorrow, not next week, maybe not next month, not until he put Humpty Dumpty back together again.

"And will your wife and daughter be joining you when you leave Cuba?"

"I've been absent. I need to send them money."

Justin told Harry that he would not only give him money, but he would also fly him to Santiago to take care of his family when things quieted down. But in this game, they were playing, there was always a whiff of duplicity.

"And why in the hell are you smiling?" asked Justin.

"This is playing out like the detective movies I watched in Newark. I studied these characters in drama class at my high school. We had a great teacher. Too bad I can't tell her I'm living in a damn play."

"You missed your calling, Harry."

"There's a lot I missed. List your cast of traitors."

Justin suspected his old friend, Juan Juan, a loose cannon who needed to be put into place. There was Norm, the pothead with enough brain parts to overhear things in the bar and enough wits to understand the implications. Ishmael, the leader of the pack, was missing. Spencer was probably drinking himself to death, but how much did he know before his wife left Cuba? Finally, there was the mystery of Charles and his connection to Lucien in the French Embassy.

"Lucien?" asked Harry.

"He's our French agent."

Each one of Justin's cast of characters had an opportunity to betray. It was an open field. But good old Leo is going to solve the riddles of the Sphinx.

"Why isn't Alberto Paz a suspect?"

"Don't worry about him," said Justin. "Alberto makes the Cuban world go around for us. He keeps the Russians at bay. Sometimes there are unforeseen forces."

"Like Felicity," says Harry.

"Unfortunate that the Russians caused her some discomfort. The night guard's appearance was a nuisance for the Russians, but being the brutes they are, they killed him. Señor Paz disposed of the body while Felicity cleaned up the mess of files in her office."

The difficulty of following the real Justin was like catching fog in a bottle.

The Russian brutes were easy to define. Killers. Morality was irrelevant.

He was back in Newark, observing the gangs in the streets. But in La Habana, corruption and crime were hidden behind closed doors. He was now in the gang. He made it to the bottom of the rabbit hole.

Must climb out.

"And where did your French files end up?" asked Harry.

"With the Russians, but Victor's dead, and I need you to retrieve the files they stole."

"That won't be necessary."

"You're not crossing me on this."

"Felicity copied our applications before the burglary."

"She does good work, but I'd still like to get the originals back."

"The originals are on the computer," said Harry. "It's the modern age in Cuba, didn't you hear?"

"I want the original paper files back, Harry, and soon."

Harry leaned against the wall at the corner of Calle Industria and Calle Barcelona, took a breath and called Juan Juan as he watched Justin return to Kirpan. As he waited for a response, Harry thought there was something not quite right about the conversation. He couldn't put his finger on it, besides the commanding order to get on with finding the traitor. Why does Justin need the original files back? If so, have Felicity run them off the computer. Then they would be the originals.

An incoming call interrupted his call to Juan Juan. It was Alma. Lovely Alma. She was in La Habana and wanted to meet. She had news about Uncle Ray. He was sick with cancer and dying.

At one time, Harry would have jumped to meet her. He was changed, not as soft, not as concerned. But her voice brought him close to his old life, to a faraway place inside himself, one that was once a place of love and respect for family. He was in his movie again, but this was another script.

Alma told him she and Ray were lovers. They had a life that was good and fulfilling. She was in La Habana to contact some of his friends, to commune in sorrow for his impending death, and to commemorate the joy that he gave to others. He had another life in La Habana once upon a time. He owned a restaurant in Habana Vieja and left a legacy that she wanted to find. It was a mission of love.

He pushed off the wall and headed in the direction of Calle San José. He tried to get his head around the fact that his Uncle Ray had another life, and he knew nothing about it. He was jolted out of his stupor when a group of drunken men crowded the intersection. They jostled each other and talked in loud bursts of obscenities. Harry turned toward the wall to blend into the street, not be noticed, but they saw him anyway.

"I've got to go, Alma. I'm in a rough section. I'll call you back."

He stuffed his phone down his pants. One of the gang pinned Harry's shoulders to the wall.

"I've got a message for you, *pendejo*." he said in a Russian accent. "You're walking dead in this city. You have no time left."

Harry kneed the kid in the groin, others came at him, but before they could beat the shit out of him, he bent his knees and slipped down the wall. The gang didn't realize they lost their target. Harry crawled out and stumbled, fell, got up, and ran down Calle San José toward Centro Habana. He ran as fast as he could, away from his life, memories of his mother, Kobe, Katrina, and Uncle Ray's imminent death. His life was receding, and he was terrified he couldn't climb out of the rabbit hole.

He called Alma back. "*Lo siento*, Alma. I ran into some drunken kids. They're everywhere in La Habana. Listen, *querida*, I want to invite you to a restaurant called Kirpan on Calle Industria. And I want you to sing tomorrow night. Come at eight, and sing your heart out. They'll love you. I need to give back to you for what you've done for Uncle Ray. I'll see you there."

Night was falling, a cool breeze picked up and engulfed the city streets. Harry needed time and space to think, to feel the impact of what the thug said. There was a mark on him by some fucking Russian.

He kept running. He was too far north of Felicity's place on Calle Gloria, so he dropped down from Calle San José, past, Capitolio Nacional, through Parque de la Fraternidad. Several teenagers were hanging out in the park smoking, along with two families and their small children playing on the jungle gyms trying to catch the last rays of light. He heard the sounds of adults fighting and children crying as he weaved his way across side streets, Corrales, Apodaca, and smelled the pungent odors of plantains being fried. It made his mouth water, and he realized he was hungry.

The lock was broken on the front door of Felicity's apartment building. The three flights upstairs were easier to take when he was fresh. His body felt like lead, a two-ton truck unable to take a steep hill. He knocked on the door. Felicity cautiously opened it.

"I knew it was going to be you," Felicity said. She hugged him with all the strength she has left in her body.

"The night guard was murdered," she said. "On the way out of the building, I saw the guard's body was gone from the first-floor room."

"Don't worry," said Harry. "Someone took him away."

He moved Felicity to the bed, kissed her lightly, and breathed deeply into her sweet-scented body.

"I need to rest. Lie with me, and maybe I can sleep."

For the first time in two days, he felt relief and some peace. As he dropped off to sleep, his last thought was about Alberto Paz.

❋

Ibrahim sat in his new tourist office in the Case Historic district of Santiago de Cuba looking out over Parque Céspedes. He was sure Justin evicted the previous renters. A ritualized hustle unfolded across the street. Young men were barking out to tourists for rides to the cigar factory, or to the road that led to the revolutionary trail, or to points further south, such as Castillo del Morro, Parque Baconao, the Parque Zoologico, or Granjita Siboney, once a key operational base for the Cuban rebels against Batista's men. Tourists loved to see the bullet holes around the white and red house that Che's guerrillas occupied to fend off government armies. Fidel's old car was parked on the surrounding farmland. Time stood still. The revolution was still happening.

Several times a day, Ibrahim checked out the competition. When a tourist accepted a planned itinerary, a manager showed up to negotiate a price. If accepted, the negotiator escorted the tourist to an old Russian car. They worked with efficiency, with smiles on their faces. But a hustler didn't always land his prey. Competition was intense and prices fluctuated.

Ibrahim was pleased that his *Cubatur* cut into the hustlers' business because of its corner location, its efficient booking, English speaking, and on-call guides who looked and sounded professional.

The terrace of Hotel Casa Granda was filling up with tourists from all corners of the world, including local Cubans drinking mojitos and watching the activities on the plaza. The crowd of gawkers sat for hours watching the boys and girls flirting, listening to guitar music, all a mix of joyous humanity.

"I'm happy for you," said William as he entered the tourist office, a huge smile on his face. "Look at you, *hombre*. The school teacher who couldn't earn a living. *Que Bueno.* Your dreams are coming true. How did it all happen?"

"I have a silent partner," Ibrahim told him firmly.

William knew that Ibrahim's good fortune came through Harry. A tourist agency was the perfect front for changing dollars into kooks. Tourists paid to escort tourists around Santiago and to the coastal end of the island. The dollar exchange worked with no added hustle. Perfect arrangement.

Satomi figured it out and sent him to Ibrahim's office to get details on how the money exchange business was working out for Ibrahim. He was always amazed at his wife's business sense.

"Do you want to work for me, William?" asked Ibrahim. William looks surprised and laughed.

"You're joking, *amigo*," said William.

"That's why you're here, isn't it?"

"*Mas o menos,*" said William sheepishly. "It was Satomi's idea, but you knew that. She is always up for a new adventure, especially when it comes to making money."

Ibrahim sat on the shiny wooden desktop, compliments of his patron. He felt fortunate that he could run the business freely. Of course, there would be favors asked, like the one in La Habana, or others, but he wasn't worried. He did the worst and lived to see another day.

William walked around the office, light-hearted, and thinking about alternatives. "And if I make extra money, I can hire a carpenter to get our Airbnb in shape faster than I do it. Then maybe we can buy another place. It's a way to expand."

"Run it by her," said Ibrahim. "Let's say your customers need local currency. I'll give you a stack of kooks so you can make the ex-

change. We keep an account of the exchanges with commissions."
They peered through the corner window and saw a young man, early twenties, doing a fast money exchange. "Can you do it that fast, Guille?"

"Not quite," he said. "But I can get used to it."

William shared with him another perk. His partner was into co-operative ventures with the Cuban government. He could manage some of his side deals. Ibrahim was hungry after the years of poverty. He had big ideas.

So did Satomi. But William was not going to let Satomi inside Ibrahim's tourist office. She would ask too many questions and confuse the issues.

Satomi was also not helpful when it came to Kobe. She wanted him to visit Kobe a few times in the last month. He did her bidding, but it was more upsetting than comforting for her. He didn't like checking up on her because Harry's emotional presence had receded from Kobe's conscious mind. He told Satomi there was a man in her life. She asked a million questions: was Kobe making friends, was she coming out of her shell, when will she be a real teacher. William answered yes to all Satomi wanted to know. She cheered Kobe's independence and maybe she had a new love. They celebrated and clinked glasses and cooked an exotic meal. William loved her craziness.

CHAPTER 13

The Art of the Deal

Waylaid by sleep, confusion, and guilt, Harry was preparing to slip out of Felicity's apartment. She looked peaceful and calm for the first time since he met her. His arms around her slim body, the warmth he provided, comforted her. In return, she allowed him to feel a sense of peace and solace he had not experienced in months.

It frightened Harry to think about what would have happened if Kobe stayed with him. His family's life would have been disrupted, and Kobe and Katrina would be collateral damage. Lovely, beautiful Katrina might be confused. Education interrupted, friends lost, surroundings foreign. He knew he could get a job in the States if political negotiations stayed fluid between the U.S. and Cuba. Then, he could fly regularly to Cuba and continue to be a father and a provider for his family.

As he walked out into the already hot, muggy morning air, Harry had no idea where to begin to look for a traitor. And with the threat of a Russian seeking revenge for Victor's murder, the stakes were higher for his survival. Instead of playing a world-class chess game, it felt like he was playing poker, with feints and tells, each player searching for strategic signs and deceptive moves to defend against capture. The game took time and patience, something Harry no longer had. His situation was more like a high-wire act.

At this hour of the morning, very few people were in the cafe courtyard of Hotel Sevilla. Light was beginning to seep through the upper windows, producing a glare that made Harry's eyes feel like burning wood. A young waiter was leaning against the coffee bar smoking a cigarette, dazed by the early morning light. His black pants and white shirt were crisp and clean. Behind the coffee bar, a middle-aged waiter was busy setting up for the day.

When he met Ishmael in the Hotel Sevilla coffee shop, he was structuring a business deal. He wasn't aware of his surroundings, and it wasn't obvious to him that Hotel Sevilla was like a forgotten old lady left to fend for herself. He didn't notice the Moorish influence and wasn't aware of its colorful history. It was urban legend that Al Capone once hired out the sixth floor for his buddies Lucky Luciano and Meyer Lansky. Everyone who loved *Our Man in Havana* knew room 501 was where Graham Greene wrote his famous novel. He learned from a tourist in Plaza Martí that the rooms were built as prison cells around a rectangular balcony. Now Hotel Sevilla was simply another Cuban partnership with a pro-business French company that substituted for the mafia.

Harry wished he spent more time in the hotel's courtyard. He didn't know the waiters well enough to start a conversation with them. Getting good information about the comings and goings was a crapshoot. He slumped in an uncomfortable chair at a table near the coffee bar. The young waiter held a small tray in his left hand and sauntered over. He had a lazy gait and hollow eyes. The waiter was on drugs.

"*Por favor*, I'd like coffee as soon as you can bring it and a pastry."

"Our pastry isn't in yet, *Señor*."

"Then what have you got to eat?"

"Toast."

"Eggs?"

"*Muy bien.*"

He watched the waiter walk away, with no hope of getting coffee or food anytime soon.

As he settled in his chair, Harry heard commotion in the lobby. A few couples were having a heated conversation. Friends and random strangers joined them. Most of the guests were speaking English. Harry was curious and listened to pieces of conversation in the lobby. The interchange was getting louder as the group grew in numbers. More tourists wandered into the lobby with their cell phones comparing notes. Soon some of the staff huddled together and talked energetically. A few waiters were crying or placing their hands over their faces in despair.

Harry heard a few words: *stranded, borders, Mexican side, wet foot, dry foot, boats, ending.* It became crystal clear to Harry what was happening. Dread.

The news was old news, but the Cubans just got it. The Obama administration announced the immediate end of the policy to grant Cubans favored status and a quick path to citizenship if they landed on American soil. No more wet foot, dry foot. Dreams smashed for millions. Not a glimmer of hope to escape. Trump would have done it anyway if he became president, but Harry didn't think it would come so soon.

Harry caught the face of the young waiter, standing in the courtyard perfectly still as he held a tray with coffee and cold toast. Tears running down his face, eyes locked in loss.

With a sinking feeling, Harry listened to the cries and wails of the Cubans in the lobby, in the kitchen, in corners around the hotel. He imagined how it affected Cubans across the island who received the news in bits and pieces or kids who searched to find an Internet connection, waiting endlessly on park benches, or in plazas. There would be a fallout from families who were split up, not able to reunite, or worse, had insufficient funds to leave and no place to land in America.

The tourists dispersed, some entered the cafe courtyard with downcast faces. Everyone felt the pain of the Cuban people who were locked in an economic vise. As the commotion receded, the residual effects were the soulful murmurings of vanished dreams. The waiter set his tray down and sat at the table with Harry.

"Cuba squeezed us inside the island so we couldn't get out," Harry muttered. "Still paralyzed. Still waiting."

"I'm sorry the toast is cold. We're out of eggs."

"Does it matter?" asked Harry. He drank the coffee in gulps, set money on the table, and collected his thoughts. The way to get off the island was to deliver the traitor to Justin, and stay one step ahead of a Russian kid who was probably offered money to kill him.

Moments of isolation and loss composed the middle of the second act. Harry's story got more complicated and conflicts escalated. Trust in Justin's process began to erode. What he did and said was not adding up. The big reveal was yet to come. Harry made a deal and Justin pulled the plug. He was still in Cuba because he was useful to Justin. He knew with an intuitive fierceness that he had no option but to stay ahead of Justin and Charles to survive until the end of the third act.

"Were you here yesterday, *chico*?" Harry asked the waiter. "Double shift, maybe?"

"The shithead waiter on duty never showed up and they called me in early to help."

"Did you see three men talking in here during the late afternoon?"

"I saw a lot of people," replied the waiter.

"Three locals," said Harry. "One of them would have been a total *singao*."

The waiter was still coming off drugs and was slow to remember anything after the devastating news he just heard, "he said. "He was loud with an American guy and another one who was always nodding off. They're always here."

"Every day?" asked Harry.

"At least once a week. The American more. He's doing business. There are kooks on the table and dollars, too. I think he stays in this hotel or one nearby."

Harry didn't want to go outside in the city streets. He imagined all hell was breaking lose. He imagined the sorrow, the disappointment, and frustrations of the Cuban people. He heard the heartbreaking conversations taking place in living rooms and in stores. There would be no demonstrations. Cubans would keep working, heads down, and suffering in silence. Anyone who started a fight with an American, or protests, went to jail.

The best thing Harry could do was hang around the hotel and hope the gang that couldn't shoot straight showed up. Time was on his side.

"Can you get me another cup of coffee, *mi amigo*?" asked Harry. "There's some money in this if you keep me supplied."

Not an hour went by before Silas appeared in the lobby looking for his contacts. He checked his cell phone several times before he saw Harry sitting comfortably in a big chair.

"Hey, dude, I wondered where you were," said Silas. "Long time, no see. What have you been up to?"

"I'm good. What about you?"

"Doing a little money changing on the side," said Silas. "Small potatoes. Got a few things cooking. Hey, by the way, I just heard about what Obama did. I know how you must feel about the news. But you'll get off the island. I'm sure of that."

"Don't worry, Silas. You've got bigger fish to fry in Cuba than to worry about us locals losing our secure path to American citizenship."

"No, wait, man, I didn't mean that in a bad way," Silas said. "It was a tough break, that's all. You're smart. You'll find a way to get out."

Harry wanted to get off this pity me dialogue and on to what Silas was doing to stay alive.

"Let's take a walk, Silas, and you can tell me your story," said Harry. "I may be able to help."

Harry felt like Justin, walking Silas along Calle Industria to find out what was inside his head. No one said anything for a couple of blocks. Harry was distracted by Cubans talking, heads down, sad faces, hunched shoulders. He knew their pain. It was his pain.

Silas stopped in front of a revolutionary war tank on a lawn in front of a glass building.

"What's this tank doing in the park?" asked Silas.

"It's the Granma Memorial, and it holds great sentimental value for those who believe the revolution was our salvation. There isn't much inside the memorial, except old weapons from the fifties."

"What's the Granma?"

"A ship that carried Fidel and Che and eighty-one revolutionaries from Mexico to Cuba to launch the revolution for the second time."

"Man, the Cuban government love their revolution," said Silas. "They can't get enough of it."

"You know this country is bullshit, right?" said Harry. "The revolution ended up enslaving its people in the same way Batista did. You probably don't know, but for most of Cubans, the revolution didn't give us way to express our truth in society. It's a shit legacy, don't you think?"

"Dude, I never experienced what you are talking about."

"What are you experiencing in Cuba?"

"I'm making contacts just as you are," said Silas. "I want to build a broadband infrastructure in the next few years."

"What's your game plan to get backing?" asked Harry.

"There's opportunity here for those who can get a foothold. I'm trying to get connected to foreign money."

Harry explained that it's not about foothold. It's about solid investors and government contacts. Silas had *nada*.

"What do you know about contacts? You hustle just like the rest of the guys on the streets."

As they walked closer to the Museo de la Revolucíon, tourists were milling around the plaza, or in small groups at the front entrance listening to their tour leaders.

"I'm asking you what you want," said Harry. "I'm not conning you. If you've got plans to build Internet service in Cuba, I'll get you to a man who can help. Cut the money man in, or there is no deal. Don't take me up on it, and you'll flounder like a half-dead fish on the beach. Take it or leave it."

"Right now, I can't think of a good reason to tell you or your moneyman about my plans," said Silas. "If I change my mind, I have your number."

Silas knew if he stuck with Juan Juan, he would stay small, or limp back to the States in six months. If he heard what Justin had to offer, he might make some real money in Cuba.

Silas checked his pockets to see if his money was still there as Harry walked off. He couldn't imagine that Harry knew anyone rich enough who could fund a tech company in Cuba. He was selling contacts, but Silas wasn't buying.

Harry knew otherwise. Silas would be back because he took the bait.

As he walked along Calle Industria toward Kirpan, Harry had a hunch. The No Name was still closed, but the back door was always unlocked. Harry entered, and in the half-darkness, he recognized the outline of a body stretched between two chairs. Spencer was dead-drunk or dead, but he hoped the merry man hadn't succumbed to a tragic end yet. He wanted to squeeze one last morsel of information from the lower depths of Spencer before he met his ignominious demise.

Spencer's face was chalky and sinking into his skeleton – forehead, cheeks, and chin almost a memory. Harry shook him lightly, then harder, and Spencer came to consciousness.

"Spencer!" Harry said, shaking him. He got a glass of water and helped him drink. It rolled down his lower lip and spilled onto his dirty, stinking clothes.

"What's going on?" asked Spencer, confused from days of drunkenness. "Did I drink everything in the bar?"

The back of the bar was littered with broken and overturned bottles. It looked like a hurricane wreaked havoc.

"Look, Spencer, I need to talk to you, buddy. We got troubles right now. You, my man, are the eyes and ears of the Kirpan organization, and you know pretty much everything that's going on. We've got a snitch in the organization. The Russians stole the French files. Did you hear me, *viejo*?"

Spencer moaned and groaned. He threw up on the floor. There was blood in his vomit.

"Doesn't look good for you, old man," said Harry. "Sit up and drink this water and you'll feel better. You'll either die of a liver that's given up working or a bullet through your head."

"I didn't snitch," said Spencer, gulping his water. "Charles knew what the French agent was up to."

"Lucien?"

"I had no contact with the Russians," whined Spencer. "The Russians offered a bribe to Lucien to get access to the French files."

"You could have told the Russians for a good price that I was working for them on behalf of Justin. Did you do that, or did the French agent set up the burglary all by himself?"

Spencer started to cough uncontrollably. It took a few minutes for him to get his breathing back.

"You are a bright one, *mon cher*. The French agent was contacted by the Russian bastards, and they bribed him to let them into the filing office to steal the French files. You were complicit. You gave Victor the name of the French company."

"I didn't think burglary was on their mind."

Spencer coughed and spit blood. He shook in pain. Through spurts of losing his voice and falling into unconsciousness, he told Harry that the French agent was a greedy bastard. Lucien told Charles the Russians were romancing him with gobs of money to get a look at the competition.

"Greedy Lucien and Greedy Charles shared the bribe. That's how it went down, I swear, Sir Harry, and that's how good I am at getting information."

Harry wasn't completely certain if what Spencer told him was the truth, the whole truth, or close to the truth.

"How did you get this information?"

Spencer couldn't control his coughing. His nose began to bleed. "Alberto Paz told me. Justin trusts that two-bit influence peddler above anyone."

Harry couldn't contemplate the next couple of weeks. The lid on the coffin just got nailed down by a demolition jackhammer. First order of business: *stay alive.*

Kirpan's lights were on. The kitchen cleaned spotless for the night's cooking. Harry knocked on Charles's office door, hoping that he might be receptive to the idea of a singer performing tonight.

"I'm sorry about Obama rescinding Cuba's special immigration status. Rotten luck."

"Cubans are now like the rest of the wetbacks. Can't come through Mexico, or sail a rubber tire to the Florida Keys."

"You might be screwed even if you get to the States."

"I'll get to the States all right, and on Justin's private plane just like we talked about with $25,000 in my pocket. And by the time I get through giving him all the information he wants and more, he'll make citizenship happen for me."

"Those are mighty powerful words," said Charles.

"Before I talk to Justin, I'd like to give you a present. My uncle owned a restaurant in Cienfuegos, and Alma Diaz was the singer. Not just any singer, but not to be believed kind of singer. I hope I didn't step out-of-bounds, but I invited her in to sing at Kirpan tonight."

"There's no money in the budget."

Harry went on about her beauty, a voice of an angel, customers would love her, Charles didn't have to pay her, and in the end, he bet anything Charles would put her on the payroll so that she could stay in La Habana.

"She's my gift to Kirpan."

Charles wasn't sure what card Harry was playing. The idea of bringing a singer into the restaurant was presumptuous. He got two beers out of his office bar and handed one to Harry.

"Look at you, Mr. Leo, entering show business as a manager. Okay, I'll see what she's got. Tell her to come in at seven tonight. Now, let's get to the point. Who's the snitch?"

"It's not clear," said Harry, knowing he couldn't tell Charles he suspected the French agent because he and the agent were undoubtedly tied together at the hip. "I think Spencer is our guy, but you don't want to hear that, except if he had a constant supply of alcohol and the offer of money, it's possible he might sell what he knows."

"What about your boys in Cienfuegos? What do they know?"

"Nothing," said Harry. "They've got hunches, that's all."

"Spencer isn't coming around here anymore. He's got two feet in the grave."

"Good, then his secrets will die with him."

"That would be convenient," Harry said. "Is Justin around?"

"He'll be back tomorrow. He went to Santiago to check out Ibrahim's travel agency. Did you find Ishmael?"

"I don't know where to look."

"Maybe he was beat up, or maybe he's in a hospital."

Charles knew more than he was letting on.

Light from the street filtered into the dining room. Beautiful Alma stood in the doorway as she adjusted her eyes. She waited a moment before walking into the room. Charles introduced himself. She apologized for arriving early. She wanted to see the setup and maybe audition, if necessary. Harry greeted her with a hug and a kiss on the cheek.

"It's an honor to meet you, Alma. I'm Charles Duran. Can we hear you sing, Alma, or do you want to surprise us later?"

He got her a glass of water from the kitchen and fussed around her.

"Of course, I will sing, *Señor* Charles," Alma said, in a voice that could melt snow. "*Por favor,* may I freshen up? It takes ages to get across La Habana."

As Alma walked toward the restroom, Charles was already smitten by her feminine charms.

"I'm going to call Felicity and have her come tonight. She could use a night out."

Harry sat on the stoop in front of Felicity's apartment. It was risky to be out in the open. He had no idea who was coming after him, who wanted him dead. While he waited for her, Harry tried to figure out the disappearance of Ishmael. If he ended up in a hospital, he would be home by now. Impulsively, he called Anna. No answer. He left a message.

Felicity approached, her slim body hunched. A new lock was on the door, and she fumbled with the key. He led her inside the apartment. It was stuffy and warm. He opened a window and the noise from the street came into the apartment. He pulled the shade up, but the outside light was smothered by the building next door. He couldn't get comfortable.

Felicity got a glass of water from the sink and gulped it down.

"A man from the French Embassy was at my office today to ask questions about the stolen French applications. My supervisor was there, too. I was questioned for more than an hour, then I told *Señor* Paz that I copied the files that were stolen. I thought everyone would be happy, but the Frenchman was still angry."

"Did you get the name of the Frenchman?" Harry asked.

"I overheard Alberto call him Lucien. He said, 'Lucien, calm down. That's all."

He held Felicity close. "Let's forget this for now. Get dressed and we'll go to Kirpan. I have a good meal waiting for you and a surprise."

✳

Alma's accompanist, Federico, played the introduction to *Montuno Favorito,* as Alma snapped her fingers and sensuously strolled onto the stage in a slinky red taffeta dress. Her beauty held the audience spellbound; she had them in the palm of her hands before she sang a note. They cheered and whistled. She smiled sensuously and began to sing and sway to the music. The crowd knew the popular song and sang along.

Harry's phone vibrated in his pocket. As he left the restaurant, he put the phone to his ear.

"How are you?" asked Harry. He paced on the sidewalk. "How's Katrina?"

"Katrina wanted you to come home," said Kobe.

"What about you?" Harry asked. "Do you want me to come home?"

The conversation was rocky, full of starts and stops. Kobe heard about the new policy of the U.S. regarding immigrants. She assumed Harry changed plans and wouldn't be able to get a path to citizenship.

"I'll never stay in Cuba," he told Kobe as he reached the corner of Barcelona. "I'm working on other ways of getting into the States and finding sponsorship, or a job that requires a green card."

Kobe wanted to know how long it would take, how long would he be in La Habana, would he see Katrina before he left. She told him she was settled, loved her job and the friendliness of Santiago. Although Satomi and William were busy, they were available for her when she needed them.

There was more. Kobe confirmed she was seeing a man. A nice man. A man with a steady job who loved the island and never wanted to leave. He was happy for her, he said, but he was angry. Guilt burned inside.

Felicity appeared in the street and saw Harry bent over, choking back tears.

"Can I talk to Katrina?" he asked.

His daughter took the phone. She was sobbing and miserable without him. When would he come home? When would she see her daddy again?

"I love you, *niña*," Harry said to her. "I love you with all my heart, and I will see you soon." No remedy for a broken heart. Too late for reruns.

The stage was empty. Harry found Alma in the back with Federico. She embraced Harry warmly.

"Charles asked us to do another set," she said jubilantly. "Isn't that something?"

"It's everything, Alma," Harry responded. He watched Federico tune his guitar with diligence.

"Federico, Viejo, you were great tonight as always." He looked up and crinkled his face with happiness. "Everybody in La Habana will be a fan."

"You are a good person," Alma said. "You have heart." Harry dropped his head in shame. "All will be well. Follow your dreams."

Harry put Felicity in a cab outside Kirpan and paid the driver to get her home. *Cuidado.*

Kirpan's patrons were still celebrating Alma as the evening extended beyond the usual hours. Charles was behind the bar cleaning alongside the bartender. Harry motioned to him.

"We've still got the disappearance of Ishmael to handle."

"We'll take care of it. It shouldn't matter to you."

"Justin asked me to find him. That's what I'm doing."

Charles had a nervous habit of drying a glass longer than necessary. It was a habitual tic. He was drying the same glass for the last five minutes.

"Get out on the streets again, hustle up those dollars." He stopped wiping down the bar. "There's an all clear in Havana with the Russians. No one gave a shit about a low-level murder."

Harry straightened up the barstools. "I haven't been paid for the job, Charles."

"Bring us dollars from the street," demanded Charles, as he closed out the cash register. "Your work with me is about collecting dollars."

The outside air hit his lungs like he had been punched in the stomach. Trying to get his breath, Harry dialed Anna's cell phone. Same story. No one picked up. He dialed Silas. He answered on the first ring. Anxious dude.

"Hey, Silas. Want to meet me some place for a drink?"

"Why would I want to do that?" asked Silas.

"I think we need to talk truth. Meet me at Hotel Inglaterra in the bar in thirty minutes."

The back door of the No Name Bar was open. He smelled death. He didn't want to turn on the light because someone from the outside might see it. There was a smattering of moonlight coming through wooden slats at the corner of the bar. Spencer was on the floor, no longer a living person. A corpse. The foul odor of human decomposition would soon be noticed from the street. It was a fitting end to the sadness of Spencer Merryman's life.

The Inglaterra was at one time José Marti's hotel of choice. Harry learned about Cuba's national hero and important literary writer and philosopher in his Cuban school, and he liked reading Marti's works, especially the history that supported Cuban independence against Spain in the last half of the 19th century. When he went to school in the States, he did more research on Martí, read his poetry, and developed a passion for his writing. If only Martí was Cuba's leader today.

Despite the hotel's age, it was hard not to admire the exquisite combination of Moorish and Colonial décor in the lobby, all cleaned up and shiny. To the left of the horseshoe shaped reception area, with its neoclassical style, was the bar-café, La Sevillana. This section was paneled with decorative ceramic tiles from Sevilla in rich patterns and colors, complemented by ornately carved archways and molding. Harry felt the lobby area was more Moroccan than Cuban.

Silas sat alone at the bar nursing a Cuba Libre, studying the grilled filigree, admiring the mood lighting, and staring into the large mirror over the colorful bar that reflected the Colonial dining room in the background.

"Cuba Libre?" Harry asked Silas as he sat on a barstool. Silas was thinner, on edge. Harry nodded to the bartender indicating the same.

"What have you got, Harry?" asked Silas.

The bartender put a Cuba Libre in front of Harry. He smelled the run, then took a long draw from the glass.

"For the record, I'm not your buddy," said Silas, ordering another drink. "And I have no long-term intention of sticking around playing this money game."

"Let me repeat. You need an insider with money and connections, and I have that person if you want your tech plan to see the light of day. You're right about one thing. We're not buddies. But I'm useful to you and you are useful to me so let's start playing this out."

"I know you work for the people at Kirpan. Norm hangs out there and he knows some shit."

"What shit?" asked Harry finishing his drink.

Harry put money on the bar. "I guess we're done. I can hire a number of tech guys who know as much about setting up a cellular service on the island as you do. They're a dime a dozen in the States. I have a card in my pocket from a higher up guy in a tech company in Silicon Valley."

Silas flashed anger and started to lunge at Harry. Harry stuck his arm out and took the breath out of Silas.

He thought Silas was a decent sort, not easily taken in, smarter than he seemed, but maybe Paula was right to leave him and go back to the States. His featured character flaw was resistance.

Silas looked defeated. He has no will to push back on what Harry told him. He took a sip of his second Cuba Libre.

"First, what about Norm."

"Norm heard the Russians applied for some competitive government contracts and how some guy named Charles was pissed and going to do something about it. And maybe he says a couple of Russians were killed. Juan Juan wanted me to find you and get the story because you wouldn't tell him."

Same story, different day. Harry wanted to introduce him to Justin, but he needed a solid Internet plan to present. He explained that going through red tape with the Cuban government was brutal. Inside contacts were crucial to success.

"Your plan better be good because Justin is a tech guy with lots of experience in the States? And he'll know if you are not prepared for your project to move forward."

Harry told Silas that he had to define the strategy and roll it out in stages, then create a definitive implementation process. Anticipate tough questions. What happens after that is Silas's business and his backer's problem.

"You're a cool one, Harry." He drew out his first smile of the evening. "And if I do that, you get points?"

"Ownership goes to the guys with money, and they get to the head of the line first. My contact is the brains of his own operation, and you'll be well compensated. He's been in Cuba a long time. You'll never have the influence he has even if you stick around for the next ten years."

Silas realized Harry had the smarts to make this happen. If he wasn't the head honcho, he could live with a good partner. Tech jobs were everywhere in the States, but he was a loner and his attitude had gotten him in trouble for his inability to work well with others. The real opportunities were in undeveloped countries. He was tired of fighting for a foothold in the U.S.

"Hey, man, what are you planning to do now that you can't go to the States the easy way?"

"That's not your worry. Focus on getting a smart plan. A half hour ago you had no tech deal. Don't screw up." Harry got off the barstool. "One more thing, and this is important for both of us. I'd like you to do a complete rundown on Justin Levitt. Who is he? What did he do? Where did he come from? I tried to Google him on a smartphone, but I got nothing."

"I'm good at that. You got it."

"Don't take more than two days to get your presentation in order. Call me when you're ready. More important, call me when you have info on Justin."

"What if Justin isn't what he seems?"

"Then we rework our deal," replied Harry. "I haven't been paid on my end, and they're stalling or selling me out.

Nothing's as it seems.

CHAPTER 14
Brothers

Harry swiped his forearm across his forehead. Sweat ran down his back. He wasn't celebrating moving Silas into Justin's camp. It was a crapshoot. He wanted to score points with Justin by sending Silas to him, but he trusted no one, least of all Justin. If it worked, great. If it didn't, Silas returned to his foxhole, and Harry was out of product to sell Justin.

He reached in his wallet for the business card from Michael Shamen, the rich tech guy sitting across Parque Plaza Hotel. Just in case.

He felt an achy tiredness in his bones, and he didn't want to walk home to his apartment. Felicity's place was closer. He had no bike and there were no cabs on the street. From a walk to a jog, he seemed to fly the rest of the way. Every step he took brought him closer to an idea about where to look for Ishmael.

Justin damn well knew where Ishmael had been. They were testing him. He had been recruited as an asset, and like any asset, he could be called upon again to do their bidding. *Where's my payoff?*

Harry stopped dead in his tracks at that thought. The idea that he was bought and paid for the rest of his life felt like he lost every value, every inch of morality that made him believe in himself. At forty, would he be worth anything as a human being? If Harry set his sights on finding a good job and having the ability to get Katrina to the States for a good education, his goals would be met. But there were miles to go before he slept. He thanked Robert Frost for the poem he learned in eleventh grade in Mr. Richard's English class.

He headed home to keep his thought clear and intentional.

⁕

Before Harry hunted down Paco at his Prado apartment building the next morning, he rode his bike to the end of the long tree-lined boulevard where the Malecón protected the Caribbean. It was a hot and dry. He smelled the salty air as he watched the sun bounce off the blue, shimmering waters that vividly outlined the soft waves, and for a moment, caused him to lose his vision.

The positive energy he felt on the Malecón was invigorating and gave him hope that his dream to leave Cuba would happen, no matter the distance he was destined to travel. He continued to peddle along the wall toward Castillo de San Salvador de la Punta, to the end of the Malecón, only stopping to admire the brightly painted old classic cars hugging the ocean curves with confidence.

Back to business.

Just as Harry was about to enter the Prado building, he saw Ishmael's old blue Moskvitch in the parking lot across the street. Ishmael didn't go back to get his car on the night of the murder.

He checked every floor and apartment being repaired in Paco's building on the Prado. He asked a few workmen if Paco was around or if they've seen Ishmael. Dead end.

Harry tried to break into Ishmael's car with all the tricks he learned from his cousins in Newark. They didn't steal cars, but they perfected the art of breaking in. That was the game.

When he randomly pulled on the door handle and it almost came off in his hand, Harry realized that the piece of crap Russian car could be stolen in a New York minute. He hot-wired the car, and the engine started quick as a Zippo lighter.

He took his bike back to his cubbyhole and headed for Ishmael's apartment. Harry entered the building, skipped up three flights of stairs with speed, and knocked on the door so as not to wake up a sleeping child. He heard Anna's footsteps approaching. Her face told him everything he needed to know. Ishmael wasn't roughed up. Anna never went to relatives. Ishmael was alive and doing whatever Justin wanted him to do for Kirpan.

"May I come in?" Harry didn't wait for her reply.

"*Lo siento,*" Anna said. "I didn't mean to lie to you. It was Ishmael who told me to do it."

"Tell me the truth, Anna."

She looked exhausted from stress and work. "I don't know everything. I know Ishmael is on business for his boss, but I don't know where. He left town for a while. He's back now."

Harry knew less than he did before talking to Anna. The only change was that finally he had wheels. If Ishmael wanted his car back, he would know who to call.

He wasted time on the streets, on a bike, walking, running, forgetting to eat, had no time to sleep. In the States, he'd have a car, a job that brings him dignity, and a life that has value. It's the life he envisioned since his return from Newark.

Kirpan was in darkness. He remembered being afraid of the dark as a child, but weren't all kids? Except Katrina. The darkness never bothered her. She said she was a witch in a former life and was used to darkness. Skinny, beautiful almond eyes, a slight yellow tone to her skin. Long eyelashes, sly smile, tiny ears.

The place was empty, but he had a hunch that Justin was alone in his office. He liked to work early in the morning. Charles checked in around noon, prepared the kitchen, and planned his menus for the night. He'd meet with Justin for business after that, or visit his government contacts.

Harry heard Justin's voice on the phone. He was speaking Portuguese. Spanish and Portuguese are not that different in structure. Similar vocabulary and syntax. Justin was speaking about Brazilian applications. Tech language was always in English. Then the magic word. *GlobalNet.* Justin was the front for Brazil's entrance into partnership with Cuba. With Brazilian money behind him, and Global-Net as a ghost company, who better to put together a cellular grid in Cuba than the guy who knew how to do it. Someone else's name was on Brazil's official application. No matter the name, Justin controlled the deal.

Classic logic: Justin wanted the original French files back to amend them, delete the tech app, or delete all bids. Then refile and reenter the bids in the computer under the Brazilian company, GlobalNet. *Brazil 1. France 0.*

Harry knocked. Justin hung up the phone.

"The Leo has returned," Justin said with a slight laugh. "Charles told me you wanted to talk to me. I'm thinking we're about to have our *come-to-Jesus* conversation."

"Charles ordered me to do my job and collect dollars."

"You are to report to me and not to Charles. Have you figured out who allowed the Russians to steal our files?"

"I have a hunch, but I have no proof," says Harry.

"I need that proof to weed out the traitors and move on to the real business of executing the future. Your future."

"The late Spencer Merryman knew a few details, but who knows if anything he said was the truth. He thought the Russians bribed Lucien Chabrol. He was also convinced Alberto Paz was part of the burglary."

"I never trust two Frenchmen doing business together."

This is a bullshit conversation.

"They're buddies. Charles put Lucien in his position at the embassy. "

"I want proof that Lucien or Lucien and Charles colluded with the Russians," said Justin.

"Speaking of mysteries," said Harry, "what was the point of misleading me about Ishmael?"

Justin walked to the portable bar and poured two scotches neat. His hand shook as he gave one to Harry and sat in a comfortable armchair catty-corner to the desk. They shared a small Moroccan table.

"I'm assessing your skills at problem-solving."

"How am I doing?"

"Your singular position gives you the freedom to operate on your own, think on your own, put things together on your own."

Harry tried again to get assurance that Justin would get him the hell off the island with his $25,000. Obama's cancellation of Cuba's pathway to citizenship upped the ante.

"You're a rich man with lots of contacts and you can make anything happen. You can get me a green card in the U.S. Or you can go through back-channels to allow my relatives in Newark to take me."

"Nothing is impossible."

Harry poured another drink and added ice. He didn't want to get tipsy, but he was nervous about getting to a resolution.

"By the way, Justin, if you want to get Spencer's stinking corpse out of the No Name Bar, you'd better send someone in with a gas mask." The nerves in Harry's body were fighting to keep him in full control.

"I own the place. How do you know about the No Name?"

Harry isn't shocked. It's futile to keep up with him.

"I stumbled on the bar while riding my bike around the neighborhood. I wanted a beer and stopped to look inside. It was a dump, no customers and one derelict bartender. I brought Spencer there the day Fidel died. I raided the alcohol to keep him talking."

"Why do you think Felicity copied the French files? Was she falling for you?"

"Has fallen for me. I'm assuming you'll take care of her. You may need her services in the future. What's Alberto's role?"

"Alberto is the cleanup man. Thanks to him the guard's body disappeared. No scandal, no investigation of the burglary or the deaths of Victor Kostroff and his flunky."

"I don't have a good feeling about Alberto. The follow-up office visit grilling of Felicity was a show. I think Alberto was involved in the bribe."

"I pay Alberto for his loyalty," said Justin as he switched chairs and sat behind his desk. He had trouble picking up his favorite pen. His hand was shaking. "If he knew what Lucien was up to, he'd tell me." Justin wrote something in a notebook.

"The only person who protected your applications was Felicity."

"You don't bring me good news. Find out who has those damn original files."

"I wasn't told to bring you good news," said Harry. "News is news. And my news is that I need money to live since I'm off the streets. Tell Charles that I'm retired from hustling."

Justin went to the safe and removed a stack of money. "You want cucs or dollars?"

"Kooks."

Harry took the money and flipped through it. "Where did Ishmael go?"

"Doing business for me, seeing to filings, meeting people."

"That was a waste of my time and worry," said Harry. "I'd like Ishmael with me for the rest of the investigation. Lucien is your headache. If I talk to him, it raises a red flag."

"You would have made a good detective, Harry."

He explained to Justin that a techie named Silas developed a broadband plan for Cuba.

"If you wanted to look at it, I told him you're the boss."

"I'm looking for a good idea for a government/private business plan in telecom. I'll listen to what he has to say. If you looked at our tech application, you noticed they weren't fully developed."

Clever man. He dropped that observation on Harry with stealth precision.

Justin poured himself his second drink. Hand shaking. "You and Ishmael follow-up with Alberto and get clarity about his relationship with Lucien. I'll keep close tabs on Charles. French bastard."

Harry left the office, saw Charles behind the bar, and passed him without a word. He hoped his asshole just slammed shut.

Dark clouds gathered in the sky. The temperature dropped, despite the mugginess. There was a storm coming. It would be a relief for Harry to feel the rain wash over him. He called Silas as he walked to the car. There was no answer.

Ishmael stood by his Moskvitch, sporting creased khaki pants, a crisp and casual striped shirt, and a gray tie. His shoes were polished, and so was his baby face.

"Get in," said Ishmael.

Harry slipped into the passenger seat.

"What the fuck is going on?"

"I got your attention," said Harry. "And I fixed your shitty door handle in this piece of crap you drive."

"Cut to the chase, and tell me what Justin wants."

"I'm glad that Anna and the kids are good. I'm glad you're safe and sound. And I'm glad you look so sharp. All professional and rubbing shoulders with the big guys. It suits you."

The car engine wouldn't start. "Piece of shit."

Harry looked under the hood and started the engine. Ishmael let out a cheer and Harry knew all was well.

"Justin wants to get to the bottom of the burglary. Charles and the French agent, maybe Alberto Paz are good suspects."

"Nasty business considering Charles is a partner in Justin's ventures," said Ishmael.

"Your air conditioner is broken, big guy. I'm sweating buckets."

At the entrance to the Hotel Sevilla, a doorman opened his umbrella and sheltered Ishmael from the torrential rain as he ran into the lobby. Harry followed and noticed Ishmael's new leather shoes were getting soaked.

"You're all fancy now, Ish. Right down to your own parking valet. How did you get to be so special all of a sudden?""

"You'll see," Ishmael answered in a hushed tone. "Keep your cool. Only talk when I direct a question to you."

They walked up a staircase and turned right on the second floor. At the end of a long corridor, carved wooden double doors greeted them. Inside, a man was pouring whisky into a Baccarat crystal glass. He was barely five feet, four inches. He wore a three-piece suit with a natty purple tie, and salt-and-pepper hair slicked back in the manner of all successful Cubans. Alberto Paz was an imposing figure. Men with money in Cuba looked like they were living imitations of gangsters in *Goodfellas*.

"Alberto Paz, I'd like you to meet Harry Cisneros," said Ishmael. They shook hands like two businessmen making a deal.

Alberto had two offices: the well-decorated office in the Hotel Sevilla for high level people – foreign visitors and embassy brass, and an office in the government building for clerks, managers, and low-level workers. The dark modern furniture looked comfortable. Alberto's desk was varnished to perfection. His desk chair must have been ordered from Amazon.

The photos on the wall indicated that Alberto was well-connected in government circles. Harry sat on the sofa to test the cushions.

"I'm going to open another window," said Alberto. "It's stuffy in here."

A cool breeze blew through the office. The rain cooled down the temperature.

"Let's get to this, Ishmael. I have appointments this afternoon. What is your business with me today?"

"What's your relationship with Lucien Chabrol?" asked Ishmael.

"He and I work together to make sure the French have preference when awarding Cuban contracts."

"And the Russian burglary?" asked Ishmael.

"What do you mean?"

"The only way the Russians could get into the application office was if they had an inside contact," said Ishmael.

"Was that someone Lucien or Spencer Merryman, who, by the way, is dead," said Harry. "Or maybe you, *Señor* Paz."

Alberto sipped his whisky. "Drinking got the better of him after his wife left Cuba." Alberto held up his baccarat crystal glass and looked closely at the amber tint of the alcohol. "Drinking is good in small doses. The minute it is consumed in volume, it dilutes the taste. I don't know how the burglary was set up."

"You are familiar with the Russian bids in Cuba?" asked Harry already knowing the answer.

"I know about Caspian Corp, and I know that Russian companies are noted for their inferior materials and workmanship," Alberto responded curtly. "*Señor* Cisneros, I am the liaison and not the spy."

"How well do you know Lucien?" asked Ishmael.

"He's a colleague. Let's move on. The Russian stooge is dead. Felicity copied the French applications, and we are in the clear."

"Justin wants all the original French files returned," said Ishmael. "Until then, your role in the burglary is still a question mark."

Alberto stood, losing all appearances of civility. "What are you insinuating?"

"You disposed of the guard's body, to cover up a murder by the Russians, stood by and watched Lucien berate Felicity for being careless. That looks bad, don't you think?" asked Ishmael.

"I removed the body so there would be no investigation." Alberto sat in his faux Eames chair. He gulped the rest of the whisky. "Charles came to visit me several times during the last six months. He wanted to know how the French applications compared to other countries, specifically the Russians, since they were always in first position."

Alberto sauntered to the window. Ishmael topped off his drink, and Harry wandered to the bookcase scanning the titles of Dostoevsky's novels and tried to gather his thoughts. He remembered a quote he read in a Dostoevsky novel too long ago to remember the title, but the quote stuck.

To live without hope is to cease to live.

"Does Caspian have an agent?" asked Harry.

"Not that I know of," said Alberto, "but I suspect that the Russians were recruiting Lucien for some time. I'm not sure if Lucien is a Russian spy, or if they knew him before, but I do know he is a *maricón,* too low on the pecking order to act alone."

Harry believed none of this story. Alberto was complicit. The Russians must have paid a fortune to Lucien to help them get access to the French application office.

"One more thing, *Señor* Paz. Why did Spencer Merryman think you were involved in the burglary?"

"I have no idea, *Señor* Cisneros."

"I think maybe you do."

✳

The rain stopped as dusk settled over the city. Harry and Ishmael waited for the Moskvitch to be brought around to the front entrance of Hotel Sevilla. Ishmael drove toward the Malecón. Harry watched the Cubans going about their business, entering office buildings, hotels, looking into shop windows, sitting on park benches, smoking and talking. He rolled down the window and smelled the cool, fresh air. Everything was normal in this big city after the death of their leader, except Harry felt anything but normal.

After reading dozens of stories about Cubans fleeing to Mexico through Brazil, Colombia, or any Central American country they could sneak in to hike for months through the Amazon, crossing crocodile-filled rivers, climbing border walls, escaping from immigration detention centers in Panama, trying to get across the Mexican border before the American government closed its borders to them, Harry had little hope for the Cuban people. How many were fleeing and failing, only to find that they were twelve hours too late, two hours too late? Doomed to a life of hunger if they couldn't find work, or worse, if they were sent back to endure harsh conditions in a Cuban jail. And if they got out of jail, they couldn't work again. The special privilege of Cuban immigration to the U.S. was dead on arrival.

America isn't America the beautiful anymore.

"What's on your mind?" asked Ishmael. They pulled up to the wall along the Malecón.

"Every Cuban is born a political prisoner, some for economic reasons and some political. Sixty oppressive years a prisoner of a mad egomaniac. And the U.S. can't stamp political prisoner on a Cuban passport anymore."

"Why do you worry about this shit?" said Ishmael as he threw his leg over the wall and stared out into the dark blue ocean. Clouds hung heavy in the sky after the rain.

"Once the traitor mystery is solved, you can go."

Not so fast.

Ishmael stretched out on the wall and watched the clouds float by. The winds were picking up. The blackish water flapped along the sandy shore and produced a rhythm straight from a Buena Vista Social Club song. *Chan Chan.*

Harry straddled the wall and mentally weighed into the end of blackness, the void. "I did what was asked of me and I want my money. I feel like I'm being held hostage."

Ishmael propped himself up on his elbows. "You'll get more than you asked for. Justin isn't taking hostages."

"A promise to pay is a promise to pay. Everything else is a lie."

"If you lose hope, your daughter will lose hope."

His real hope was that Katrina wouldn't settle like Kobe. Katrina had a big imagination and was wise beyond her years. Harry wanted his daughter to reach higher than she ever thought she could. Cuba won't bury her.

"Leo, Leo, Leo, don't despair." Ishmael breathed in the cool night air and expelled his breath with measured determination. "You were accidentally born a Cuban. You got a bum deal. Maybe I did, too. Let's get the hell off this island. Let's be brave for the rest of the time we're together. We'll be like lovers forging our path in the world, staying true to what we believe in."

"Do I hear you right? Are you talking about leaving the island, with Anna and the kids? Justin won't let you go."

Ishmael hopped off the wall, hugging himself to ward off a cool breeze. Harry jumped up, put his body in front of Ishmael and grabbed his shoulders.

"This idea is insane for you, chico. You don't need to get off the island. You've got a good life with Justin. If what we think about Charles is true, then you're next in line to run his business."

"It's not any more insane than your wanting to leave. Why can't I?"

"Sounds great, but nothing is that simple," said Harry. "You end up living from visa to visa in the States, six months back and forth to Cuba if everything is normalized. What kind of life is that for your family?"

"Right," said Ishmael. "We've got other things to figure out first. And since we have no crystal ball, we have work to do. Prove Lucien is a double spy or just a stupid bastard who got greedy and took a bribe from the Fat Man before he died."

Before I killed him.

The situation that Harry found himself in – as Justin's private detective – reminded him of how his mother used to make soup. He remembered that the soup started with chicken broth. She added vegetables and potatoes, anything she could beg, borrow, or steal in Cienfuegos. It was a mystery how this soup tasted so delicious without a recipe. One day, he asked his mother to share her secret.

"There is no mystery, *niño*. Add as many vegetables to the broth as you can find, and when the carrots float to the top, the soup is ready because they are the heaviest vegetables, and take the longest to cook. Everything else sinks to the bottom."

It was genius. His mother's secret to making great soup was the way he would finally solve the mystery of Kirpan's traitor.

CHAPTER 15
The Snitch

Harry was amazed by the breadth and scope of the Plaza de la Revolucíon. His fourth-grade teacher taught the class about José Martí. She said he was Cuba's most important revolutionary figure. A student asked if the statue in the Plaza de Revolucíon in La Habana was José Martí. The teacher smiled and said it was true, and that the plaza was the one of the largest squares in the world. It was considered the seat of the Cuban government and the Communist Party. All the students clapped.

Harry stopped in front of the statue of Jose Marti and wondered if Marti were alive today, what would he think about how the Cuban revolution played out.

José Martí said that *to be cultured was to be free.* His quote was splashed all over Cuba. Either Cubans didn't read it, or they ignored it. Culture wasn't just about art and artifacts, museums and revolutionary monuments. Cuba had great artists and writers, but its *culture rested in the hearts and in the soul of its people.* That's how Gandhi defined freedom – *to have a heart and soul.* He would like to tell Martí that Fidel and his communism washed away the heart and soul of Cuba.

Harry rode around the exterior parameters of the plaza looking for a place to hide his bike. He saw old and battered trash cans at the back of the Capitol. There was an avalanche of garbage and debris. He hoped Justin's company would do a better job of trash collection than the Cuban government. Harry guided his bike behind one of the big containers and locked it onto a corner leg. The garbage stunk so bad that he ran out from behind the container holding his breath.

Felicity was surprised and happy to see him. She gathered her purse and sweater and left her office cave. The afternoon air was unusually cool. To maintain propriety, they kept their distance as they walked along Avenida de la Independencia.

"How did you get here?" Felicity asked.

"I rode my bike. I locked it behind one of the disgusting garbage containers in the back of the Capitol."

Felicity laughed. "Only rats go near the garbage bins."

They approached Café Laurent on Calle Aranguren.

"Is this a restaurant?" Felicity asked. "There's no sign."

"I know. That's its charm. You don't see it from the outside, but there's an old lift that takes you up to the fifth floor where you'll be surprised."

They rode up the rickety lift and entered a new post-Fidel Castro reality. The dining room was intimate with a French flair. Starched white cloths were spread smoothly on the tables. Flower- patterned plates, crystal glasses, and a vase of roses decorated each table. Gauzy, see-through drapes covered large panes of glass surrounding the modern interior and kept the sun from glaring onto the diners. The waiter seated them near a floor-to-ceiling window with see-through vistas of La Habana.

"Let's have the lamb stew," said Harry. "The restaurant is famous for it."

"This is beautiful, Harry," Felicity gushed. "How did you know about it?"

"One of the men I work for told me about it. This view of the city makes Cuba look heavenly."

Harry asked for two glasses of champagne. The waiter removed the cork, and Felicity was delighted. She took Harry's hand.

"What are we celebrating?" asked Felicity.

"You've been helpful to me. Let's toast to that."

They touched their champagne glasses and sipped the bubbly sweetness.

"It's like a fairy tale. I want it to last forever."

"It's been a roller coaster with us, and I want it to slow down. To do that, I'd like to know a few details about you that will keep us both safe. Is that all right?"

The waiter brought bread to the table and organized the place settings. Harry ordered lamb stew for both of them.

"What do you want to know?"

"How well do you know Alberto?"

"Very well. He's my cousin, and he got me my job."

Harry kept his face neutral, although he was surprised by her answer. "Do you know why Alberto and this man, Lucien, from the French Embassy, entered your office and questioned you about the Russians?"

Felicity hesitated.

"Alberto works with the same people as I do," said Harry.

"The Russians?"

"Do you think Alberto works with the Russians?"

"I don't know. It's not my business. I just file applications. But I'm not blind. Bribes and shifting loyalties are everywhere in government."

Harry told her that he worked with a French group that wanted to partner with the Cuban government. Her cousin gave the French help as their applications were reviewed. Alberto and Lucien were making sure his employer came first when bids were handed out. And then the burglary happened.

The lamb stew arrived at the table and the lovely smell made Harry and Felicity forget about business for a moment. They ate their food and enjoyed the atmosphere.

"It must be exciting for you that Cuba is changing. The island is going to build a large service sector connected by a Wi-Fi network. They'll be many more goods and service jobs."

"I've got the figures, Harry. Cuba has about 500,000 entrepreneurs involved in businesses. And the latest statistics show that four million people visit Cuba, six hundred thousand of them are Americans."

"What the numbers mean is that everybody's expectations about how prosperous Cuba could be in the future are changing."

Forks down, champagne glasses empty. And a silence stretched between them.

"What is it, *mi amor*? You can ask me anything."

"Do you think it was Lucien's idea to come to your office that day, or Alberto's?"

"Alberto called to warn me that Lucien wanted to question me about what happened with the Russians, but that he would be there to protect me. Lucien asked me why I copied the French files. I fumbled and never gave an answer. He got angrier and said, 'Damnit! This compromises me.'"

Felicity picked up her fork and pushed her leftover food around the plate.

"You didn't tell me that before," said Harry.

"I didn't know what Lucien meant. But after Alberto apologized for the ugly scene, my cousin told me he was there to see how Lucien handled the situation and to protect me."

"Alberto was protecting himself as well as you."

"I've been in the application office long enough to know the Russians want to be number one in getting Cuban contracts. They think they deserve it for supporting Cuba during the Soviet years. Alberto knows I'm useful in my position because I speak and understand Russian."

"Do you remember hearing anything more when the Russians took the French files, anything about someone tipping them off or conversations with other people? Maybe Lucien or someone named Charles?"

"I told you all I know."

"Please don't talk to Alberto about this. Don't bring my name up. I don't want him to link us together. It might be dangerous for Alberto to know we talked."

"We haven't talked since Lucien came into my office."

Harry kissed her on the cheek. She returned his affection with a light kiss on the lips.

On the way back to Felicity's office, Harry's phone rang. Felicity dug into her purse and pulled out a souvenir key ring with Che's image.

"How did it work out?" asked Harry. "That's great. I knew it would be a good fit. Talk later about the other thing I asked you to do."

One vegetable sunk to the bottom of the soup pot. Silas was in the clear. But he wasn't sure what game Justin was playing with Silas. The Brazilian company he represented had a sophisticated and well-thought-out plan to provide broadband in Cuba. Silas's Internet pitch couldn't compare with it. Justin's technology, if accepted by the Cuban government, would take time to roll out. And who in Cuba was sophisticated enough to understand the structure and how it would work? Justin would have to bring in Brazilian techies. He decided to show the Brazilian bid to Silas.

"This is the first time I've seen you relax in a while," said Felicity. "When you smile, you look like a kid. *Querido,* I have a present for you." Felicity gave him the key chain.

"Is this the key to the hiding place?" asked Harry.

"My apartment may not look like much, but it has its advantages," said Felicity. "One day, while I was making the bed, I found a piece of the wall had fallen away from behind the bed. There was a safe inside the wall with a key sticking in the keyhole. That's where the copies of the Brazilian files are located."

For ten years, Harry thought about getting back to the States. When Cubans lost their special status, he lost all hope. Anger took his focus, but Felicity brought back his resolve. She was a gift, his way out. He planned to leave Cuba no matter what happened with Justin.

It felt harsh to tell Felicity that he would be leaving Cuba, but honesty was the only way to handle the moment.

She turned away, wiped her tears, and walked ahead of him.

"I didn't expect we'd be so close. It's come as a surprise to me. Please stop and look at me. Felicity, wait. Let's not imagine the future. We don't know what's going to happen."

Felicity kept walking. The movement helped control the pain in her chest. Her breath shortened. She had hope for them.

Behind the garbage bin, Harry tried to unlock his bike. The lock caught on the inside of the leg. Pulling out the bike was impossible. His lungs were filling up with rotten garbage. The muggy humidity added to his nausea. He vomited and wiped his mouth with his sleeve. He broke the lock, rolled his bike to the corner of Avenida de la Independencia and Salvador Allende and called Ishmael.

"I need a ride and I need a fucking car. I can't do this on a bike anymore. I'll meet you at the French Embassy. The address is Calle 312 Miramar Playa. I Googled it! How the fuck else do you think I know the address?"

Harry's bike was trashed, but his spirits were lifted as he headed toward the sea. He smelled the salt water from miles away. Even though his body was overheated and salty sweat poured down his face, he felt a brief sense of elation. Delivering the truth to Justin and exposing the traitor was a double-edged sword. There was Justin, the traitor to his own band of thugs. And the men who took a bribe and double-crossed Justin. There might not be a winner.

The ocean spray hit Harry in the face as he threw his bike over the wall and watched it land in the sand. Piece of crap. Several kids came up behind him and leaped over the wall to get a look at the bike floating in high tide. They ran along the wet sand, pinwheeling past the rocks jutting out from the shore. He jogged to the French Embassy, feeling lighter than ever before.

The French Embassy was two blocks from the Malecón and was one of the more picturesque landmarks on Miramar Playa. A tall iron fence surrounded a faded white two-story structure. The beautifully crafted tall wooden front doors, one a deep Chinese red and the other a vibrant yellow, gave the edifice an artistic distinction that was perfectly in keeping with the colorful neighborhood. The building, made of sturdy, durable stone, had decorative corners, which were diminished by a series of iron grates on every window facade. A large French flag flew atop the embassy, waving lazily in the soft breeze.

The car windows were down in Ishmael's car. He was on the phone, but Harry couldn't make out what he was saying. His gestures were strong, almost angry.

"*Pendejo, cabrón.* What do you want me to do about it? *No te preocupes.* It'll blow over."

Ishmael saw Harry and closed the phone.

"What the hell took you so long?" asked Ishmael.

"I dumped my bike and walked. Who pissed you off?"

"It was Charles who called wondering where you are. What's up with him lately? Why do you think he's got an axe to grind with you?"

"Because I'm getting close to the truth."

Ishmael opened the car door and wiped his forehead with a clean handkerchief.

"What truth?" asked Ishmael.

"Who's the traitor. Who's in bed with the Russians."

"You've got no proof," said Ishmael. "We know nothing for sure. Better not open your mouth."

"Here is the situation. You set me up to kill Victor, and I took the fall. If you're my buddy, why did you go along with using me as a sacrificial lamb?"

"It wasn't my call. Charles suggested to Justin that they take the Russians out of the picture after the burglary and get the original files back. I suggested you were the guy to take out Victor because you could get close to him."

"Anyone could have been the hit man. It was a money opportunity, but I didn't get paid. I was stiffed and now I'm held hostage to that payment. It's fucked."

"Let's climb off this subject. We'll get the original files for Justin and we walk away from this, your payment included."

"No one is walking away from this."

There was a small park next to the embassy. A large rubber tree provided shade for a bench next to a water fountain.

"A few vegetables are still missing from my soup pot."

"What the hell are you talking about?" asked Ishmael.

"When my mother made soup, some vegetables immediately sank to the bottom, and some floated to the top. Top veggies are the most important because they are the most nutritious."

"Okay, I'll play your game. Silas has no flavor and isn't an important vegetable, so he lands on the bottom. The traitors stay floating on top because they are the bad dudes."

"You learn fast."

"My mother made the same soup," said Ishmael. "What about Alberto? What's his position in the soup pot?"

"I don't know yet. So far, it looks like Lucien accepted a bribe from the Russians and gave them access into Felicity's office, but that's too simple. Alberto has *mucho dinero* and he wears it well."

"I suppose Lucien couldn't take money from the Russians in the French Embassy. It had to be delivered by someone from the outside."

"Here's my two-bit theory," said Harry. "Bribe money was delivered to Charles first, then someone took the bribe back to Lucien. But you already know that, don't you?"

Ishmael lights a cigarette and begins to pace.

"How would I know that?" said Ishmael avoiding Harry's eyes. "Jesus, Harry, you're off base. I take my orders from Justin. Not Charles."

"You take your orders from Charles, and we both know it," said Harry as he walked back to the car.

"I didn't mean to put you in that spot," says Ishmael. "You have to believe me."

"Right now, my list of vegetables includes, in no order, Lucien, Charles, Alberto, and you."

"Why the hell am I a vegetable?"

"Because you know more than you're telling me," said Harry. "And if you're not going to find out what happened to the stolen French files, I will, because that's my job. I work for Justin and he wants to have them back."

Ishmael hung back as Harry opened the car door.

"You're not going to do anything stupid, are you?"

"Not now, but you owe me. We have a common purpose. Deliver Charles and Lucien on a silver platter to Justin no matter what part you played in the bribe and give him back the stolen files. Got any ideas besides getting me a car?"

✣

Felicity walked deliberately around the Plaza de la Revolucíon. The high humidity made her lethargic. Her worst fears had been realized. Harry was going to leave Cuba.

Alberto should not have gone to her office with that awful Lucien. She never liked him. He was rude to her, always putting her on the defensive. Recently, he would go through the French applications to make sure they were in their proper place. That's why the Russians could steal the French files with speed. The break-in lasted no longer than seven minutes.

Alberto's secretary was not at the reception area. Felicity walked into the interior office and didn't see Alberto sitting behind his desk. Felicity was confused because she expected to see to her cousin. She looked out a small window facing the plaza. Cubans were mingling without concern.

Alberto walked in the office and put down a pile of files. *"Hola, mi carina."*

"Cousin Alberto, I'm sorry to be here, but I'm concerned." Felicity sat in a chair in front of Alberto's desk. She noticed that he was sweating as he sat behind his desk. The air conditioner was not functioning properly. She took off her sweater and folded it neatly in her lap.

"Do you know a Harry Cisneros?"

"Why do you ask?"

Felicity gave her cousin background for clarity. Harry came into her office and asked to look at Russian files. He was nice, and she let him inside the file room. He came in a second time, and when he left, she saw that the French files were not put back properly. She thought if she did Harry a favor, like copying the French files for safety, he would like her more.

Felicity pulled a loose string from her sweater and watched it unravel.

"Está bien mi cariño," said Alberto softly. "It's a game these countries play. It's competition. Who has the highest and who has the lowest bid on contracts with our government. But it gets dangerous because there are too many spies. Especially the Russians. They would like to get rid of all the countries who want to partner with us."

"I'm in my position because of you, and I need to know if you are part of the burglary."

"I go over the French applications before they are filed. But I had nothing to do with the burglary."

"Señor Lucien is not a nice man and you shouldn't trust him. Did he say anything to you after you left my office?"

"He was fuming. Very angry with you, and he began to take it out on me because he knows we are related. He wanted me to find out more about why you copied the files."

"No one will ever understand why I copied those files."

"I told your father that I would watch over you and be your guardian, and I won't let you or him down. I'm sorry that you were involved."

"Con permiso," said Felicity. "I think you must stay away from Lucien and stay away from this business."

❖

Harry got the shit detail. Ishmael told him to follow Lucien. Ishmael would hang with Charles. On the way back to Ishmael's apartment, they stopped at a garage to get Harry a loaner car. The old Russian Moskvitch 408 was in a dilapidated state. He hoped the washing machine engine could hold out for a few weeks until they decided what to do.

Harry staked out his position across the street from the French Embassy where he met Ishmael that afternoon. Trying to park in reverse was unworkable. He pushed the car into the curb. It stuck out into the street. The heat in the car was unbearable. He wiped his face and choked on the muggy air.

The phone rang. Ibrahim started talking a mile a minute.

"Slow down. Say that all again."

He wanted Harry to come back to Santiago and get involved in this tourist business. He needed him, good looks and all. They've got more American tourists than they could handle. This was his chance to be with Kobe and Katrina.

"Did you see my wife and daughter?"

"I saw them last week. William and I went to eat at Ezra's place. They look great."

"You must know she has someone in her life," Harry said. "She's moved on."

"Sad for you, I know. But Katrina is beautiful. Smart and growing up fast. Kobe's working long hours at the school but, with all the responsibility, she is doing well."

"I'll call you when I'm out of this darkness."

Fuck waiting at the French Embassy for Lucien who may not leave the building for the rest of the day. It was bullshit.

Harry stood in front of Victor's apartment building on the Prado where the agonizing saga began. It was like yesterday translating for Victor and three lawyers. The Fat Man with the stained purple shirt conducting business as if he owned Cuba.

The phone rang. *Silas.*

"I can't talk right now. Call when you can meet me."

A Russian entered the building. Harry wasn't sure if he was the man who watched Victor bleed to death at the restaurant. He waited until the man walked up the stairs before entering.

Harry followed him. Even at a distance, he smelled of stale cigarettes and rancid body odor. The damn Russians never showered. Harry stopped at the top of the landing of the third floor and watched the Russian knock and enter Victor's apartment.

A half hour later, Harry went back up the stairs to the third floor. He wore a baseball hat pulled down tight around his ears, large sunglasses to obscure his face, and a dirty tee shirt. He was carrying food in plastic bags.

"You order food, Vladimir?" asked a Russian at the door.

"No, we no order food," responded Vladimir.

Harry recognized Vladimir as the man sitting next to Victor at the restaurant. Two other Russians were playing cards. He felt a close familiarity with the apartment.

"We take it anyway," Vladimir said. "How much?"

Harry put the bill down on a table. He didn't know which smelled worse: the Russians or the stink from cabbage soup boiling on the stove. He stifled the urge to vomit. The Russian reached for his wallet and Harry saw a gun on his left hip. He took the money and left.

Just as Harry reached his car, one of the Russians left the building and walked along Paseo de Marti toward the Malecón.

Harry followed him toward the colonial fortress, Castillo de San Salvador de la Punta, which jutted out from the rocks in the Bay of Havana. His mind flipped to the other defensive fortress in Santiago de Cuba built about the same time in the 1600s. He liked the fort in Santiago de Cuba better.

The phone jolted Harry out of Cuban history.

"Ish, I can't talk. Where are you?"

The Russian was on the wall, talking to another man who gave him his fishing rod.

"You still there?" asked Harry, as he walked closer to the fortress. "I need to go back inside Victor's apartment and look for the stolen files. It's Prado 314. I'll be outside waiting."

In half an hour, Ishmael showed up and parked in his usual space in the lot across from Paco's building. He grabbed several thick ropes and a roll of duct tape from his trunk and stuffed it in a duffel bag.

On the third floor, Ishmael smelled garlic and cabbage. He held his nose and gagged.

He knocked and Vladimir cracked open the door.

"Anybody speak English here? Or Spanish?" asked Ishmael. "We've got a problem with the building maintenance. I need to check your plumbing in the bathroom."

Ishmael and Harry pushed their way in and the Russians stood back, willing participants to the repair.

"I show you," said Vladimir in pidgen English. "Serge, get out of bathroom." Serge walked out smiling.

"Holy shit, it stinks," said Ishmael as he walked into the kitchen. Harry was left to examine the bathroom.

"Thanks," said Harry. "You're all heart."

Vladimir and Serge resumed their card game. Several minutes passed in silence until Ishmael coughed and Harry came out of the bathroom. Ishmael threw Harry a rope, and both men flipped over the chairs of the Russians, and tied them up like Christmas turkeys. Ishmael pulled a knife out of his belt and held it to Vladimir's neck.

"This can be easy, or deadly. Where's Victor?"

"Dead," said Vladimir.

"If he's dead, what are you two doing here?" asked Ishmael as he shoved the knife deeper into Vladimir's neck. "You should be on your way back to the motherland."

"We wait for money. Money for our job," said Vladimir screaming.

"Where are the files you took?" asked Harry.

Harry didn't wait for an answer. It would take too long to torture him. Harry ripped through the apartment, opening every drawer, pulling blankets off beds in both rooms.

The hiding place was predictable. He found the original French files under a mattress in the second bedroom.

"The fisherman returns," said Ishmael.

"Who is supposed to bring you money?" asked Harry, shoving the files into an empty, greasy pizza box.

"A French man," said Vladimir.

"What color is his hair?"

Ishmael pushed the knife deeper into Vladimir's sweaty neck and drew blood. He screamed in pain. "Brown. *Marrón.*"

"We robbed the office and he gave us nothing," said Serge. "We want money. He bring it tonight."

Ishmael gave one last kick in the ribs to Vladimir, and they left the apartment, barely missing the Russian fisherman coming around the top of the staircase. The Russian entered the hallway preoccupied by a fish that slipped off the newspaper and onto the floor. He bent over to pick it up as Ishmael and Harry turned a corner and ran up a stairwell to the sixth floor. They faced a fire escape.

CHAPTER 16

Great Art
Percolates

Harry opened the glove compartment, rifled through it, closed it, then opened it again.

"What are you looking for?" asked Ishmael.

"Where are your cigarettes?"

"You don't smoke."

Harry found a pack of cigarettes in the glove compartment and lit one with shaky hands.

Ishmael pulled over to the curb and dialed his phone.

"Tell me where to meet you," said Ishmael. "Give me twenty minutes."

Harry inhaled and choked on the smoke.

"You're all grown up now," said Ishmael as he clicked off his phone. "Live with the fear. Live with uncertainty. That's the dangerous state of life as we know it. Go back to your car and meet me at Museo Nacional de Bellas Artes. We're going look at art."

When Harry first met Ishmael, he thought of him as a kind and generous family man trying to make some extra money. He didn't know him anymore. His friend showed a willingness to take risks like it was a badge of courage. Harry didn't see it coming. It must have been there all the time. Paco trusted him with his buildings, his workmen, and to show up every day. It was predictable work. He wondered what changed Ishmael. And what changed him?

The last time Harry came to the Museo Nacional, he came with his mother. He was eight years old. That was the day his father left and didn't come home again. Instead of getting angry and throwing pots and pans, his mother took him to Cuba's most famous cultural arts museum – two buildings that displayed the history of fine arts from primitive times to the present. Harry thought that it was the biggest, grandest palace in the world. Sometime later, he forgot about his father.

Regina told him that museums were places of culture and helped preserve Cuban history. He was too young to understand the historical significance of artifacts and artists, but he spent the day in awe of his mother who pointed out her favorite sections and favorite artists.

Leaning against a column on the ground floor of the museum's parking garage, holding a greasy pizza box, and waiting for Silas, Harry thought he must look like a comic figure in a Fellini film.

A taxi entered the garage and Harry got into the cab.

"What did you find out?" asked Harry.

"Justin Levitt doesn't exist. No such person ever lived with that name or resembled the person known as Justin Levitt. I hacked into every government website I could think of, every tech company's roster, Intel, where he said he worked, global searches for tech corporations. *Nada.*"

"Who is he?" asked Harry.

"A phantom spy who disappears with different names without a trace. No date of birth, lived nowhere, no parents, no kids, no photos. He probably operated through front companies or corporate cutouts in tech or land deals. Maybe he gets rich by money laundering, guns, or controlling commodities markets, or turning drug profits into real estate or science research."

"We've been played," said Harry.

"He's sending me to the States to work on my Internet plan. We're going to be working together."

"Not so fast. We're working together, but not in the way you think. If you take Justin's deal, you'll end up in the gulag."

Harry told Silas about Justin's Brazilian connections, the private company, GlobalNet, the many file boxes outlining the full range of a cellular system to wire the island. It was already designed and probably in production. Harry had the files. He also had the original French files, which included a basic Internet operation for Cuba.

"I don't get it. Why did he say he was sending me to the U.S. if he has all the goods from Brazil?"

"He wanted to see what you had in the pipeline. He's double-crossing all of us, especially Charles, who is double-crossing Justin. We're being set up from both sides."

"You mean, I'm not going to the U.S. to work for him?"

"Unless you're sure there is warm weather on the other side," said Harry. "Justin wants the original French files so he can delete the Internet plan the French proposed."

"Sounds like Justin wants to merge all French bids into Brazil's GlobalNet."

Harry left the pizza box with Silas and got out of the cab.

"I don't have to tell you to keep this to yourself. You lose this pizza box, you lose your future and mine. After you've gone over them, put the files in the Hotel Sevilla's safe.

"Are we going to work together someday?" Silas asked.

"I'm counting on it."

Walking the two blocks with Ishmael to the museum, Harry told Ishmael not to mention finding the original French files to anyone. Play dumb.

They passed into the pre-Columbian room, perfectly organized in cases of categorized artifacts. Justin, movie star handsome in up-scale casual GQ, was studying a case of primitive weapons as Harry and Ishmael entered the section.

"Did you know that this building was once a presidential palace?" Justin said. "It was constructed between 1913 and 1920. Tiffany did the interiors. It's a splendid building. I can see you're fascinated by this history, so tell me what you have."

"Victor's Russian gang are waiting for their cut for the burglary," said Ishmael. "A French man is to deliver the money."

"They could be waiting a long time," said Justin. "Fill in the rest of this story."

Harry rolled out the way the bribe was likely handled.

"Two carriers were involved in the bribe: one to deliver the Russian money to Charles, and one to take the money, minus what Charles took out for his cut, back to Lucien. There was no money left to pay the Russians for the burglary."

"What did you find out from Alberto?" asked Justin.

"My money is on Alberto delivering the money to Charles," said Harry.

"Don't jump to conclusions," Justin explained. "Alberto has a difficult job in the Cuban government. Everyone has secrets, but I am also sure he wasn't involved in the burglary until Charles asked him to get rid of the guard's body."

"Alberto knows more than he is telling you," said Harry. "He saw Russians visiting Lucien months before the burglary, and Charles was pushing Alberto to tell him about the contents of the Russian applications. That sounds like collusion to me."

A group of school children neatly dressed in navy blue and white uniforms and their teacher walked through the room, eagerly eyeing the artifacts.

Justin returned to studying the primitive tools. He could spend all day and night in the museum, believing that art reached the soul. Great art was imagination at its extreme. It was a shame that communism saw art primarily as a vehicle for propaganda. On the other hand, the glories of Russian culture would always be preserved through its artists.

"I'm thinking about Norm," said Harry to Ishmael, "taking money to Lucien."

"Norm is a nothing. A stoner. He can't put two and two together."

"Norm is a dangling participle," interrupted Justin. "Get confirmation of the mules. More important, get the original French applications back to me."

The meeting went nowhere. Waste of time. Spinning wheels. Victor was dead and Felicity was the hero of the day.

He was swimming with sharks.

⁜

Harry was not happy that Norm provided another plot point in the mystery, especially because the only way to start his search was with Juan Juan. He'd rather walk to the Malecón and enjoy the cool breeze, or lounge in bed with Felicity, or spend time in the Bellas Artes. He parked at the end of the Prado, walked to the wall, and called Juan Juan. Again, there was no answer.

He made another call to Alma, asking if he could see her that night at Kirpan. For safety, he asked for her address. She told him she was busy, and it would be better to talk at the restaurant. Charles was with her. Why should he be surprised? Charles was predictable.

The blue waters of the Caribbean were choppy. Afternoon winds picked up. He thought of the Mariel boat people. Over time, the refugees became iconic heroes who were revered by those who didn't have the means or the courage to leave. Most of the eighties generation were old and forgetful. They left their memories behind long ago.

Harry spotted a man stumbling on the beach, dragging his feet in the sand, head down, longish, matted hair, faded tan, turning lighter every day.

The disheveled man turned to the wall and saw Harry. He dug his feet into the sand and walked toward him, hand held out in a begging gesture. Begging was not allowed in Cuba. It was a desperate move.

"*Hombre,*" said Harry. "*Cual es su nombre?*"

"Rafael," he responded, slurring his words.

"Where do you get your drugs, Rafael?"

"Everywhere. Mostly weed. You can get anything you want."

Harry knew drugs were plentiful on the island, part of the black market and as permanent as the rehab clinics in the neighborhoods of La Habana. The upper classes also participated in the drug culture. It was a status symbol of wealth. But as prices went up, the marginalized got left behind, and the fallout was that the poor took the brunt of policing and ended up in jail.

Raúl Castro told the world that drugs didn't exist in Cuba. It served as effective propaganda for tourists. But the truth was that marijuana, psychotropic drugs, and different varieties of cocaine were sold and consumed. The drugs came in from the waters adjacent to the archipelago, especially Jamaica and the Dominican Republic. When the Coast Guard approached drug traffickers, the smugglers threw their drugs overboard. Residents of coastal regions hunted for stray packages that washed up on shore and had a field day.

"*Conoces a un hombre llamado* Norm?" Harry asked, knowing it was a long shot.

"*No se. Tal vez debajo* el Castillo de San Salvador de la Punta. *Ellos fuman ahí.*"

Harry handed him a handful of kooks.

The man walked to the shoreline and headed toward the fortress. Harry made another call to Juan Juan.

"Where's Norm?" asked Harry.

"No small talk, right? *Está bien.* Norm told me he wanted to stay in La Habana. We had bad words because he was pretty strung out. I tried to shove him into my car, but he fought me. I had to let him go, poor bastard. I told him he better find his sister and get some help. He mumbled something about not knowing where his sister was. Then he disappeared."

"What's Norm's last name?" asks Harry.

"Salcedo. He might go back to Kirpan to see if he can scrounge money for drugs. That was his thing lately."

"You're a good guy after all, Juan Juan."

"*Singao.*"

The odds were slim that Harry would find Norm. Needle in a haystack. Harry remembered something Uncle Ray told him if he wanted to solve a problem: *The lower you go, you find the truth.* The truth started with Norm.

Before Harry went to Kirpan, he checked out the place under the San Salvador fortress. The ruins of the fort were perched on the end of the Malecón and provided a natural inlet into the Bahia de La Habana port. Harry wandered around the fortress a few times since he moved to La Habana. There wasn't much to see from the outside. Most of the time the fortress was used to throw a fishing line into the sea.

He climbed down among the rocks below into a cave impervious to onlookers, especially the police. The rocks were slippery with moss and the smell of rotten fish permeated the stifling surroundings. A few potheads were smoking. When they saw Harry, they were too stoned to worry about being caught. He smiled and waved. They smiled and waved back to him.

"*Hola. Conoces a un hombre llamado* Norm?" he asked.

The men were oblivious to Harry. Some nodded out.

"He's a friend and his mother died. I need to find him."

One man responded with slurred speech. "He was coming here the last couple of months, *pero ya no.*"

"Didn't he have a sister or a brother in La Habana?"

Another man remembered. *"Una hermana. Ella vive en Habana Vieja."*

"Did she ever come looking for him?" asked Harry.

"Una vez. Yo creo." He reached into his tattered pocket and pulled out a crumpled piece of paper. He was stoned, but not too stoned to know that something of value was coming his way.

"Ella me dio esto." He waved the paper in the air. Harry was slow to move toward him.

He patiently played the pantomime game and took a few kooks out of his pants pocket. The man grabbed the money as Harry deftly lifted the water-stained paper from his hand.

Rita Salcedo lived a few blocks away from El Capitol and Plaza Vieja. Walking through the plaza, Harry noticed tourists engaged in the busy social life. The colonial and rustic buildings were old but appealing. Plaza Vieja and every plaza in La Habana, needed a white-washing. Inside the barrio, the streets became narrower, dirtier, pockmarked, resembling a shantytown or a war zone. An eco-skeleton of a car pushed to a crumbling curb complemented the architecture.

Harry wasn't familiar with this section of Habana Vieja. Remnants of La Habana's few industrial factories that produced small amounts of commercial goods back in the sixties receded from the sidewalks. Rita's neighborhood was overdue for renovation, but he knew it wouldn't happen for many decades.

He approached the three-story tenement. It was surrounded by trash. Odors of rotten food permeated the street. Lines of clothes hung on makeshift ropes. The ground floor door of Rita's building was open, begging for a breeze. Air conditioning was a non-starter for the poorest of Cuba's citizens. The dwellings were similar – small and narrow, consisting of a living room and a bedroom, old wooden floors pulling away from the dirt beneath, and something that resembled a kitchen sink that couldn't possibly be working.

Harry walked up to the third floor on rickety, wooden stairs. He hoped they held his weight. He looked for numbers on the door, but there were none. The search for Norm's sister was more trying than he expected, but what hasn't been exhausting and demoralizing on his journey?

He knocked tentatively on several termite-ridden doors. No Rita. At the fourth door, a woman opened the door just enough to identify the intruder. A line of ants moving efficiently up the door frame held his attention briefly before he answered.

"*Hola,*" Harry said nervously. "I'm Harry Cisneros. I'm a friend of Norm's." Rita was confused and fearful.

"How did you find me?" snapped Rita.

"Please excuse the intrusion. I'm a friend of your brother."

"Why do you want to see him?" Rita asked.

"I know him from Cienfuegos. I haven't seen him for some time, and I'm worried about him."

"That makes two of us. Come in."

Harry entered the shoddy but clean-living room. He didn't know where to sit, afraid to break a chair or be gouged by a coiled spring sticking up from the dilapidated sofa.

"I'm sorry to bother you."

"You already said that."

Rita Salcedo was attractive. Older than Norm by about ten years, tall, thin, and neatly dressed in a tight skirt and colorful blouse that, although vintage, was still respectable. What passed for furniture had been picked off the street, a dented stainless steel table with faded red Formica, four chairs in various states of collapse, and an old couch that saw better days twenty years ago. A small bedroom was tucked away in the back, windowless and drab. Flies hovered around what passed for a kitchen sink.

"Want a drink? I've got rum."

"No, thanks." She was slightly drunk. "But go ahead." He watched Rita down a shot of rum.

"Sit down."

It dawned on Harry that Rita was a prostitute. The rum was compliments of a customer. She swayed over to him with an interesting grace that belied her status.

"When was the last time you saw your brother?"

"Maybe three weeks ago. He was going to get me some money so I could get out of this dump and back to Cienfuegos. He never showed. When I asked him where he lived, he told me under the El Salvador fort. I didn't know he was an addict until I went looking for him a week or two ago and left my address with one of the pot-heads." Rita poured another shot. "Norm isn't around, he is?"

"I'll take a shot if you don't mind." Rita dripped a thimbleful of rum into a glass that had a prominent crack on the rim. Harry gulped it down. "Has anybody come by looking for him?"

Rita ran her hands though her dirty straight hair and took a drink from the rum bottle.

"About three weeks ago this man with a French accent knocked on my door. I thought it was a customer, so I let him in. He was good-looking. Sweet-talking me. Turned out he was looking for Norm. I didn't know what to tell him. He slapped me around trying to get something out of me that I didn't know. He hurt me. I thought he was going to kill me."

"What did you tell him?"

"What you already know about the caves under El Salvador." Rita was already grieving. "What did I do?"

Rita's degrading life made his stomach turn. "Do you remember his name?"

"I'm never getting out, am I? I'm going to die here, old and lonely and starving to death. That's what Cubans expect. We live hopeless." Rita tried to get control of herself. "I've got someone coming over. You have to leave."

"I need a name. Did you get the name of the man?" Harry patiently waited for her answer. "If you want to know what happened to your brother, I need a name. If not a name, can you tell me what he looked like?"

"Tall, brown hair, curly. Wore clean clothes. He smelled good. Expensive cologne, but had mean devil green eyes."

"Glasses?" Charles didn't wear glasses. Rita shook her head.

The lower you go, you find the truth.

Harry pulled a stack of kooks from his pocket and handed them to Rita.

✣

Charles looked up as Harry entered Kirpan. The restaurant was lively. The bartender couldn't make the drinks fast enough. Charles managed the kitchen and made sure the stage was ready for Alma and Federico. Harry leaned against the back wall and studied Charles in all his glory.

Alma took the stage with all her radiant grace and beauty. She was wearing a floor-length, body-hugging gown of turquoise taffeta with a decorous décolletage, long sexy rhinestone earrings, and a red rose at the nape of her neck. The customers quieted down as Alma sang a popular tango that began her set. The first phrase of the tango, *Malena,* was greeted with applause. Her expressive phrasing, deep and melodious sensual voice brought back his life in the uncomplicated city of Cienfuegos, his wise, loving, and concerned Uncle Ray and the elegant simplicity of his life.

Alma spotted Harry walking to the bar and nodded his way with her Mona Lisa smile. He felt special.

"What's on your mind?" asked Charles.

"Norm."

Charles continued to tidy up after customers.

"Is he still around?" asked Charles.

"Maybe. He has a sister who is worried about him."

"He's probably in Cienfuegos."

"He's not. He's nowhere. Any ideas?"

"I'm not concerned about a pothead. He came around looking for a handout, and I sent him on his way."

"Right. Good idea. Get rid of him." Harry got off his barstool and headed to the restroom. Charles followed him down the small hallway.

"What's up your ass?" asked Charles. "If you have a problem, tell me. The kid was a punk and a liar."

"Does that mean he knew too much about what was going on with the Russians?" Harry asked.

"I don't know what he knew, and I don't care. Think what you like because you'll be off this island very soon."

Harry thought not.

Harry waited for Alma to come off the stage. She saw Harry in the hallway and embraced him. Charles watched from a distance.

"We need to talk in private. No Charles."

"He takes all my time. I don't know how to get away."

"Get sick and go home," suggested Harry.

"We live together."

Expect the unexpected.

"What happens after your last set? Do you have to wait around for him to close?"

"Not always. I can tell him my throat is sore and I need medicine. He might believe me. Meet me at Cafe Madrigal in Vedado at midnight. I have a contact, the manager. He wants me to sing."

A waiter, wiry and tall, dressed in black, familiar to Harry, slowed down and squeezed by them. His canine black eyes sent a shiver down Harry's back. Same guy who threatened him on the street while he was on the phone with Alma, minus his drunken gang. Harry wasn't as tall as the waiter, but he could hold his own if the Ruski made a move on him.

"Want to tell me what's on your mind?" asked Harry.

"You'll know soon enough."

"Who sent you? Is he serving drinks at the bar?"

"I'll get you." The Russian moved past them.

CHAPTER 17
Treason

Café Madrigal took Harry away from the dirt and grim of his life. It was a magical setting. Alma would be a perfect addition to this dimly lit romantic restaurant. The bar was famous. A sign on the wall told its story: a Cuban movie director, Rafael Rosales, who was famous for his elegant and visually exciting movie sets, created the bar scene. It was right out of one of his movies. The French art on the walls gave the bar a feeling that customers were part of the bohemian crowd in the Paris Latin Quarter during the twenties.

Harry settled down on a barstool and looked through the open dining room and onto a beautiful terrace where several couples were talking and eating. He ordered a chicken and vegetable basket, tapas style, and decides to splurge for a daiquiri. Money was running low, but Harry wanted to be a part of this experience even if he left without a kook in his pocket. If Harry had to stay in La Habana for the rest of his life and work for Justin, he decided to eat at Café Madrigal twice a week with Felicity on his arm.

Alma entered carrying her beauty like a work of art. She blended into the elegance.

"What would you like?" asked Harry.

"I can't talk long. I have to see the manager."

"You have to get out from under Charles. He won't let you leave Kirpan."

"Please don't lecture me, *querido*. I know exactly where I am in my life. A good place and a bad place. The owner of Café Madrigal wants me to sing here, but I have to get away from Charles. Tell me what you want, please."

"Have you heard anything about a man named Norm?"

"He ran errands for Charles for a while. Then he disappeared. I heard them arguing one day. Norm wanted more money and Charles told him their business was over."

"What else do you remember?"

"Charles told him that if he left, he was on his own."

Alma ordered a Compari, took a sip, and relaxed.

"It's suffocating out there in the streets, but it's lovely in here, isn't it?"

"Did he mention someone named Lucien?" asked Harry.

"How do you know this name?"

"It doesn't matter. Just tell me what you know."

"Something about Lucien and Norm. And money. I think Norm took money to Lucien."

"What about a man named Alberto?"

"He was rather rotund but a nice-looking man. Beautiful dark suit. He brought a package to Charles. I saw him open it, count money, remove more than half of the stack, and put it under the bar. I thought it was part of the money changing game. He gave the rest of the money back to Norm who left Kirpan."

"Does Charles know you witnessed this transfer of money?"

"I was hiding in a dark corner on the balcony," Alma said. "He almost saw me. I had to stand in the shadows until he left."

"Don't go back to Charles."

A handsome man of medium height with wavy dark hair, penetrating dark eyes, walked over to the bar and introduced himself to Alma. Mr. General Manager, Aaron Garcia. Harry put his hand on

Alma's shoulder and squeezed it with affection. *Señor* Garcia shook Harry's hand.

"Be good to her," said Harry. "She is a woman of value and talent." Harry reached for his wallet, but *Señor* Garcia picked up the check. On his way out, Harry gave Café Madrigal one more admiring glance to a time long past.

Tired of going around in circles with his posse, Harry called Ishmael as he left the hotel lobby.

"Why are you calling me in the middle of the night?" asked Ishmael in a sleepy and defensive voice.

"You better tell me the truth. Face-to-face tonight. I'm sick of this shit with you. Meet me outside your apartment. I'll cut you a break. You don't have to drive."

Before he could get to his car, Harry's phone rang.

"He was a coder," said Silas.

"I'm fifty years behind the tech curve. Explain."

"Justin's not just an ordinary coder. He created his first computer code at six, his first hack at ten, by the time he was twelve, he was making million-dollar apps, and by the time he was eighteen, he did his first covert operation. He knows every coding language, which means Justin can build any kind of website in the time it would take you to take a piss. He's a coding artist, a sleight of hand guy who can write code so beautiful that it makes everyone gnash their teeth in envy."

"Get to the point," said Harry. "I'm late."

"I had to find this guy somewhere. Only by dumb luck, I found his name buried decades ago in a list of old coder names with a company called MathLab. A math-based company that generated a shitload of codes for hardware platforms, desktop systems, even embedded hardware. Justin was a genius at integrating the generated code into important projects like source code, static libraries, and dynamic libraries. The highest of high tech stuff. As soon as I found his name, it was deleted."

"Holy shit. He's a high-tech phantom who sold himself to the Brazilians under another name. He wants the original files back because he's jumping ship with the French."

"I don't get it. If he wrote the software for the Cuban government, he can hack into the computer and delete the French files digitally," said Silas. "He doesn't need anybody to do that. Get the paper copies and burn them."

"Justin doesn't know we have the original French files, and that's the paper trail he wants to destroy."

"Don't worry. They are in Sevilla's hotel safe."

"I want you to study the Brazilian files from GlobalNet," said Harry. "You'll understand the tech bids. Stay by the phone. We'll set up a meeting place."

Harry clicked his phone off as he leaned against his car. He wiped the sweat off his forehead with the tail of his shirt.

Harry pulled up outside Ishmael's building. He was smoking and pacing. Harry parked and Ishmael stomped out his cigarette.

"What the fuck is this about?"

"You, Charles, Lucien, Norm, Alberto. The gang that couldn't shoot straight."

"How does Norm play into this?" Ishmael shuffled and lit another cigarette.

"There's an old saying: Go where the silence is. You didn't want me to look for Norm because Norm was missing. Know anything about that?"

"How would I?" asked Ishmael. He looked like a lion locked in a cage too small for his body.

"I'm sick of getting yanked around and threatened. Everybody's playing off everybody, and I'm the most disposable."

Ishmael takes a long drag on his cigarette.

"Not talking?" asked Harry.

"Get off my case. I thought you were going to talk to Alma tonight?"

"Did I tell you that? I didn't tell you I was talking to Alma. Be straight with me for once, because before one of Charles's guys kills me, I'll tell Justin everything I know about you and your expensive wardrobe courtesy of the Russian burglary."

"Are you throwing me under the bus?" asked Ishmael.

"You're already under the bus. You knew Charles was involved in the Russian bribe, he and his buddy, Lucien, and I'm guessing you know what happened to Norm. By the way, nice scene you played with Alberto in his office. You know he took the bribe money to Charles."

"I didn't know that. You have good spies."

"How much was it?" asked Harry.

"A million. That fuck Charles got most of it."

"Did Charles ask you to kill Norm?"

"He was half dead when I found him stumbling around El Salvador fortress. He fell and hit his head on a rock. I took the body away."

"Where did you go after you set me up to kill Victor?" asked Harry.

"I went to Santiago, talked to Ibrahim. They made it seem more important than it was. The trip was to get me out of the way. So I learned more about his operation. It has more possibilities for making money than I thought."

Harry leaned against the apartment wall. Clouds covered the sky like dark moss. No stars. Inky black. Like Harry's mind. Like Rita and her life and the lives of those Cubans who never had a chance to escape.

"Let me guess. I'm next on your kill list."

"I can't. I won't kill you."

"Who's the Ruski that keeps threatening me? Tall, skinny Darth Vader. Waits tables at Kirpan. The hustler du jour."

"I'll take care of him," said Ishmael.

"No way you come out of this shitshow alive, Ish. You're too compromised."

"And no one is helping you get off the island. Justin had no intention of following through."

The anvil drops.

If you were in the club, the gang, the mafia, you never saw the big picture. You were dealing with minutiae all day, running errands, following orders. No thoughts. No questions asked.

That's how Harry went down the rabbit hole. He knew how the government did business, how Cuban officials answered to money, how foreign investments were at the top of government handouts, and Harry refused to see the big picture. He was one of the guys who helped grease the wheel. He didn't just commit murder, he helped the bad guys get a foothold in Cuba.

Everything went along fine until it didn't. Victor got cute, spread a bunch of money around, and pulled a burglary with the help of Charles, Lucien and Alberto. Harry got squeezed, killed the Fat Man, and the tripwire was pulled. Spencer Merryman was right.

Nothing's as it seems.

Ishmael snuffed out his cigarette. "I'm sorry, *comprade*. I got you into it, and you don't deserve what came down."

"It's best you keep me alive if you want me to save your ass. I'm your lucky charm."

"If I don't kill you, I'll be the next dead man. Darth Vader will burn on me."

"Stay away from Charles. Don't take calls. Think fast on your feet and stay out of the plazas. You'll be followed, so call me every hour."

Ishmael pulled out his phone and called his wife. He handed Harry a cigarette, lit it for him, and did the same for himself. They inhaled deeply.

Ishmael heard a *psst* sound from the third-floor balcony. Anna lowered a stack of money. He caught it and threw it to Harry.

They were a team again, even though Harry was now the quarterback.

"I didn't have your back. I betrayed you. The worst thing I could do."

"We've all betrayed each other and ourselves. It begins with money and ends with money. But for Justin, it's about absolute power. He's the Wizard of Oz."

�֎

It was late and Harry was exhausted. Almost to the end of the line. Almost to Felicity. He needed to climb into bed with her, hold her, be safe with her for one more night, but he couldn't, he won't because he knew Charles would find out where she lived and hold her hostage. He had every reason to fear the unknown.

A few blocks away from Felicity's place, the streets were quiet in the hours after midnight. A car drove slowly down the street. He darted in and out of doorways until he arrived at the back of Felicity's building. He climbed up the fire escape to the first floor and tapped on the window.

Darth Vader pulled him inside and held a gun to his neck.

"Where is she?" asked Harry.

"Tied up in the bathroom."

Harry knew Felicity was leverage for Charles. First Alma, then Felicity. Justin was not behind this kill. Collateral damage doesn't interest him. He betrayed everyone for the power that came with moving Cuba into the 21st century.

Harry told Darth Vader he wasn't getting paid by Charles, just as he had no intention of paying off the Russians for the burglary.

"Shut up. I've already been paid."

"Must be nice. How much?" asked Harry.

"A thousand."

"He stiffed you. The Russians paid Charles a million for allowing Victor's crew to steal the French files."

"I don't know anything about that."

"You should. You should be smarter than you look."

"I've got a thousand and you have nothing."

Harry felt the Russian relax, soften. He recognized that Darth Vader wasn't a killer. He was equivocating. Mentally stumbling. Harry knew about killer instincts. He killed and didn't stumble. Dark Vader's softness was an opportunity to grab his gun, and turn it on him with force.

"You're not a killer," said Harry. "You just look like one. I don't look like one, but I'm a killer. Funny, huh?"

"You killed Victor?"

"Shit, yes. Now untie the girl and get her out of the bathroom."

Felicity came out of the bathroom rubbing her wrists. She didn't come near him.

"I lied. Charles didn't give me any money."

"At least he's consistent. How about you disappearing? Wherever you came from, go back."

"Can I have my gun back?" he asked.

"I'll keep it for a souvenir of our friendship. And don't go near Ishmael. He's set to kill you."

It was a threat but one that scared the shit out of Darth Vader. The Ruski climbed out the window as fast as a lion chasing his prey.

"Are they going to kill you?" asked Felicity.

"Not if I stay one step ahead of them."

Harry told Felicity to go to a relative's house until she was out of danger. Leave in the early morning. Take enough clothes and don't tell Alberto anything. Say you have termites or the plumbing is out. Easy enough to believe in Cuba.

"*Mi amor*," Harry whispered. "I'm going to stay with you tonight for your safety, and I'll take the Brazilian files out of the wall safe tomorrow morning when I leave."

She opened the safe with her key, removed the files, and wrapped them in a paper bag, easy to carry.

Felicity whispered lovingly, "Don't forget the knife you left in the refrigerator. It might keep you safe."

❈

The sun was rising as Harry gathered his things to leave Felicity's apartment. He kissed her tenderly one more time, told her to get out soon, took his knife out of the refrigerator, and taped it to his back. He left through the window. There was no time to think of all the things he should have done.

This was a Mexican standoff between greed and power. Between dark and darker. Between Charles and Justin. The stakes were high. Charles had no idea about the global power that Justin possessed. Justin bought and sold information to the highest bidder. He betrayed everyone who got in his way. That was his game, his global chessboard. Every player was a pawn. Time and patience and brains were on his side.

Charles got greedy, didn't play by the rules, and fouled Justin's plans by allowing the burglary to happen. The cover-up was a bust. He didn't pay his people. Even worse, he didn't know that stealing the original French files was his biggest mistake. There was no turning back for Charles. He crossed Justin.

Driving along Avenida Simon Bolivar at the intersection of Padre Varela in the early morning, Harry turned his car into Calle San José and parked. He took out his old flip phone. Safer to call Silas on a phone that can't be traced.

"Come up to my room," said Silas.

The pass-off of the Brazilian files to Silas happened in room 501. Graham Green's room. Harry saw this as a sign of luck. He confessed to Silas that Justin had no intention of helping him off the island, nor sending Silas to the U.S. The third act was in full swing. It was time to make clear choices about surviving.

"Analyze this technology file and tell me if you can do what Justin is proposing," said Harry. "Don't talk to Justin, don't get near him. I'll call you when I can."

The day that Justin gave Harry a smartphone, he gave him a piece of paper with a special number. He put it in his wallet for safekeeping, never looked at it because he knew it was for life support. That was a joke. He suspected it was meant for something more sinister. He called and no one answered.

It was still early in the morning and he was close to Hotel Parque Central on Calle Agramonte and Paseo de Martí. He felt energized walking into this luxury hotel. A fighter getting ready to enter the ring.

A staircase out of *Gone with the Wind* took front and center in the lobby. Lush green ferns and colorful hydrangeas in expensive designer pots decorated hallway entrances and white columns. Shiny marble floors extended for what felt like a mile in every direction. Comfortable sofas covered in white linen, flower-colored lounges and stuffed chairs arranged in conversation areas were set around ornate coffee tables, bringing tourists together in friendly contact. Harry felt he deserved this five-star experience.

His clothes weren't the best, but not any less casual than those of the early-rising American and Canadian tourists who were avidly reading their morning newspapers on their iPads or phones. Harry could be in any luxury hotel in the States. No one looked at him as he headed to the coffee shop.

Before he entered the cafe, he noticed that coffee was available on a side table for the hotel guests. Who was to know he isn't a guest? He poured a cup for himself and sauntered over to a sofa, put his cup and saucer down on a marble side table, and picked up an American newspaper. Two days old. Damn! Cuba still lived in the 20th century. He read it anyway: Trump talked anti-immigration as the first order of business should he become president. One small step for mankind. But that was a temporary condition, because Trump had bigger plans to keep everyone who wasn't white and Christian out of the U.S. Harry passed for both, but what good was it if he still needed a visa and a reason to stay in the U.S.? Someday Trump would be gone and America's best interests would prevail.

A small article caught his eye on the bottom right column: Trump would overturn Obama's easing of trade and travel restrictions for Cuba. Hey, Trump, what happened to the fifteen or so American companies who already set up shop in Cuba? Raúl doesn't give a rat's ass if the U.S. resets to the old sanctions. He's got plenty of European and South American countries investing in Cuba.

Harry's phone rang. It was too loud and a few tourists glanced at him with hostility.

"I see you are in the lobby, Leo, my boy." Justin laughed and Harry almost jumped out of his skin.

"I'm behind the palm tree next to the bar," Justin said. "Is it too early for you to have a drink?"

Harry laughed out loud. The guy lived in the hotel. Leave it to Justin to sense the irony in this moment. *Of course, he lived in a hotel. He was invisible. Left no trace.*

Justin was ordering coffee and brandy. "And one of these for my friend here, please, Julio."

"You never cease to amaze me, Leo. This is serendipitous because I was calling you back to meet me here. And, voila, you are here! This must be important. You used the lifeline. Is someone going to kill you?"

"Funny you should ask," said Harry, taking a sip of his coffee. "And since you are all-knowing, do you know who that might be?"

"Charles is first in line. You are the biggest threat to him. Tell me all you have and this time don't hedge your bets."

This was a no-win, one-way conversation. Justin knew everything. He planned this moment. He could make Harry go away in the blink of an eye. Keep it simple.

He told Justin about looking for Norm, meeting his sister, and confirming his role as the go-between who brought bribe money from Charles to Lucien.

"May I remind you that you used the emergency number, so there must something more urgent than Norm."

Harry gave up Ishmael. Justin won't care about Ishmael finishing off Norm. Just another loose end tied up. Perversely, it might put Ishmael in a better light.

Moving on.

"Was meeting Victor a setup or just dumb luck?"

"Dumb luck. I'm good, but not that good."

"Did you think the Russians could bribe your people? Your crew gave you up for money."

"The alchemy and greed between Charles and Lucien was palpable. They're history."

Justin sipped his coffee and the cup shook in his hands. He scanned the bar area, the tourists in the breakfast room, and beyond the lobby.

"Who are you looking for?" asked Harry.

"You never know who is watching," Justin responded. "And by the look on your face, you'd be a lousy poker player. Want to get something off your chest?"

"First, I want to ask you about why your hands shake."

"I was born with the neurological disorder that causes shaking in different parts of the body. In my case, it's my hands. When I code, it's under control."

"Do you still code?"

Justin ignores the question. "Alberto."

"You trusted him too much," said Harry. "He took the bribe money from Lucien and gave it to Charles."

"I refused to suspect him. That's good information."

"Everyone's for sale."

"Except you."

"That doesn't exempt me from the inevitable."

"How little you think of yourself," said Justin. "Where are the original files?"

"Don't know, and even if I knew, I wouldn't tell you because that would be considered leverage."

"Clever boy."

"Most people in your situation would be happy with the copies. But you're not most people."

"Is there more then?" asked Justin.

"More is when I see my money, when my exit date is fixed."

"Enemies never treat you fairly, dear Leo."

"That's comforting. Except Charles told Ishmael to kill me, or he's a dead man walking. To his credit, he couldn't do it. I call that treating me fairly."

"You are in no danger of being killed. To the matter of Ishmael, I owe him for bringing you into Kirpan, and if you need Ishmael, if he makes amends for his sins by helping you corner Charles, get the files, then redemption is at hand."

"Did you know all this?" asked Harry. "Was this a rat maze I went through so we could meet at the Hotel Parque Central and compare war stories?"

The bartender poured a brandy for both men.

"You were the catalyst, my Leo. But after you killed Victor, you were expendable to Charles. You stayed in the game because I needed you to make the pieces fit together. Alberto is a disappointment. Trusted soldier falls. Good detective work."

Harry smelled the brandy and gulped it down. It felt warm as it traveled through his body.

"Charles is planning his last act," said Justin. "Find him and get the original files. I'll take care of the rest."

"The deal was over when I took Victor out. No more extensions."

CHAPTER 18

Leaving Cuba

The sun was high and blazing in the cloudless sky as Harry left the Hotel Parque Central.

This next phase, this last phase of planning was more suited to Ishmael. It sounded too much like the *Gunfight at the OK Corral*. Harry saw that old movie while living with his uncle and cousins in Newark. He loved western movies, but the problem with westerns was that the good guys and bad guys were presented in black and white. In real life, people lived in the gray area, where emotions and actions were complicated.

Out of nowhere, Harry was engulfed in the smell of garlic and stale cigarettes. A hand went over his mouth and he was forced into a car. Shit! He should have used valet. He tried to fight the men off, but the two big, disgusting bears were angry and determined. So much for watching old westerns.

Ishmael was tied to a chair inside Victor's apartment. Harry's entrance made him more like an angry lion in a cage. Payback was a bitch. Harry assessed his surroundings. He knew the apartment well. No way out. Charles was holding them hostage, for leverage, money, but not for sport killing.

Without anything to do, the Russians drank, went out for a smoke, a walk, got food, and lost track of time. The big bears got cranky and forgetful. They were no match for Ishmael and Harry, who shared a history and kept their eye on the ball. Ishmael won't take a dive at this point.

❖

At nine, Justin sat behind his desk. He called the shots, made the plans, and executed. But today was complicated because there were too many variables. Best outcomes: Charles could kill Harry and Ishmael, and there would be no proof of the Russian bribery. Or, Charles could take Harry and Ishmael as hostages and extort Justin for money. *Not going to happen. They're expendable.* Or, Charles could blow the whistle on him with Cuban authorities, taking control over Kirpan enterprises, a position he always thought he deserved. *Again, won't happen.*

Charles interrupted his thoughts.

"You're here early. I'd like my hour of contemplation."

"Alma decided to sing at Café Madrigal. She left two nights ago and never came back."

"That's not the way we do business. Bring her to Kirpan. She sings tonight. She either wants more money, or she's sick of you controlling her life. Whichever it is, make it right."

"How the fuck do I know where she is," Charles said.

"You took a bribe to allow the burglary to happen, lost my files, tried to cover it by setting up Harry to kill Victor, and now you think you still work for me. You're finished. I want my files back. I don't care what you do with the rest of the crew. That's your deal. I don't need them anymore.

Charles poured himself a drink, gulped it down.

"You have no leverage left," says Justin.

"What if I get rid of them?" asked Charles. "Worth anything?"

"'*Let me tell you, Cassius, you yourself are much condemned to have an itching palm.*' You should have read your Shakespeare."

"If you want your lapdogs to disappear, you'll have to pay for it."

"Didn't the Russians pay you enough? You need more money to get back to France?"

"A million for the files," says Charles. "And Alma."

✳

The staleness of Victor's apartment was overwhelming. Harry felt nauseous and desperately wanted to vomit, but couldn't because he was gagged. Choking to death was a terrifying thought. Ishmael vomited into the tape covering his mouth. Vladimir removed the gag and wiped Ishmael's mouth with a dirty rag. Ishmael hyperventilated. Vomiting was contagious. He gagged several times. Breathing deeply through his nose didn't help.

The room was filled with stench. Even the Russians were revolted. An open window didn't help. Vladimir ran into the bathroom to relieve himself. Serge stuck his head out the window and tried to breath clean air. The Russians were fed up with their assignment.

"Pull the gags off, Vladi," said Charles as he entered the apartment. "It stinks in here. Leave the door open. And clean up this vomit."

Charles circled the chairs with taunting movements. "Ishmael, you're a real disappointment. Your friend Harry is obviously alive. What did I ask you to do?" Ishmael doesn't answer. "That's not an answer."

"What's your game, Charles?" asked Harry, with the calmness of a priest hearing confession.

"You two are on your way out of Cuba in a body bag. Justin has no more use for you. You're not even worth ransom."

"I need to take leak," said Harry. "You don't want to add the smell of urine to this disgusting hole."

"One at a time, and hurry up."

"Is the Russian going to hold my dick?" asked Harry. Vladimir yanked Harry out of his chair, unzipped his pants, and pulled down his briefs. He looked up and winked at him.

Ishmael was hyperventilating. Vladimir unzipped Ishmael's pants with excruciating deliberateness and checked out his boxers. Ishmael screamed in fear.

Harry hopped into the bathroom. He didn't try to control his urine. He tried to get the knife taped to his back, but he didn't have a free hand. He opened a drawer under the sink with his teeth. He found a pair of scissors, and used his teeth to get them out of the drawer and onto the counter. He turned around and hid the scissors inside his hands, leaving the drawer open for Ishmael, hoping he would find a weapon to use.

He banged on the door with his head. Vladimir opened it and kicked Ishmael on his naked butt into the bathroom.

As Serge pulled up his pants, Harry dropped the scissors into the back pocket of his jeans.

"Original," said Harry to Charles. "Driving us to a secret place and holding us hostage until you get blood money from Justin. I think you've seen too many American gangster movies. Usually, the French movies are subtler."

"Shut up, kid. You've never seen a French film in your life."

"I'm looking forward to being shoved into a car, blindfolded, driven to an undisclosed spot, and tortured," said Harry. "Or, as in French movies, talked to death."

Ishmael came out of the bathroom. Vladimir pulled up his pants in disgust as Ishmael drops something into his back pocket.

"Why do all this when Justin doesn't give a shit about us?" said Harry. "Kill us here."

"Not what I have in mind," responded Charles.

To Harry's surprise, Charles didn't ask about the files. He had no idea they ended up in Victor's apartment, under the mattress. Charles obviously lacked basic management skills.

Harry fidgeted in the back seat of the car. Ishmael was drenched with sweat and had trouble breathing. No one was talking on the drive to nowhere. Twenty minutes went by in silence.

Harry remembered his psychology teacher in high school, Mr. Gregory, who discussed the profile of a psychopath. The characteristics were illusive and hard to identify. Psychopaths appeared normal, but their impulses to kill people made them feel superior. They felt no regret and killed again many times to feel the power high.

Mr. Gregory also told the class about another kind of personality who hid behind charm and who appeared normal. That type of personality could be as manipulative as the psychopath, sometimes passive and sometimes aggressive. They didn't have an impulse to kill, but they got the power high in other ways like lying, cheating, and causing others harm. People in both categories justified their cruel behavior in devious ways to obscure their true intentions. They looked appealing on the outside, but when challenged by a remark or an opposing opinion, they raged and acted out.

Charles drove to the far reaches of the desolated outskirts of La Habana where no human set a footprint in decades. Harry wondered why they weren't blindfolded. He memorized a few landmarks in case they were able to escape. The area was deserted of population and the ground had lost its usefulness, ravaged by caliche and hard rock. No growth, no water.

During the repetitive dullness of the drive, Harry amused himself by thinking that the two Russians in the car, Vladimir and Serge, were the reincarnation of Saddam's sons, Uday and Qusay. They portrayed almost a comic effect of two gangsters who could only act on the orders of their boss. They had no original thoughts. Anything was possible. Anything could happen.

Charles stopped at a dilapidated farmhouse, the only sign that civilization had existed on the hard land. Uday and Qusay dragged them out of the car, into the musty, mildewed house, and shoved them down in a corner.

Alma sat straight as an arrow on a couch made of sticks, looking disheveled, hands tied in front of her. She had been crying, but she was relieved to see Harry. He tried to reassure her with a timid smile.

Charles checked his watch. Then, like in a French B movie, he kissed Alma on the cheek. "I'll be back soon, *ma cherie*, and everything will be back to normal. We'll go to Paris, get our second chance, and you'll live a happy life." He whispered something to Vladimir, glanced back at Harry, and left.

Harry started coughing. He fell onto his side and rolled around on the floor. His face turned red as the coughing continued. The acting was Leonardo DiCaprio level. A total pro, but the Russians were unmoved by the performance.

As he rolled up to a sitting position, he slipped the scissors to Ishmael. Then Harry looked pleadingly at both Russians, as he continued to cough. They walked outside laughing. The unrelenting gagging and coughing became a cover as Ishmael started to cut through his ropes.

Outside the front window, the Russians smoked and kicked an old, deflated soccer ball around. Amateur hour. Uday and Qusay had the attention span of gnats.

Ishmael stopped slicing the ropes with the scissors and indicated that Harry should reach into his pocket and get what he removed from the bathroom. Harry couldn't see it, but he felt something sharper than scissors. He couldn't believe Ishmael's luck. It was a small, sharp knife. Harry gave the knife to Ishmael, and he continued to cut quickly through Harry's ropes.

Harry monitored the Russian movements through the front window as he freed his hands. He pulled off Ishmael's ropes, then cut the ropes around Alma's hands. She knew to rewrap the ropes around her wrists pretending she was still tied up. Harry pulled the tape off his mouth.

"You're bigger and stronger," said Harry to Ishmael. "Get on the other side of the door. Whoever enters first, slam him. I'll lunge for the other one and wrestle him on the floor."

Harry lifted the back of his shirt and pulled tape off a knife. Ishmael couldn't believe Harry still had the knife he used to killed the Fat Man. With Che's image, no less. Dumb luck. He'd take it.

"Alma, look at me," said Harry.

She was immobilized by fear. She had wet her dress.

"Alma! Look at me! Stay where you are until they come in. They'll look for you when they don't see Ishmael. Do you hear me?" Alma nodded.

"I don't suppose there is any rope in this place," said Ishmael.

"Use the venetian blinds to tie them up," said Alma with a stone face. "Maybe they'll be sharp enough to cut their necks."

Just as Harry put the tape back over his mouth, the door opened. Serge entered first. That's not what Harry hoped for. He shook his head *no* to Ishmael. Luckily, Serge was missing a few crayons from his brain because he didn't get the full picture of the ambush. Vladimir pushed him inside and Harry lunged at Serge and grabbed his legs. He stuck his knife against Serge's neck.

With perfect timing, Ishmael slammed the door on Vladimir as he forcefully pushed into the door. Ishmael pushed harder and sent him flying to the floor. Ishmael pulled his knife out and leaped on Vladimir, stabbing him in the arm.

"Alma!" yelled Harry. "The venetian blinds. Back bedroom. Not the ones in front."

Serge pushed back on Harry and accidently ran into the knife that Harry held at his neck.

"I think I hit an artery," said Ishmael as he headed for the kitchen. "Stop squealing like a pig, Vladi. You'll live."

Alma brought two sets of venetian blinds. "Give a pair to Ishmael and go fix yourself up if you want."

"The only fixing I want is for Charles to be flushed down a toxic sewer in payment for his sins."

Ishmael put on a tourniquet Vladimir's arm and tied him up.

"How does that feel, *pendejo*?" asked Ishmael. "Payback's a bitch."

They tied up Serge and dragged both Russians into the back bedroom. Harry noticed that Serge's shoulder was bleeding.

"Ish, give me those rags from the kitchen. And find tape to gag these guys."

"They were going to kill us anyway. Let him bleed out."

"You can do what you want but tape their mouths," said Harry. "We have a shitstorm to face when Charles comes back and finds the files gone from under the mattress."

"Stay in the bedroom." Harry climbed out the window.

An eerie silence descended over the desert. Harry waited patiently under the hot sun on the side of the house. He had no clue how to proceed. A walking dead man had few options. Staying alive was the first priority.

A car approached. A door slammed shut. Harry headed to the back of the house. Charles peered through the front window, saw no one, and walked around the perimeter to the bedroom window.

Harry grabbed him in a chokehold, one arm around his neck while the other hand held a knife to his back.

"Welcome back, Charles."

"If it isn't wonder boy," said Charles, struggling to get his words out.

Charles was no match for Harry as he pushed him around to the front door.

"Open the door, Ish."

"*Compay*, come in," said Ishmael as he let them inside.

Harry gave Charles a hard push, and he fell to the floor.

Alma spit on the floor in front of Charles. *"Hijo de puta."*

Charles smiled, further angering the singer. Before Alma could recover from the insult, he pulled her leg out from under her, grabbed her, and pointed his gun to her head.

Harry drew his gun on Charles as Vladimir came into the living room holding the venetian blinds in the air. Ishmael put a choke hold on Vladimir from behind. He was no match for the Russian's brute force. He knocked Ishmael to the floor and used the venetian blinds as a weapon, beating on his body.

Harry turned the gun on Vladimir and shot him in the leg, then turned the gun back on Charles.

"Put the gun down, Charles, and let her go," said Harry.

"Look at you," said Charles. "It's the Wild Wild West."

Charles kept his hold on Alma. "Where are the files? Tell me if you want her to live."

"You don't have the guts to kill her."

Harry shot the gun out of Charles's hand. Alma pushed him away with all the force she had left in her body. He stumbled and fell.

"Lucky shot," said Ishmael impressed. "Take me to target practice sometime."

Charles was defenseless, bleeding, and for the first time, frightened.

"Blood drawn. I picked the right guy to kill Victor."

"All you and Justin had to do was honor the agreement," Harry said.

"Have some patience," said Charles. "Let's have a meeting of the minds. We can solve this."

"I thought you were a smart guy, but you didn't see it coming either. We have no value to Justin anymore. That was the deal from the beginning."

"What are you talking about?" asked Charles.

"You're expendable to Justin. The situation changed. He has other plans for Cuba, and you're not included."

⁜

The French Embassy was bustling as Justin entered the reception hall. There was always an active energy to the place. The French were proactive about selling their culture to the Cubans. Every time he and Charles made applications under the French moniker, they were being educated into the French lifestyle. The real problem with the French was understanding their motives. Sneaky bastards.

Justin walked up the stairs to the second floor and found Lucien talking on the phone. More than likely, he was talking to Charles. Panic covered his face like a blanket, and he abruptly hung up. There was a noticeable tic in his left eye.

Justin extended his hand without enthusiasm. Lucien had a limp wrist. No strength in his arms nor upper body. His face was lined with crevices of a man twice his age. Dirty blond hair receding from his forehead.

"To what do I owe this visit, Justin?" asked Lucien.

"We have a problem, Lucien. You took a bribe from the Russians and gave them permission to steal our applications."

"What would you like me to say? You are already privy to the transfer of funds."

"You are resigning as of now. Alberto has your papers ready to sign. Charles won't protect you. There are no second acts in this drama. In the meantime, let us look for someone to replace you. Your recommendation is crucial to your good health. Do you understand?"

Lucien was beaten, finished in Cuba, and he had to comply with Justin unless he wanted to spend the rest of his life inside an infamous Cuban jail.

"What did you do with the money that Victor Kostroff paid you to give his thugs access to our files?"

"I still have the money. Charles got most of it though.

"Where are the original files?"

"I don't know. The Russians got them, but I was supposed to get them back and give them to Charles."

"Write down three names of people you trust in this embassy to be our next French agent."

Lucien wrote down three names and handed the paper to Justin. He gave the names back to Lucien.

"I'll take the woman. Rene Albert. Set up an interview. Your last duty to my company. It's not a good day at the French Embassy, is it Monsieur Chabrol?"

❉

Charles sat in a chair, arms behind his back. A blood-soaked rag wrapped around his hand. The Russians were in bad shape.

"Got any ideas?" asked Ishmael.

The rabbit hole was endless.

"I think we should leave them all here," said Ishmael.

So far, Harry stayed ahead of the game, kept it underwraps because every moment had to be orchestrated and precisely executed. The full impact of Justin's betrayal, his lies, promises, his unending con sweetened with concern and support, took him down a path that wasted his time. He was betrayed and he betrayed himself. The anger was eating him alive. If he could get inside that anger, into the eye of the storm, he might be able to calm himself. There was still the end of the third act to write.

"I don't suppose that I can beg for my life," asked Charles.

"You are a liar," said Harry, "and you are a liability. You and Justin are the other side of the same coin. And you've cannibalized each other. Either he'll kill you or we will kill you. *No hay honor entre los ladrones.*"

I'll get you off the island," says Charles. "I've got money and a plan."

The door opened. Ibrahim stood in the doorframe, backlit by the late afternoon sun.

"Shit, man, are you the villain, or the savior, or the school teacher from Santiago?" asked Harry.

Harry trusted no one. Ibrahim could be nothing but a pawn in Justin's game, or he could double-cross the man who set him up in business. It was difficult to read the answer. Where does the line of betrayal begin and end?

Ibrahim closed the door. "Looks like everything's under control, Harry. You did well."

"Why are you here, Ibrahim?"

"To get Justin's original files back from you."

Game on.

"And if I don't have them?"

"I kill you anyway."

Ishmael lets out an audible sound of disbelief.

"And me?" asked Charles. "What's to be done to me?"

"You're dead. Contract null and void," said Ibrahim.

"Justin can't do that. We're partners. We have contracts."

Ibrahim, with his cool head and academic intellect, faced off with Charles. *Where did this man come from?*

"He's already drawn up the papers. Your partnership with Kirpan and businesses involving the Institut Français des Aquatiques is over. They'll be no severance."

Off with his head.

Ibrahim's knowledge of English astounded Harry. Cuba lost one of its outstanding English teachers because they didn't offer him an honest wage. He finally understood irony.

Ibrahim took out papers from a file folder he carried under his arm. Just like a lawyer.

"Get him on his feet, Ishmael," directed Ibrahim.

Ishmael pulled Charles to his feet and walked him to a rickety table near the door. Since his hands were tied in front, Ibrahim forced a pen in his good hand. Charles signed in defeat.

Ibrahim took Alma by the arm, led her outside, and into the car. "Wait here. Please don't worry."

Harry walked outside and confronted Ibrahim. "What are you doing here, Ibrahim?"

"Justin sent me to get the files and to kill you and Charles. Otherwise, I'm out of business. I'm trying to think how to end this. Why does Justin want those files?"

"He's jumped ship. Works for the Brazilians now. A phantom spy with no borders, no footprints. Never had loyalties. He disappears when there is a better deal. French applications no longer viable. He'll transfer the French bids to Brazil."

"What should I tell him?"

A gunshot was heard from inside the house. Harry and Ibrahim raced inside. Ishmael held a gun in his hand. Charles was dead.

"I asked him where the money was for the bribe and he wouldn't tell me," said Ishmael. "How does this guy get to keep close to a million?"

"Now we'll never know," said Ibrahim. "What do we do with this mess?"

"Set it on fire," said Ishmael. "I'll come back in a couple of days and do it. I can't do it now. Not in front of Alma."

CHAPTER 19
The Phantom

The ride to Kirpan was exhausting and interminable. Harry worried about Alma, how the strange odyssey would affect her life, her future. And what was to become of Felicity? What did Justin do about Alberto? How was he going to take care of his family?

Ibrahim stopped in front of Kirpan. Harry encouraged Alma to go to her apartment, get some rest. Ibrahim would drive her.

"I'm going back to Cienfuegos and will take over Ray's restaurant. He's dying and I want to be with him. A small life is better." Harry embraced her. "You always have a home here if you change your mind."

The front door was open, and Kirpan felt empty. They grabbed a beer and tore the place apart looking for the money. All drawers were locked, but Ishmael was expert at getting into them. They pored through Charles's accounting books, through Justin's ledgers.

It was obvious. Right in front of him.

Alberto kept the money.

"Get the money from Alberto, Ish. Lucien's money may be in the mix. That's ours, too."

"Simple plan. The money gets you get off the island. Better yet. Take Justin's private plane. Illegal is better than nothing."

Harry had a bigger plan. He didn't want to think of the outcome, but he had no choice except to pursue the inevitable. He was going to become Justin Levitt or whatever name was on the Brazilian applications. Assume his identity.

The rest was fate.

"Where did you get that gun?" asks Ishmael.

"Remember the Russian I wanted you to get rid of? You didn't get him off my back, and he followed me to Felicity's. I took his gun as a souvenir."

"Is there such a thing as bad karma anymore?"

Harry felt his breath return. A profound sense of relief followed, although he doubted the grinding guilt would ever be truly over.

Ishmael went back into Justin's office and came out with a small booklet. "This is the pilot information. His name is Ruben. I know him. He's a good guy. He flew me to Santiago when I disappeared. All he cares about is being paid for his work."

"Are you ready to take over Kirpan and the currency exchange?" asked Harry.

"I was born ready." Ishmael embraced Harry. "Jesus, Harry, I'm sorry I put you in danger. *Por favor, todavía hermanos?*

"*Claro que si.* No one knew Justin. How could we know?"

"I'll put the pilot on alert for you to go to Santiago when the time comes. The plane is going to wait for your return."

He hands Harry several large stacks of kooks. "Tell your wife she should pick up money once a month at Ibrahim's travel agency. She'll never go without, as long as we're in business."

Harry knew what this meant. He and Ishmael forged a bond. Maybe this was the deal from the beginning. The trade-off. Harry didn't see it coming.

Ishmael smiled, white teeth, bearing straight. There was long distance in that smile. His smile stretched for decades.

Ibrahim entered Kirpan, exhausted but trying to maintain the adrenaline that propelled him the last few days.

"How is she?" asked Harry anxiously.

"I bought her a *cortado* and something to eat. I'd like to tell you that she won't go back to Cienfuegos, but it feels like she wants to keep Ray's memory alive. Alma must forgive herself for falling for Charles's line of shit. Nobody likes to be used."

Ishmael handed Ibrahim a beer and headed for the door. "I'm going to pay a visit to Alberto."

Harry told Ibrahim to call Justin and tell him he would deliver the original French files to him at Parque Central.

"Tell him to have a plan to get him off the island," said Harry. "And wait for my call."

Felicity's apartment was empty. He looked to see if the safe in the wall behind the bed was closed.

Felicity entered and looked as if she had seen a ghost. They embraced quickly.

"Something bad happened," she said.

Harry confirmed that Alberto was involved in the burglary. She half-expected it. Justin came to the office and threatened Alberto, but he told her cousin that he was still useful to Justin's plans. Alberto was to merge the French files into the Brazilian contracts.

"Alberto must find the original files, or he will no longer have a position in the Cuban government." said Felicity. "That means I'm going to merge the files. *Señor* Levitt thinks I might know where the files are located."

"I have them, and I'm going to bring them to Justin."

"Alberto tried to make amends by giving *Señor* Levitt his portion of the bribe money," said Felicity. "It was settled that my cousin would keep the money safe for now."

Harry was not ready to talk about the future with Felicity. He had no idea whether Alberto would be around to see the end of the saga. He hoped Felicity would stay in her position with the government. Until then, she would be his greatest ally.

Harry sat on the windowsill and called Ibrahim. "I have one stop to make, and then I'm on my way."

He closed his phone and Felicity took his hands. "Be careful, *mi amor*. We are in dangerous territory."

✣

On the way to Hotel Parque Central, Silas called Harry. He was up the last twelve hours reviewing and analyzing the Brazilian files.

"That fucking Justin is a genius. I just got my doctorate in tech design and coding from that Brazilian file. Jesus! Harry, this thing is a monster plan."

"Can you implement it? Can you be Justin and talk it through to the Cuban government?"

"Are you shitting me?"

"You can't be an American and pitch this," cautioned Harry. "We have to work that out with the Brazilians."

"But we also need a Cuban who knows more than I do to talk me through it."

"Getable. I have a guy that can find you someone."

Ibrahim.

Throughout this journey to freedom, Harry was projecting a soft landing, easy and civil, not the struggle, not the crime, not a big-bang ending.

"Meet me in the Hotel Sevilla lobby and give me the French files."

As he entered Hotel Parque Central, it was clear to him that the end would be a crucible, a trial by fire with challenging elements, leading to something new. This was the moment of truth.

Ibrahim saw Harry pouring coffee at the side table for the hotel guests, files wrapped in a brown paper bag, tucked under an arm.

He was determined to maintain the adrenaline that propelled him the last few days.

Ibrahim told Harry he'd like a cup. No cream or sugar. They gulped down the black, sticky liquid in morbid silence, and took the elevator to the twelfth floor. At the entrance to the room, Harry patted his gun. Ibrahim indicated he had a knife, the same knife that he used when he killed the Russian at the bar the night Victor was killed.

Harry knocked. Justin opened the door, and without a word, he handed the bag of files to Justin and sized up the room. Beautifully decorated and appointed. Lush green plants scattered around. White walls, white furniture. Fluffy pillows. Sunlight drawing into the pristine scene. Ibrahim stood back toward the door.

"I'm taking your leverage away, Leo," said Justin.

"I don't need it anymore."

"Be careful what you say."

Harry walked past Justin and edged his way onto the balcony. The vista of La Habana in the distance was stunning in the afternoon light.

"Charles once asked why I didn't stick around Cuba and participate in doing business on the island. Cuba's not about freedom, but I've been thinking that Charles might be right. I should stay, hang around. I'll get to the U.S. eventually."

Justin walked toward the balcony, wondering at the change in Harry. He came up to the railing and faced Justin.

Ibrahim moved into the room, inching closer to the balcony. He and Justin made eye contact, understanding what was to come.

Harry extended his gun into Justin's stomach. The unexpected had happened. Ibrahim charged into Justin, who thought Ibrahim was going to be his savoir. With adrenaline surging through Harry and Ibrahim, they lifted Justin over the balcony and watched him drift through the air, plunging downward onto a concrete sidewalk.

✳

Harry once again made his climb up the steps of Padre Pico to find Kobe. It was late afternoon and Los Lobos was not busy. The quiet took the edge off his anxiety.

He asked a waitress for a beer and a plate of fried fish. Harry checked his phone to see if there were messages from Ibrahim or Ishmael. Ezra came out of the kitchen and wiped his hands on his apron, an unconscious movement that he made about a hundred times a day. He seemed to have lost weight, but Harry couldn't be sure. The man appeared older and walked slower.

"Hello, Harry," said Ezra. "How are you?"

"I'm hoping to enjoy your fried fish."

The waitress brought Harry a beer. He sipped it with relish and anticipated a good meal.

"You're looking for Kobe, I suppose," Ezra said stoically.

"Yes, of course, Ezra," said Harry. "Do you know when she will be home?"

"She and Katrina don't live here anymore."

Harry put down the beer. He was afraid to ask Ezra where she lived, who she was with, what she was doing, or even if she still lived in Santiago. The waitress brought him the fish, but he had no appetite.

"Eat up, Harry. It's not as bad as you think. You knew that Kobe was seeing someone on your last visit. It can't be a surprise now. She and Katrina have moved in with the nice man."

The nice man.

Harry stood up. Panic set in.

"Sit down," commanded Ezra. "She knew you'd be back. She didn't know when, but life goes on. You love her and she loves you, but you cannot be together because you are choosing to live different lives."

Harry picked at his fish.

"Please be sensible. Eat and enjoy and listen. There is an old Jewish saying: *Keeping good silence is harder than talking good.* I will get word to her at four o'clock today that you are in Los Lobos. I will ask her to come to my restaurant and bring Katrina and then you will have your meeting. At five o'clock, Los Lobos will have its first customers. You'll have an hour to talk."

Ezra lumbered back to the kitchen. Harry tried to breathe calmly to shake off his feeling of dread, but the fear wouldn't go away. He couldn't stop the gnawing in the pit of his stomach.

He left the restaurant walked east to Parque Céspedes through a maze of narrow streets that jutted into the main square. Everything began and ended in Parque Céspedes, where at all hours of the day and night the benches were filled with people in conversation or musicians were playing *Vente Anos*, a favorite song from Buena Vista Social Club. Kobe and Katrina would never be alone, as long as people talked and laughed and shared life.

He sat on a bench in the plaza. His life had changed forever. He had to keep moving. With focus and strength, Harry headed southwest to the Balcón de Velázquez. He gazed out over the corner viewpoint at Calle Mariano Corona and Bartolomé Masó. The smooth bay calmed him. He was not anxious about his future because he would able to provide for his family.

Fear and shame: the twin evils of life. Harry encountered the twins far too frequently since he left Cienfuegos. He wanted to embrace Kobe and take his daughter in his arms and tell her she was strong and intelligent and that her life mattered to him. Someday she would come to America, live with him, and get an education. She would have a choice in deciding how she lived her new life. His old life was receding.

He couldn't remember when the split happened, when he decided to journey in another direction, when his feelings and needs separated from Kobe's. He had loved her so much. And then, there was the passage of desire and time.

He couldn't go back.

Harry caught a glimpse of Kobe and Katrina through the front window of Los Lobos. He marveled at how Katrina fit perfectly next to her beautiful mother. He held out his arms to embrace them with love and strength. He was ready to talk about a future.

"I'm not angry, Kobe, with your new living arrangement. I'm happy for you. I want you to always be happy."

"Daddy, Daddy," said Katrina excitedly. "You look so different. You are older."

"Yes, my love. I'm older but still the same."

"It's good to see you, Harry," whispered Kobe. "You look different, but calmer and stronger."

"I am." Harry paused to collect his emotions. "I want you to be happy, and I didn't make you happy in the end. But I will always love you and Katrina." He handed Kobe a package. "This is for you to take care of Katrina and yourself if you wish. I know you want to teach school and are happy in your position, but, if you choose not to, you have the means."

"I don't need this, Harry. I'm doing well."

"The first of every month, please go to see Ibrahim at the travel agency where William sometimes works and pick up what I have arranged to leave for you. If you don't want to use it to live, please save it for Katrina's college education, or you can send Katrina to the States. I want her to go to high school like I did. I'll take care of her."

"Yes, Daddy. I want to do what you did."

"You'll visit me often either in La Habana or in the States. I'll always take good care of you."

Kobe would never lose her love for Harry. She took his hands and kissed each one. "You will always be my life."

Harry returned her kisses. Their foreheads touched. Katrina embraced her father with all the strength she had in her body.

"You will always be in my life," repeated Harry.

Harry walked down the steps of the Padre Pico with some peace. He pushed from his mind everything he had lost. If he gave in to the emotion of what he was about to do with his life, he would lose himself in bitterness. Life in Cuba as he once knew it was over. He was a different man with a different name.

He cut across Aguilera, past the Casa de Diego Velázquez, and jogged down into Parque Céspedes where the Hotel Casa Granda dominated the plaza. Kitty corner was the *Cubatur*, Ibrahim's pride and joy. His tour agency was bustling like bees in a hive.

William embraced Harry. Ibrahim stood to shake his hand.

Harry's extended family looked prosperous and happy. Guille was all smiles. His Airbnb business was growing. Soon he and Satomi would have another room to rent.

Harry directed Ibrahim into the back office. "I've got to leave soon, but you know about the money that Kobe is to pick up monthly. If she doesn't come to the office, please take it to her. William knows where she lives. Try to get the money to her without the man knowing. Maybe she'll want you to keep it for her. I didn't suggest that. I don't want to be suspicious."

"Don't worry, Harry. I'll take care of it. And we won't speak of it again."

"Be her guardian angel. Be to her what I should have been: a safety net against evil in the world." Harry embraced Ibrahim. "One more thing. I'm going to need you more in La Habana. Train Guille to do your job, give him more responsibility. We're all a team now. I can't do this without you."

On his way out, he embraced William again with unspoken devotion. "Say good-bye to Satomi for me."

Harry flew back to Havana with Ruben, the pilot that once worked for Justin. It is an uneventful flight, but he was anxious.

When Harry entered Kirpan, he poured himself a whisky to steel himself against what was to come.

"How was the flight?" asked Ishmael. "You look tired."

"The flight was good. Seeing my wife and daughter was wonderful and difficult. I'm trying to be at peace with what I've done."

Ishmael told Harry the bribe money was in Alberto's wall safe. He handed it over after he knew there would be a change in management. He was shocked, but he pleaded to stay in his government position. I also told him that Felicity was to merge the files of the French and Brazilian companies as soon as possible. She may need the assistance of a man named Silas who understood the software.

"Other loose ends?" asked Harry.

"I put the money in Justin's safe, but you need to make a decision soon. It's up to you where you want to stash it. Confer with Ibrahim if you want. And Lucien already left Cuba."

"More than anything we've discussed, we need the most expert tech person in Cuba to work with Silas to build the cellular service infrastructure around the island," said Harry. "It's better if he comes from Brazil because this a Brazilian will be on the applications and approved by the Cuban government. Check in with Ibrahim and start the interview process. We need a wide net for this and it's our first priority."

"I'll send for him tonight."

An excited Silas entered. He reported on further modifications in the contract with Brazil's GlobalNet. He worried the work that had to be done should come from the States and not Brazil. And the work can't be done in Cuba because there is not enough Internet bandwidth.

"We'll send you first to Brazil to check it out, and work with the GlobalNet group," said Harry. "If Justin put the deal together, GlobalNet can get it done. But you can't leave until you help Felicity merge the French and Brazilian files. Can you hack into the software program?"

"It's basic stuff," replied Silas. "And by the way, my friend, you need a crash course in computers. You have to get up to speed."

Harry told Ish to get his money exchangers together and improve the system. It needed to run more efficiently. Do a better job of vetting the runners. And increase the percentage for the workers.

"And you?" asked Ishmael. "What is your role?"

"Silas, what's the name that Justin used to sign the Brazilian bids?"

"Eduardo Cadu."

I'm now Eduardo Cadu.

Harry's gaze fell on the colorful ties hanging in a straight line from the railing of the upper balcony. He found them comforting, as he began to think about the next chapter of his life. Since he was a young boy, he wanted more out of life, more for himself, more freedom to think, and more space to grow into who he was meant to be. The accidental Cuban was not leaving immediately, but in time, he would become an American.

✣

*My gratitude to the following who cheered me on
with insight and support*

�֍

Michael Noll, Program Director, The Writers' League of Texas
Chesley Nassaney
Emily Chase Smith
David Boucher
Pat Jackson

Joan Moran is an author, motivational speaker and expert on health and wellness. She teaches management, employees and business leaders how to think creatively, implement innovative ideas, adapt to change, achieve work-life balance, and live a life of optimum wellness. She has developed the idea of stretching the mind at any age into an art form.

Joan combines 25 years of theater experience, teaching, and writing textbooks on acting. She founded and was the artistic director of Nevada's first professional year-round theater. After attending American Film Institute, she became a screenwriter and producer.

She spreads her knowledge and energy as a writer and blogger for *The Huffington Post* and as a contributing writer for *Sixtyandme*. Joan's idea of a happy life is to roam the world dancing Argentine tango.

Joan is the author of her humorous and incisive memoir, *60, Sex & Tango: Confessions of a Beatnik Boomer, I'm The Boss of Me! Stay Sexy, Smart & Strong At Any Age*, and *Women Obsessed. An Accidental Cuban* is her latest novel.

Web: www.joanfrancesmoran.com

Twitter: @joanfmoran

Email: joan@joanfrancesmoran.com

www.ingramcontent.com/pod-product-compliance
Lightning Source LLC
Chambersburg PA
CBHW060027030426
42334CB00019B/2217